PETRIFIED FOREST NATIONAL PARK

George M. Lubick

PETRIFIED FOREST
NATIONAL PARK

A Wilderness Bound in Time

The University of Arizona Press   Tucson

For Diana, Robert, and Nancy

The University of Arizona Press
Copyright © 1996
Arizona Board of Regents
⊗ This book is printed on acid-free, archival-quality paper.
Manufactured in the United States of America

01 00 99 98 97 96 6 5 4 3 2 1

Library of Congress Cataloging-in-Publication Data

Lubick, George M., 1943–
    Petrified Forest National Park : a wilderness bound in time /
    George M. Lubick.
        p.   cm.
    Includes bibliographical references and index.
    ISBN 0-8165-1604-9 (cloth : alk. paper).—ISBN 0-8165-1629-4
    (paper : alk. paper)
        1. Petrified forests—Arizona.   2. Petrified Forest National
    Park (Ariz.)   I. Title.
QE991.L84   1996
333.78′4—dc20   95-32549
                                                    CIP

British Library Cataloguing-in-Publication Data
A catalogue record for this book is available from the British Library.

CONTENTS

FIGURES

ACKNOWLEDGMENTS

A good number of friends and colleagues have contributed to the completion of this study. Andrew Wallace of the History Department at Northern Arizona University has generously shared his copies of Whipple's diary and other materials and also read and commented on early chapters. Sidney Ash, of Weber State University, took time from his research at Petrified Forest to discuss aspects of the park's geology and to guide me to several sites, including, perhaps, John Muir's "Sigillaria Grove." Similarly, David Wilcox of the Museum of Northern Arizona shared his knowledge of the archaeology of Petrified Forest, and Dale Nations of the Geology Department at Northern Arizona University was a helpful and encouraging colleague. Personnel at Petrified Forest invariably were generous with their time and made research trips to the park library a pleasant undertaking. In particular, I wish to thank Superintendents Michele M. Hellickson, Gary Cummins, and Edward Gastellum as well as District Ranger Terry

Maze. The National Park Service Western Regional Historian, Gordon Chappell, was a good source of information, and I thank him for his support. Sarah J. Hillyer, the NAU History Department's efficient administrative assistant, not only proofread chapters but, more important, provided expert guidance through the mysteries of word processing.

Northern Arizona University provided organized research grants that facilitated research at the Huntington Library, the National Archives, and the Hayden Library at Arizona State University, and the staffs at those institutions expedited research tremendously. Karen Underhill and Laine Sutherland at Archives and Special Collections at Northern Arizona University's Cline Library were invariably helpful, and documents librarian Sean Evans guided me to much material that I otherwise would have missed. Susan Olberding and Carol Burke were most helpful in securing photographs and illustrations at the Museum of Northern Arizona. I owe a special thanks also to Suzanne Schafer at the University of Arizona Press.

Earlier research appeared, in different form, in two journals: "Soldiers and Scientists in the Petrified Forest," *Journal of Arizona History* 29 (Winter 1988): 391–412, and in "Protecting Our Forests of Stone," *Plateau* 61, no. 4 (1990): 24–31. I am grateful to the editors of both for permission to repeat here information published in their journals.

To all of the above, thank you.

PETRIFIED FOREST NATIONAL PARK

INTRODUCTION

"Yessir," the traveler drawled, "Away out there in the petrified forest everything goes on the same as usual. The petrified birds sit in their petrified nests and hatch their petrified young from petrified eggs."

Treasury of American Folklore

Among America's national parks, Petrified Forest has existed as something of an anomaly. Americans value their parks as scenic wonderlands, and places like Yellowstone, Yosemite, and the Grand Canyon set the standards for our definition of national parks. Monumental scenery, varied recreational opportunities, extensive campgrounds, and even resort hotels like El Tovar and the Old Faithful Inn all contribute to shaping the American vision of these national vacationlands. When the first Park Service Director, Stephen Mather, described these great national parks as the country's "crown jewels," he chose a particularly appropriate phrase.

The country's first parks owed their existence, at least in part, to an enduring sense of cultural anxiety. Nineteenth-century Americans worried about the new nation's seemingly meager artistic contributions in comparison to those of Europe. Particularly distressing was the lack of remnants of a glorious past; the United States could boast of no castles or

cathedrals, no monuments of Western Civilization. "The shadowy gran-
deurs of the past," to use Washington Irving's often quoted phrase, were
missing from the New World. For these cultural traditions Americans substituted monumental scenery, particularly after the Civil War, as they became increasingly familiar with the American West. The Yosemite Valley,
the Sierra Redwoods, and Yellowstone's geysers and canyons, among other
scenic wonders, became this country's emblems of national identity. The
idea of national parks originated in response to this cultural anxiety, historian Alfred Runte has noted. From the beginning, Americans valued
their national parks largely for their scenic impact.[1]

Such attributes as monumental scenery do not adequately describe Petrified Forest, which became a park only after a long tutelage as a national
monument—a separate category of scientific, historical, and archaeological sites established by the 1906 Antiquities Act. Its history has not always
paralleled that of other parks. From its inception in 1906, it was large for
a national monument (only a few others embraced more acreage), and,
because of its location only a few miles from the Santa Fe Railroad's main
line, it was easily accessible to travelers. Railroads often supported the establishment of national parks and hastened to serve them. Petrified Forest
was among the few monuments to enjoy the benefit of transcontinental
rail service. Later, Route 66 would bring even more tourists, and their
numbers would reach nearly a million annually by the 1980s.

The ancient stone trees, which towered over Triassic swamplands more
than 200 million years ago, suffered at the hands of visitors; protecting
them was the sole reason for establishing Petrified Forest National Monument in 1906. Though the responsibility was an important one, it was for
a long time interpreted and executed very narrowly. Even as paleontologists and paleobotanists unearthed from the Triassic Chinle Formation
around Petrified Forest more and more remains of ancient plants and animals, Washington officials retained a single-minded obsession with preventing vandalism and theft of petrified wood. Attempts to develop a
thoughtful educational or interpretive framework for this unique landscape were sporadic. Congress did not authorize the National Park Service
until 1916, and even then the agency did not address interpretation systematically for years. The exception was at Yosemite, where Joseph Grinnell

of the University of California's Museum of Vertebrate Zoology pioneered such activities as early as 1914.

The need to educate visitors was particularly pronounced at scientific sites like Petrified Forest. These monuments, like archaeological and historical ones, embody an essentially educational commitment that reflects the discoveries of field research and the ingenuity of interpretive specialists. Nowadays we acknowledge that parks comprise more than simple recreational sites. As Paul Tilden, editor of National Parks Magazine, has observed, they also are "units of a national educational institution which offers informal classes in the architecture and history of the earth." Similarly, geologist William Matthews describes parks as "outdoor geological laboratories" that provide visitors with an opportunity to see how natural processes have sculpted the landscape.[2]

Geologic processes shaped the magnificent scenery at Grand Canyon, Yosemite, Yellowstone, and other places, but visitors easily take the landscape for granted, never considering the physical forces that produced the spectacular terrain around them. People often overlook interpretive programs and are fully content to take in the scenic vistas. For decades this simple truth operated to the detriment of Petrified Forest. Visitors often delighted in the subtle hues of the Painted Desert and enjoyed wandering among the giant petrified logs; but they really had no framework for understanding the phenomena they witnessed, nor did they perceive the role of national monuments among the country's reserves. Consequently, visitors too easily categorized Petrified Forest as merely a curiosity or a collection of oddities.

Beginning in 1916, a number of national monuments—Lassen Peak, Grand Canyon, Bryce, Mukuntuweap (to become Zion), Mt. Olympus, and others—made a quick transition to national parks. All of them possessed obvious scenic attributes, and their original establishment as monuments represented a temporary status along the way to their elevation to parks. Petrified Forest did not then make the transition, even after the addition of the Painted Desert in 1932 gave it a unique scenic dimension. For several decades, the reserve remained something of a Park Service stepchild—scenic, larger, and more heavily visited than its sister monuments and some parks, but lacking the dramatic scenery that would make it park material.

As a result, for much of its history Petrified Forest existed on the administrative fringes of the Interior Department's responsibilities. Most of the national monuments shared the same fate, but because of its size, the number of visitors, and the vulnerability of its scientific sites, Petrified Forest demanded more attention. Washington's focus invariably was on the parks, and when civilian administrators proved inept, the Park Service resorted to the army—as in Yosemite and Yellowstone prior to World War I. For the monuments, though, Washington often relied on voluntary custodians, eventually paying them a nominal one dollar a month to prevent theft and vandalism.

The administrative history of Petrified Forest in the early twentieth century is a case study of the Interior Department's relationship with the national monuments and the problems of relying on volunteers or very poorly paid custodians. Near Petrified Forest the little railroad town of Adamana boasted the Forest Hotel as the gateway to the reserve, and its owners typically took on the responsibilities of monument custodians. From the 1890s through the 1920s, Petrified Forest was a one-man operation—the domain of whomever owned the Forest Hotel at the time. These custodians were expected to patrol the various deposits of petrified logs, preventing theft and deterring vandalism. Often these men also repaired roads, built bridges, constructed rudimentary shelters, and installed primitive water systems, all the while receiving little direction or compensation from officials in Washington. For custodians at Petrified Forest, it was usually Frank Pinkley, superintendent of the Southwestern National Monuments, who provided encouragement and instructions and often interceded on their behalf with Park Service administrators in Washington. Pinkley was the only contact that many custodians ever had with the agency's administrative hierarchy until the 1930s.

With the inauguration of Franklin Roosevelt's New Deal programs in the 1930s, the national monuments attained a degree of parity with the parks and received more attention from Washington. Petrified Forest benefited immensely from federal remodeling and refurbishing, thanks to the Civil Works Administration, the Public Works Administration, and the Civilian Conservation Corps. By the end of the decade, Park Service officials acclaimed it as the country's outstanding national monument. A full-time naturalist joined its meager staff and immediately initiated paleontological research projects and planned exhibits. Scientific work had gone on there—albeit intermittently—during the previous decades and had resulted in important discoveries. Scientists actually were piecing together the components of the Triassic environment that existed in the area 200 million years earlier. In so doing they were gradually defining a crucial time in the earth's history.

The role of scientists was not unique to Petrified Forest. Since the 1860s, scientists had explored and surveyed the mountains of the American West, and their illustrations and descriptions shaped the popular image of national parks. At Yosemite, Josiah Whitney, Clarence King, and John Muir not only identified the impact of glaciers in shaping Yosemite Valley, they also developed the concept of the geological sublime that gave meaning to the region's spectacular scenery. Similarly, much of our appreciation of Yellowstone and the Grand Canyon rests on the exploration and descriptions of John Wesley Powell, Clarence Dutton, and Ferdinand V. Hayden.

Scientific discovery also constitutes an essential ingredient of the national park experience at Petrified Forest, and it defines the reserve's unique characteristic. The huge petrified trees are novel remnants of an earlier time, and it is precisely that ancient environment—the time of the-codont reptiles and early dinosaurs—that is most important. Translating the scientific information into interpretive experiences that will capture the interest of visitors has been a critical responsibility for the Park Service at the reserve, but it has often proved difficult. Without some appreciation of this ancient environment, visitors have found Petrified Forest lacking in specific focus. Too often, causal tourists have viewed the place as a colorful roadside attraction—one of a great many along Route 66. In reality, the panoramas of the Painted Desert and the "forests" of stone trees are remnants of a 200-million-year-old ecosystem. The raw materials for an expansive science park were there to be employed, but Park Service personnel were slow to develop them.

Petrified Forest made the transition from monument to national park in 1962, more than a half-century after its founding. The new title recognized the reserve's expanded and upgraded facilities, the scenic landscape of the Painted Desert, and the vastly increased number of visitors—nearly three-quarters of a million—who arrived annually by Route 66. Scientific discoveries continued throughout the 1960s and 1970s, and a new visitor center allowed for more sophisticated interpretive exhibits. Finally, in the 1980s, park officials actively encouraged research by paleontologists, paleobotanists, and archaeologists, among others. Their work culminated in assembling a scientific advisory committee and ultimately in plans for an expanded scientific and interpretive center at the park—one designed to draw visitors into the unique world of scientific discovery in the Triassic Chinle Formation.

Park officials now propose to expand Petrified Forest's boundaries to include the remainder of the globally significant Chinle outcrop that cuts across the park. This is far more than a simple land acquisition, for they envision a program to introduce visitors to the geology, archaeology, and history of the park. A new management plan sets forth a combination of research center and visitor center overlooking the Painted Desert. The natural backdrop itself is an exhibit of the natural processes that shaped the area, and this panorama demonstrates how the contemporary landscape reflects events that occurred 200 million years ago. The close relationship between research and interpretation for visitors recognizes Petrified Forest's origins as a scientific site and provides a sense of continuity with the past.

Today, the petrified trees remain to provide a glimpse of an earlier environment—one that seemingly bears no relationship to the arid high plateau that surrounds the park. Modern visitors can now, in fact, "visit the Triassic," as the park's advertising proclaims, and carry home not purloined specimens of petrified wood but a perception of the area's ancient environment and perhaps an appreciation of man's humble place in the realm of the earth's history.

Petrified Forest still does not quite fit the popular image of national parks as expansive vacationlands located in places of scenic grandeur, graced with resort hotels and rustic campgrounds, and offering diverse recreational opportunities. Instead, Petrified Forest has been a daylight park for several decades; visitors stay but a few hours before resuming their journeys along Interstate Highway 40.

Although lacking some of the characteristics of its grand and scenic sister parks, it nevertheless remains an important environmental site that preserves 30 million years of the earth's history. In this respect, Petrified Forest contributes a unique dimension to the national park idea. To evoke an image in contemporary popular culture, it is a Triassic Park that exhibits and interprets an ecosystem that flourished in the region when the earliest dinosaurs made their appearance. Then, the stone trees that now lie scattered and broken on Arizona's high desert stood alongside lakes, swamps, and wandering streams that were home to phytosaurs, primitive fishes, and small dinosaurs like *Coelophysis*. Here was an ancient wilderness that modern man has come to know only gradually as erosion has freed its fossil plants and animals from the encasing rock matrix.

Petrified Forest requires visitors to confront geologic time—"deep time," as John McPhee labels it in *Basin and Range*. To think in terms of millions, or hundreds of millions, of years is a novel concept for most people. Few ever truly comprehend deep time; at best their minds can only measure it. Visitors to Petrified Forest National Park encounter the fossil remains of an ecosystem that sustained a diverse population of plants and animals hundreds of millions of years ago. A human lifetime, in contrast, is reduced to "a brevity that is too inhibiting to think about," McPhee notes. Nonetheless, he concludes that "a sense of geologic time is the most important thing to suggest to a nongeologist: the slow rate of geologic processes, centimeters per year, with huge effects, if continued for enough years." [3]

In proposing the expansion of this science park, the National Park Service has taken on a substantial challenge, hoping that visitors will choose a park experience that is educational rather than recreational. Over the past few decades, the definition of national parks has broadened considerably to embrace a variety of new reserves, and that diversity can also accommodate parks that preserve and interpret geological time and other natural phenomena. Such sites will never replace the crown jewels of Yosemite, Yellowstone, and other scenic places; they simply add another dimension to our understanding of the earth's history and changing environment.

1

CHINLE TIMES

When you come to the Petrified Forest—well, one guess may be as good as another! The greatest geologists, the greatest botanists, have bumped their inconclusive heads against it in vain. . . . It is the prime mystery in geology—the hardest nut, and the hardest wood, in the world.

Charles F. Lummis, southwestern writer, 1912

A few scientists and topographical engineers passed through the petrified forests in northeastern Arizona in the late 1850s, but their visits typically were brief and their examinations of the terrain cursory. From time to time, specimens of petrified wood were dispatched to schools and museums on the East Coast and in the Midwest, but no thorough scientific survey of the region occurred until the end of the nineteenth century, when the United States Geological Survey examined the region known as Chalcedony Park as a possible site for a national park. Local residents had given that title to the extensive deposits of petrified wood in the vicinity of the agate bridge. The mystical stone of the Greeks, chalcedony is a translucent milky or grayish quartz distinguished by slender fibers of microscopic crystals arranged in thin parallel bands. Chalcedony Park was never precisely defined and today is included in a section of Petrified Forest called Crystal Forest.

During the following decades both amateur and professional scientists explored the area's colorful badlands terrain. Most of them, like the naturalist John Muir, came at their own expense. But federal funding supported research by scientists from the Geological Survey and the National Museum. Such institutions as the Museum of Northern Arizona in Flagstaff, the Laboratory of Anthropology at Santa Fe, and the Museum of Paleontology at the University of California underwrote additional research at Petrified Forest. With the expansion of graduate education at the end of World War II, scientists could rely on the assistance of growing numbers of well-trained students. Throughout much of the American West, estimable scholars led their young charges to isolated sites in search of potsherds and other artifacts of prehistoric cultures or of the fossil remains of ancient creatures that had once inhabited the area. For graduate students, this fieldwork might amount to no more than an exercise in manual labor under the watchful eye of a renowned authority. But, at best, such excavations could result in the inclusion of the budding scholar's name among the coauthors of a brief scholarly article—the publications characteristic of contemporary refereed journals.

For Bryan Small, a graduate student at Texas Tech University, fieldwork at Petrified Forest National Park in August of 1984 culminated in a once-in-a-lifetime discovery. Small was working with a group of paleontologists from the University of California and other institutions that summer, examining the terrain near Chinde Point in the Painted Desert for plant fossils. In a small valley he came across an ankle bone, recognizably that of a dinosaur, which summer rainstorms had partially exposed. Small summoned his colleagues, and further inspection revealed other bones still in place in the soft rock. Members of the party removed enough material to verify the find, but further work had to be discontinued temporarily. August was too late in the season to begin excavation, so the site was covered with plastic, tarps, and layers of dirt to secure it against the elements. That winter at the University of California in Berkeley, researchers determined that Small had discovered not just a dinosaur but a new genus and species.[1]

Led by Robert Long of the University of California's Museum of Paleontology, the contingent was back the next spring, anxious to learn more about the new dinosaur. Excavation revealed a remarkable find. On June 6, 1985, the paleontologists removed from its 225-million-year-old burial

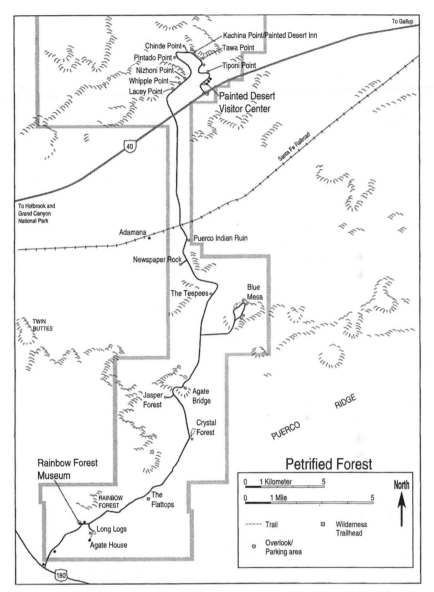

Petrified Forest National Park (Map by Ronald Redsteer, courtesy of the Bilby Research Center, Northern Arizona University)

ground the skeleton of a small dinosaur, about the size of a large dog. Given the fanciful name of "Gerti," this newest dinosaur was the oldest articulated dinosaur fossil from the area that could be dated with some degree of accuracy. Along with the relatively intact skeleton of Gerti, further digging revealed the remains of several other small dinosaurs. The discovery, Long explained, represented "the first definite evidence that dinosaurs lived as long ago as 225 million years or more"—in a time called the Upper Triassic period, when dinosaurs were making their first appearances.[2]

Researchers covered the collection of bones with tissue paper and burlap soaked in plaster, preparing it for removal from the site. A powerful Sikorski helicopter was used to lift the bundle from the floor of the Painted Desert to Chinde Point. There the 1,200-pound slab of Triassic earth and bones encased in twentieth-century burlap and plaster was loaded into the craft's cargo hold for its flight to the Museum of Paleontology at Berkeley.

The rocks that yielded Gerti's skeleton belonged to the Chinle Formation, which was deposited 220 to 225 million years ago near the end of the Triassic period of the Mesozoic era. The Chinle is hardly composed of exotic elements. "To begin with," one geologist writes, it is "nothing more than an accumulation of mud and silt along with a little sand and gravel."[3] More specifically, a variety of sedimentary rocks make up the Chinle formation; most of them are soft, fine-grained mudstone, siltstone, and claystone, compressed by the passage of time and overlying rocks that have since eroded away. Beds of harder and coarser sandstone and conglomerate also occur, and near the top of the Chinle is a series of limestone beds. The name of the formation comes from the Navajo village of Chinle near Canyon de Chelly, where, in 1917, H. E. Gregory first described well-exposed deposits in Chinle Wash. In the vicinity of Petrified Forest, the formation is more than eight hundred feet thick.[4]

The colorfully banded rocks, so characteristic of the Chinle, exhibit a subtle spectrum of pastel colors. In the Painted Desert, the section of Petrified Forest National Park north of the Puerco River, the dominant colors are shades of pink and red, but combinations of minerals and other substances produce muted tones of blue, gray, brown, and even white. Iron oxides are responsible for variations of red, decayed plant and animal remains contribute to grays, and gypsum accounts for the white. Elsewhere in the park are softly rounded hills, ranging in color from chocolate hues to purple and gray. At some locations, the muted shades of badlands slopes stand in vivid contrast to stark brown or white sandstone ledges.

Even after a comparatively brief time, erosion can transform the Chinle into badlands—arid terrain virtually devoid of any vegetation. No stable soil mantles the variegated colors, and in this "landscape of destruction," as one observer describes the Painted Desert, the surface is always new, always in the process of creation. Here, geologist Matt Walton writes, "only form and living process are stable and substance is transitory."[5] Rainfall at Petrified Forest, only about nine inches annually, often comes as torrential cloudbursts that produce raging flash floods. The murky water is heavily laden with abrasive rock fragments and surges through normally dry arroyos, slicing the land into intricate mazes of narrow ravines, crests, and pinnacles. Because of the rapid erosion, few plants establish a foothold; no roots develop to bind the soil together. The ground itself contributes to erosion; not only does the earth here lack organic material to sustain vegetation, but soft, porous bentonite also is abundant in the strata. This clay absorbs great amounts of water, then disintegrates into a fine, flowing mud. When dry, it again hardens, only to be sculpted away by the next torrential rain.

Water continues to shape the surface of the Chinle in the winter, when rain or melting snow seeps into cracks and crevices in rocks. Upon freezing, the water expands, widens the crack, and further weakens the rock. Eventually a portion breaks away, tumbling into a gully where later runoff will wash it away. Wind, too, has shaped the landscape of Petrified Forest. Spring's blustery winds sweep across the area, transporting fine sand and dust over considerable distances. At some locations, steep-sided buttes and mesas rise from the surrounding flat terrain; their cap rocks of sandstone or lava resisted the wind while the softer, underlying rock eroded much faster. Blue Mesa and the Flattops owe their appearances to such phenomena.

The cycle of erosion continues year after year. The steeper slopes in the park lose about a quarter of an inch of soil annually. Less than half that amount disappears from the gentler hillsides, and still less is blown from level areas. The Puerco River and its tributaries unceasingly wash away bits of the Triassic landscape, and much of the sediment is deposited in the ephemeral river's broad valley. Over the years, some of the material has been swept into the Little Colorado River and then through the Grand Canyon, eventually ending up in the Gulf of California.[6] Within the park, erosion has exposed more and more of the petrified logs for which it is famous. And those thousands of huge stone trees attest to a climate virtually the opposite of the high desert of contemporary northeastern Arizona.

Early in the age of dinosaurs, 225 million years ago, Arizona was a tropical lowland and was located some seventeen hundred miles closer to the equator than it is today. According to the theory of plate tectonics, the earth's present continents once had been joined in a supercontinent that we call Pangaea, meaning all earth. From it, today's land masses eventually separated and drifted off to the positions they now occupy. In the Triassic period, just as the drifting began, present North America rested far to the south of its present location, at about the same latitude as Panama.[7]

Northeastern Arizona was then a broad, relatively flat coastal plain, dotted with swamps and ponds and laced with muddy streams. Its tropical climate sustained a rich growth of plants. To the south and southeast rose a chain of volcanic mountains, the Mogollon Highlands, while much of present California and Nevada were inundated by the sea. Numerous streams arose in nearby mountains and meandered across the plain, gradually depositing sediment in their channels and floodplains. Trees and logs washed down from the highlands and over the years became mired in mud and covered with sediment. At other places floodwaters carried trees beyond riverbeds. The collections of trees eventually became waterlogged, sank to the bottoms of marshy lagoons, and were buried in the Triassic muck.[8]

Seeds and leaves from local plants accumulated as well, and some of that material found its way to the bottoms of shallow lakes and shifting streams. As Mogollon streams continually deposited loads of sediment, burying additional plants and animals, the Chinle Formation grew thicker. Like trees and logs, animal remains were fossilized and exposed by erosion centuries later. This slow and nearly continuous accumulation of sediment went on for millions of years, and the Chinle was the result.

The precise course of events in Petrified Forest following the deposition of the Chinle Formation remains unclear, because erosion has removed much of the evidence. Periods of deposition alternated with periods of erosion, and, as paleontologist Sidney Ash notes, the presence of marine strata in nearby places indicates that the sea probably covered the area in the Cretaceous period. For a time in the early Cenozoic, Petrified Forest experienced deep erosion, but conditions changed near the end of that era. The Chinle was buried beneath another formation, the Bidahochi, which consists mainly of soft, light-colored sandstone, claystone, and siltstone, and some hard beds of lava. At about the same time, volcanic eruptions occurred sporadically, covering the earlier strata with lava and ash. These, in turn, were later covered by sediment deposited by streams. Erosion then eventually removed most of the Bidahochi Formation within Petrified Forest and cut into the Chinle, too, exposing vast quantities of petrified wood and other fossils.[9]

Environmental conditions—temperature, moisture, oxygen, content of sediment, depth of burial, and other factors—all determine the rate of fossilization. Most of the wood and bones in Petrified Forest were in fact petrified, that is, turned to stone by a process in which practically all of the organic matter is replaced by minerals. The fossil retains the external shape of the object but little of its internal structure.

The process of petrification is a complex one that is not completely understood, but the following chain of events occurred. Once buried in waterlogged sediment, the trees underwent a process of replacement. As silicon-rich water percolated through the logs and bones, the silicon came out of solution and combined with oxygen to produce minute crystals of quartz within spaces in the tissue. In most of the fossil logs, the tissue was filled or replaced by quartz, and the trunks were completely petrified. In some instances—in hollow logs or in cracks of otherwise solid pieces— the growth of quartz crystals was not restricted. Such cavities within the wood might be lined with large crystals of amethyst, rose quartz, smoky quartz, or rock crystal quartz. Nineteenth-century treasure hunters particularly prized such finds, often using dynamite to dislodge the valuable crystals. The silicon-rich water also contained other elements that gave the fossil wood a variety of colors. Iron yielded shades of red, yellow, brown, and even blue. Carbon, sometimes manganese, added black; cobalt and chromium, though rare, produced blues and greens. Manganese also provided varieties of pink.[10]

The process was a slow one, and the Triassic swamplands proved ideal for the transformation of the fallen logs into brightly colored silicified trees. The key to the change was the volcanic ash—the natural source of silicon. Its breakdown yields large amounts of silicon in solution. "Time and slowly moving stagnant water did the rest," a geologist comments.[11] Most small items, such as leaves, seeds, cones, pollen grains, stems, and even fish scales, have been preserved as compression fossils—thin films of carbonaceous material that remain when a leaf, for example, is buried in sediment and flattened by the weight of overlying rocks. When the encasing rock is split, the fossil appears as a thin layer of black paint on the surface. Such fossils exhibit considerable detail and are valuable aids to scientists in their reconstruction of ancient plants and animals.[12]

Petrified trees are, of course, the region's best-known treasure and easily the most visible plant fossils in the park. Most of the logs are conifers—cone-bearing trees—and they normally grew to a height of eighty to a hundred feet, with trunks measuring three to four feet in diameter. Some attained heights of two hundred feet, and their diameters reached ten feet. None of these ancient trees are now standing—to the disappointment of visitors who anticipate groves of stone trees. No complete tree from roots to crown has ever been found within the park. In fact, trunks invariably are battered and worn. No limbs are evident, and there is little or no bark, indicating that most were carried some distance by streams before being buried and petrified. A few upright stumps have been found at different locations in Petrified Forest. They are only a few feet tall, and the roots clearly extend downward into the ground. Their existence suggests that small groves of trees were growing in the area when the Chinle Formation was deposited.

Most of the petrified logs and stumps are *Araucarioxylon arizonicum* and are related to the modern Norfolk pine and Monkey Puzzle tree, both of which now are used widely in decorative planting. Well-preserved trunks of *Araucarioxylon* show clearly that branches were restricted to the very tops of the trees. At Blue Mesa, groups of petrified stumps, some of them five feet in diameter, indicate that these ancient trees grew only ten to fifteen feet apart. Consequently, shading by neighboring trees suppressed branch growth, producing a dense, closed canopy of trees with small crowns. The ancient *Araucarioxylon* forest very likely resembled modern redwood forests along the Pacific Coast.[13] Two additional types of silicified trees, *Wood-*

worthia *arizonica* and *Schilderia adamanica*, occur in small numbers in the Black Forest in the northern part of the park, as well as at other locations. *Schilderia* typically were small, growing to heights of only twenty to thirty feet. *Woodworthia*, in contrast, were larger, perhaps fifty feet tall with trunks three feet in diameter.

As colorful and impressive as the petrified logs are, they are not as important as the less visible fossils, such as stems, cones, seeds, and pollen grains. Dr. Sidney Ash of Weber State University has studied the area's paleobotany for years and notes that petrified logs account for only a small percentage of the area's ancient plants. Of two hundred species of plants identified, seven are based on petrified wood, while sixty have been identified on the basis of compressed leaves, seeds, stems, and cones, and the rest from pollen grains, spores, and other minute parts. All of the plants that flourished in Petrified Forest in the Upper Triassic are extinct, but modern descendants of some of them live in humid, tropical parts of the world. With the exception of flowering plants, which appeared on the earth later, most of the major plant groups are represented in the Chinle Formation. Some of the ancient plants resemble their modern descendants; others are unfamiliar and sometimes bizarre.[14]

Horsetails, or scouring rushes, commonly occur in the Chinle at a number of places; both the fossil and the living plant in this group have straight, jointed, hollow stems. Some of the ancient horsetails grew twenty to thirty feet high and had diameters of fourteen to sixteen inches. (Today's horsetails, in contrast, rarely grow beyond ten feet.) Ferns also were abundant throughout the Chinle, as were cycads—primitive tropical plants that resembled a pineapple with palmlike leaves growing in a top cluster. Scientists have found abundant leaves from a similar plant, *Bennettitales*, an extinct group that may have been related to the cycads. Other plants have proven difficult to classify; one of them is designated *Dinophyton spinosus*—the "terrible spiny plant."[15]

Insects and their relatives were abundant throughout the ancient landscape. The cockroach, so well known and detested in the twentieth century, also was at home in the Triassic, as indicated by compressions that scientists have found. Various beetles, too, made their homes there. Some petrified logs bear the holes and scars left by wood-boring insects, and some fossil leaves appear to have been nibbled on.[16]

Analysis of plant fossils has provided information about the size and habitat of the original plants as well as data about the climate. Growth rings on petrified trees indicate the length of growing seasons, for example. In addition to plant fossils, scientists have found remains of clams, snails, clam shrimp, horseshoe crabs, crayfish, fish, amphibians, and several kinds of lizards, not to mention early dinosaurs. The study of fossilized animal remains has provided clues about the dimensions of some extinct creatures and information about their environment. The size and shape of leg bones indicate how an animal moved; teeth suggest the nature of its diet and also its size.

The shallow waters of streams and ponds were home to shoals of clams and other freshwater mollusks. Above them swam a variety of fishes, most of them primitive species, generally less than a foot long and covered with rectangular or diamond-shaped scales. Some, like Turseodus, were elongated and tapered at both ends, similar to today's sturgeons. Others, such as Hemicalypterus, were narrow and deep-bodied like the modern Mississippi gar. With its heavy enameled scales, the gar provides an impression of the body covering typical of Triassic fishes.[17]

A close relative of the modern Australian lungfish inhabited the region's streams and lakes. Named Ceratodus, it was widely distributed in Triassic time, and its habits were similar to those of its modern descendants. When streams and ponds dry up and the remaining water stagnates, lungfish (which indeed have lungs) surface to gulp air and thereby survive. The presence of Ceratodus suggests that the region's climate then alternated between humid seasons and dry months when streams and lakes were low.[18] Researchers have found remains of two kinds of sharks, neither of which was particularly large. Undoubtedly the most formidable of the fishes in the region was Chinlea, which one scientist describes as "the top of the food pyramid among the fishes in the Chinle." Chinlea could grow to five feet in length and weigh as much as 150 pounds, although most were less than two feet long. Regardless of its size, Chinlea's dominant characteristic was its complement of large, sharp teeth, which made it a feared adversary.[19]

Among four-legged animals, only amphibians and reptiles have been found thus far in Petrified Forest's Triassic landscape. Metoposaurus resembled vaguely a giant salamander and was one of the more common amphibians of the region. It grew to a length of six to eight feet and was

Phytosaurs were common in the ancient environment of Petrified Forest. The smaller, lightly built figures in the foreground are sphenosuchian reptiles, direct ancestors of today's crocodiles. (Illustration by Doug Henderson, photograph courtesy of the Petrified Forest Museum Association)

possessed of an inordinately large, flat skull. Its jaws held numerous small, sharply pointed teeth, indicating that *Metoposaurus* was a fish eater. Weighing about half a ton, its heavy body and great head obviously taxed its short weak legs, which could not bear its weight on dry land. Typically, *Metoposaurus* spent its time sprawling in mud and water—a habitat to which it was better adapted. Researchers occasionally have come across large concentrations of this giant salamander-like creature, usually in water holes where they died when the water dried up.[20]

The dominant inhabitants of the waterways were phytosaurs, crocodile-like reptiles that averaged about seventeen feet in length, with the largest reaching thirty feet. Their long jaws were equipped with numerous sharp, conical teeth, and they probably ate anything they could catch. Fish as well as any animals that lived near the water were their natural prey. Despite the

Metoposaurs were among the largest of the ancient animals in Petrified Forest. These giant amphibians spent much of their time in marshes awaiting prey. (Illustration by Doug Henderson, photograph courtesy of the Petrified Forest Museum Association)

superficial resemblance to modern crocodiles, phytosaurs were not their direct ancestors. The body and tail of phytosaurs were covered with heavy, bony plates. Nostrils were located on a dome just ahead of their eyes—an arrangement that allowed these animals to remain submerged for long periods of time while patiently awaiting their prey. Fossil remains of phytosaurs found in Petrified Forest are identical to specimens discovered elsewhere in North America, Germany, and India. Similarly, the bones of *Metoposaurus* are duplicated by fossils uncovered on this continent and in North Africa and Germany. The similarities, E. H. Colbert points out, represent additional evidence of the juncture of western Europe and Africa (to which India then was joined) with North America in Triassic times.[21]

A variety of reptiles, both herbivores and carnivores, inhabited the higher ground around the lakes and streams. *Typothorax* and *Desmatosuchus* were thecodonts related to phytosaurs. Both of these plant eaters reached lengths of ten to fifteen feet and were armored with large plates. Also, sharp lateral spikes protruded from their bodies, perhaps as defenses against their phytosaur cousins. The dominant herbivore of the time was *Placerias*—a member of a reptile group called dicynodonts that once ranged over much of the world's land areas. By the Triassic period their numbers were dwindling, and *Placerias* was one of the few remaining large members of the species. It was about the size of an ox and was among the largest animals living on land at that time; the largest dinosaurs had not yet made their appearance. Like most herbivores, *Placerias* had a broad, barrel-shaped body and was likely an awkward animal, one authority speculates. Most of its time was spent foraging for vegetation.[22]

In contrast to the region's plant eaters, the carnivores *Hesperosuchus* and *Coelophysis* were small creatures that probably fed on small game and even insects. Clearly they were no threat to a brute like *Placerias*. A small thecodont, *Hesperosuchus* was equipped with sharp teeth and was an active predator, capable of walking on its hind legs while using its long tail as a counterbalance. Its small forelimbs had facile hands that were used in foraging. *Coelophysis* was one of the earliest dinosaurs—a miniature edition of the giants that evolved later. Six to eight feet long, it weighed only forty to fifty pounds. It walked in a semi-erect position, its long, slender tail effectively balancing the weight of its body. Strong hind legs ended in a three-toed foot that left an imprint similar to the footprint of a bird. Its forelimbs were small and equipped with tiny clawed hands that allowed *Coelophysis* to catch and hold its prey. Its backbone was supple and its neck comparatively elongated. In short, *Coelophysis* represented a "typical example of the ancestral dinosaurs from which the great giants of the later Mesozoic Era evolved," according to one expert on the region's dinosaurs.[23] It was the first dinosaur found within the boundaries of Petrified Forest National Park. Its fossil remains were recovered in 1982, and a half dozen dinosaurs, including Gerti, have been discovered since.

Coelophysis is similar to fossils found in Connecticut, and it also has a close counterpart in the Upper Triassic deposits in Rhodesia. As in the cases of the lungfish, phytosaurs, and large amphibians, evidence suggests a close relationship among fossils found in Arizona, eastern North America, Africa, central Europe, and India. All of this buttresses the validity of the theory of plate tectonics and drifting continents, Colbert argues, and the fossils of animals found in the Chinle Formation in Petrified Forest have contributed significantly to this new view of the earth.[24]

Fossilization is a hit-or-miss proposition. The creatures that inhabited the swamps and streams of the Chinle Formation were preserved only occasionally. Preservation of the remains of such animals requires that they die in a place that is inundated with sediment before the carcass decomposes. Normally, when an organism dies, its remains decay or are eaten by other animals. Even when fossils form, they can be destroyed by floods, earthquakes, volcanic eruptions, or other natural occurrences. A great many fossils were formed in Petrified Forest simply because the right conditions were present.

The Triassic trees and organisms lay entombed in rock for millions of years. Then, beginning 60 million years ago, episodes of mountain building created the Rocky Mountains and the Sierra Nevada, giving western North America its modern form. The violent and complex movements in the earth's crust also affected the area that is now northern Arizona, which was raised slowly thousands of feet above its original sea-level location. With the change in elevation came an equally pronounced change in the climate. The onetime tropical lowland became part of a high desert—an extensive uplifted area called the Colorado Plateau. Forces of erosion soon were operating; and in time rain, wind, and frost began reducing the surface rock. As the Bidahochi and Chinle Formations gradually eroded, the ancient stone trees weathered out of the surrounding rock.

We know today what early visitors could not—that Petrified Forest's ancient environment was a crucial time in the earth's evolution. Early dinosaurs were just making their appearance, replacing earlier thecodonts that had dominated the landscape. Every new discovery, whether the unearthing of an early dinosaur or the meticulous screening of soil for spores or grains of pollen, adds incrementally to our knowledge of the ancient ecosystem. Today's national park preserves not just an unspoiled portion of America as it existed before humans arrived in the area. Petrified Forest protects an environment that existed before people even appeared on earth. The gradual erosion of the Triassic Chinle Formation provides us with an imperfect view of the earth long before humans could alter its environment.

The first people to observe the clusters of petrified trees were ancestors of today's American Indians. When Navajos moved into the Southwest several hundred years ago, they came across numerous ruins that ancient inhabitants had abandoned. These prehistoric pueblos clearly were not the work of the Navajos' own ancestors, and they consequently referred to the ancient dwellers of the region as Anasazi, a term that translates roughly as "enemy ancestors" or simply "ancient ones."

Archaeologists adopted the Navajo name and still use it to describe the prehistoric people who settled in Canyon de Chelly, Chaco Canyon, Mesa Verde, and other places throughout the four corners region. Anasazi cultural development spans as much as fifteen centuries. Archaeologists designate the earliest Anasazi sites as Basketmaker II (from as early as 100 B.C. to A.D. 500–700)—a time when the Anasazi typically lived in caves and grew crops of squash and corn while also engaging in hunting and gathering. Their culture became increasingly sophisticated over the centuries. The designation Basketmakers, of course, derives from their expertly made baskets, although the Anasazi began making pottery as early as the sixth to eighth centuries. From the eighth to the fifteenth centuries, their culture was based on pueblos. Initially, houses simply were clustered more tightly, often sharing adjoining walls. By the eleventh to the thirteenth centuries, the Anasazi were living in large masonry villages with buildings sometimes reaching several stories high. These centuries represented the high point of their architecture, basketry, and pottery, and were a time of extensive trade with neighboring groups. Even larger villages became common in the following two centuries, when settlements housed hundreds, perhaps thousands, of people.[25]

As early as the twelfth century, though, the Anasazi began moving south, often to the mountains of present Arizona and New Mexico. By 1300, the San Juan region had been abandoned completely, and in the following centuries the migration continued as the northernmost Anasazi joined relatives living in the Hopi mesas, along the little Colorado River, near Zuni, and along the Rio Grande. The Spanish intrusion, beginning with Coronado's arrival at Zuni in 1540, marks the beginning of the historic period.

The Anasazi were not the only prehistoric people to settle around Petrified Forest. The lower Puerco River Valley lies in a geographic frontier region between several cultures. Not only the Anasazi but also the Sinagua and Mogollon peoples left their impact on the land. Whereas the Anasazi primarily inhabited the high plateaus and canyons around the Four Corners, the Mogollon were mountain dwellers along the present Arizona–New Mexico border. They raised some corn, beans, squash, and, later, cotton, and probably engaged in more hunting and gathering than did the Anasazi. Until about 1100 the Mogollon settlements consisted of pithouses; settlements were small and long-lasting. After that date, the Mogollon settlement patterns changed, although not consistently, and the people also built surface structures. Population tended to converge into fewer but larger settlements along major drainages. By the middle of the fifteenth century, the Mogollon had abandoned their earlier sites, and remnants of the groups went off to Zuni and Acoma.[26]

The center of Sinagua culture was some distance to the west of Petrified Forest, near the present site of Flagstaff, Arizona. Although only a few Sinagua sites have been excavated, evidence indicates that these people lived in small settlements consisting of pithouses. Their population grew dramatically after Sunset Crater erupted in 1060, covering the earth with a layer of cinders that increased soil fertility and productivity. The Sinagua also underwent significant cultural change as they interacted more fully with nearby peoples.

In the twelfth century, Sinagua settlement patterns changed, as did those of the Anasazi and Mogollon, and large pueblos replaced pithouses. Although population had peaked during those years, after 1200 it declined rapidly and the Sinagua departed the Flagstaff area settlements for the Verde Valley to the south. By 1300–1350 the former area was virtually abandoned; the only remaining large northern Sinagua pueblos were located around Chavez Pass.[27]

Although Petrified Forest was the site of significant cultural mingling, it never emerged as any kind of a cultural center. Such blending, archaeologist Yvonne Stewart explains, "is not uncommon, but it has rarely been studied and is poorly understood." Archaeologists have analyzed the influence of cultural groups upon one another around Petrified Forest, an area that one researcher describes as a "frontier" between cultural groups. They generally agree that such interaction is evident from the time of the earliest settlement to the latest.[28]

The oldest habitation site within the present national park is Flattop Village, which the Anasazi occupied prior to A.D. 500. This collection of pithouses located on a mesa in the southern part of the park was probably only a summer residence—a place for the Anasazi to live while they farmed adjacent land. On the valley floor about six miles to the northeast is Twin Buttes Village, which was inhabited from the sixth to ninth centuries. Pottery and a few items made from shell indicate that the residents participated in regional trade that extended as far west as the Gulf of California.

A small Pueblo III site (1100–1250) is perched on a low knoll in Rainbow Forest near the south entrance to the park and is called, appropriately, Agate House. It is constructed entirely of blocks of petrified wood, as are a number of other ruins in the vicinity. Agate House contains only a few rooms and probably was used only for short periods of time, archaeologists believe. Another site from the same period, also in the southern part of the park, is a Mogollon campsite near Jim Camp Wash.

The thirteenth century was a period of widespread drought in the Southwest, and important changes in Indian cultures occurred as inhabitants adapted to the new environment. Despite a general lack of rainfall, some areas retained enough moisture to sustain agriculture. Puerco Indian Ruin is one such location—a 125-room pueblo that was first occupied in the twelfth century. Its residents farmed the floodplains and terraces along the stream, growing beans, squash, and corn. At its height, the village sustained perhaps sixty to seventy-five people, and it had cultural ties with settlements to the west. Its residents left during the drought, but the pueblo was occupied again during the fourteenth century. Rainfall had increased by that time, but precipitation was heaviest in the winter months. The meager summer rainfall came in short, violent thunderstorms that eroded the terraces along the Puerco River and flooded the adjacent farmland. As food production fell off, inhabitants systematically departed by 1400. Investigators have found no evidence of violence or epidemic to suggest that the people were driven away from their pueblo. According to Hopi tradition, the Puerco people moved northward and took up residence on the Hopi mesas. The archaeological sequences indicate that the area now embraced by Petrified Forest National Park was a cultural melting pot. Located between the Anasazi's high plateau and the

Mogollon Rim, the region experienced a variety of influences from surrounding cultures.[29]

When Europeans viewed the region for the first time in the sixteenth
century, the confines of the present Petrified Forest National Park were
devoid of any settlement. In July of 1540, Francisco Vásquez de Coronado
and Fray Marcos reached the Zuni village of Hawikuh. From there Coronado dispatched parties to investigate the surrounding territory. One such
contingent, led by Don Pedro de Tovar, was the first to reach the Hopi
mesas in northeastern Arizona; another detachment followed García López
de Cárdenas westward to the Grand Canyon of the Colorado. Neither
group turned up any evidence of great wealth, as Coronado had hoped
they would. The only evidence of the Spanish presence near Petrified Forest is a brief reference to *Desierto Pintado*.

If other white men passed through the area before the middle of the
nineteenth century, none left an account. Petrified Forest eventually passed
into American ownership in 1848 as part of the Mexican cession following
the U.S. war with Mexico. Little time elapsed before the new American
owners were methodically exploring and surveying their new domain,
and in the process their soldiers and scientists came across the deposits of
petrified trees that wind and rain had uncovered during the previous
centuries.

2

"QUITE A FOREST
OF PETRIFIED TREES"

I've trapped beaver on Platte and Arkansas, and away up on Missoura
and Yaller Stone; I've trapped on Columbia, on Lewis Fork and the
Heely. . . . I've trapped in heav'n, in airth, and h——; and scalp my
old head, marm, but I've seen a putrified forest.

Moses ("Black") Harris, mountain man

Lieutenant James H. Simpson of the United States Corps of Topographical Engineers was the first to record the discovery of petrified wood
in the Southwest and to provide a description of the rock that encased it.
His 1849 discovery occurred not in Petrified Forest but in similar terrain
about one hundred miles to the north in Canyon de Chelly. Simpson was
no scientist and found the specimen simply by chance. He provided only
a brief description of the fossil, including it with his expedition report.
Modern scientists, having read the account, acknowledge that the Canyon
de Chelly fossil was of Triassic age.[1]

Two years later, another topographical engineer led a detachment
through northern Arizona and New Mexico, this time in search of a new
route across the Southwest to California. Captain Lorenzo L. Sitgreaves had
orders to explore the course of the Zuni River to its supposed confluence
with the Colorado and to report on the general characteristics of the region
as well as on the river's potential for navigation. In September of 1851,

Sitgreaves traveled from Zuni Pueblo westward to the Little Colorado River, making camp twice on that stream only a few miles south of the present park boundary. On September 28 the captain abandoned the soft, muddy terrain along the river for higher ground, where his men soon came across "masses of what appeared to have been stumps of trees petrified into jasper, beautifully striped with bright shades of red, blue, white, and yellow." Much of the area, he reported, was strewn with pebbles of agate, jasper, and chalcedony.[2]

Samuel Washington Woodhouse, the thirty-year-old physician and naturalist with the expedition, also commented on the petrified wood. One of the trees, he noted, was broken into pieces as if it had fractured in falling, and its roots faced uphill. Neither Woodhouse nor Sitgreaves offered any explanation for the origins of these fossilized trees, and Richard Kern, who served as the expedition's draftsman, penned only the laconic observation "Fossil tree purple color."[3] Woodhouse, a member of the Academy of Natural Science in Philadelphia, selected three specimens of petrified wood during the expedition's brief visit to the site and in 1859 presented them to the academy. Two of the pieces were lost over the years, but the third still rests there among the institution's collections.[4]

Along the Little Colorado, the Chinle Formation is exposed extensively, giving the terrain around Petrified Forest and Painted Desert its characteristic range of pastel colors. For centuries, wind and rain had slowly uncovered the immense deposits of petrified wood, and Sitgreaves and Woodhouse were among the first Americans to venture into the region. If anyone can be designated as the "discoverers" of the Petrified Forest, that title ought to go to Sitgreaves and Woodhouse. Their discovery of the petrified wood was, of course, incidental to the main task of their expedition, and that perhaps explains why the men commented so briefly on their find. The captain would have missed the trees entirely had he not led his contingent out of the riverbed in search of higher and firmer ground on September 28.

The Sitgreaves party focused on exploration, but the next expedition to visit Petrified Forest operated under a much broader mandate. In an attempt to resolve the intense debate over the route of the country's first transcontinental railroad, Congress in 1853 sought an impartial solution by establishing the Pacific railroad surveys. The legislation placed the surveys under the aegis of the Corps of Topographical Engineers and directed reconnaissances along four potential routes. Of these, a southern road along the thirty-fifth parallel led through northern New Mexico and Arizona, proceeding from Albuquerque to Zuni and then westward through a portion of the Little Colorado River Valley.

Because Congress wanted extensive information about the terrain along the routes, each survey included expert scientists. Individual commanders typically chose their civilian scientists after consultation with Secretary of War Jefferson Davis and his special assistants, Major W. H. Emory of the Topographical Engineers and Captain Andrew A. Humphreys, head of the newly created Bureau of Western Explorations and Surveys. But the Smithsonian Institution, various learned societies, and leading scientists also had a voice in determining the scientific contingents. Louis Agassiz secured the appointment of his colleague, the Swiss geologist Jules Marcou, to the thirty-fifth parallel survey. Similarly, on the recommendation of the great Prussian geographer Baron Alexander von Humboldt, Heinrich Baldwin Möllhausen joined that survey as an artist and topographer. Rounding out the civilian contingent were a physician and a surgeon, both of whom doubled in scientific capacities, an astronomer, engineers, surveyors, and a computer who recorded distances.[5] Leadership of the thirty-fifth parallel survey fell to Lieutenant Amiel Weeks Whipple of the Topographical Engineers.

Whipple left Albuquerque on November 8 and began the trek across northern New Mexico. By the end of the month, his contingent had entered the eastern part of present-day Arizona, and on December 1 they crossed the Puerco River. On the following day the party moved on westward, stopping for the night on a low ridge above a nearly dry streambed that Whipple named Lithodendron Creek. The terrain around the camp was strewn with pottery fragments, and Whipple commented on the numerous pueblo ruins in the area. During their short stay at the site, the men partially excavated the walls of one of the "stone houses." If these remnants of an earlier civilization temporarily engaged the members' imaginations, the discovery of "quite a forest of petrified trees" further intrigued them. None of the trees were standing, and most were buried in red marl, as Whipple described the soil. Some of the logs appeared charred, as if they had been burned before petrification. The main portions of these trees were a dark brown color, Whipple reported, while the smaller branches exhibited a reddish hue. Smaller fragments covered the surface for miles around.[6]

Whipple had led his party into the Black Forest—a deposit of petrified wood located in the Painted Desert in the northern reaches of today's national park. Though fossilized wood is plentiful here, it lacks the diversity and colors exhibited in the park's other "forests," such as Rainbow Forest and Crystal Forest. Still, Whipple wrote that the colors were "as rich and bright as I have seen."[7]

Baldwin Möllhausen, for whom exploration of the West took on the aspect of a romantic adventure, was much more effusive in his description but also remarkably perceptive. "We really thought we saw before us masses of wood that had been floated hither or even a tract of wood land where the timber had been fallen for the purpose of cultivation," he wrote in his diary. Petrified trees of all sizes were scattered over the terrain, including some stumps "with roots that had been left standing."[8] The German's comments are significant. His observation that the petrified logs appeared to have floated into Lithodendron Wash agrees with standard explanations about their origins. Möllhausen was also correct in reporting standing stumps among the more numerous prostrate logs. Later discoveries of such stumps in various locations of the park confirmed that some of the fossil trees had in fact grown in the area.

Möllhausen noticed that most of the long, petrified logs appeared to have been cut into shorter pieces, many of them only a few feet in length. After examining the trees more closely, he concluded that over the years, torrents of water rushing through Lithodendron Wash had left the logs virtually bare of limbs. In his diary, he explained that many of the larger ones were hollow and looked burnt. They were mostly of a darker color, but it was still possible to discern the bark, burnt areas, rings, and cracks that had occurred in the pieces. Whipple had made no provisions for hauling the huge logs, so the men had to be content with collecting fragments from as many different fossil trees as possible. The pieces, Möllhausen wrote, indicated the variety of petrifications in the area, and he regretted

This sketch of Petrified Forest was made by Baldwin Möllhausen during the Whipple Expedition of 1853–1854. Note the stump in the lower right-hand corner, suggesting that some trees were growing at the site. (From Möllhausen's *Diary of a Journey from the Mississippi to the Coasts of the Pacific*, photograph courtesy of Museum of Northern Arizona)

that there was no way to convey the dimensions of the blocks of petrified wood.[9] His own sketches had to suffice to depict the size and characteristics of the fossil logs.

Significantly, the party searched in vain for impressions of leaves and plants but found only some "tree-like ferns." The area contained little vegetation of any kind, and consequently the men passed a cold night encamped near Lithodendron Wash. Nearby were what looked like masses of wood, but "they were the kind that one could only get a spark out of by means of a steel," Möllhausen complained. When the expedition followed down the streambed the next day, the men observed additional deposits of petrified wood along the route. And, like twentieth-century tourists, they could not resist the temptation, Möllhausen wrote, "to alight repeatedly and knock off a piece, now of crimson, now of golden yellow, and then another, glorious in many rainbow dyes." [10]

More sophisticated than Mollhausen's account was the description by Jules Marcou, who had earlier published a controversial geological map of the United States. Although Louis Agassiz had praised the work and recommended Marcou as a geologist with the Whipple survey, the map had engendered harsh criticism from geologists James Dwight Dana and James Hall. W. P. Blake of the Office of Railroad Explorations and Surveys also disputed some of Marcou's findings. [11] Marcou's "Resume and Field Notes" in French were published in parallel columns with Blake's translation in the third volume of the railroad survey reports. His observations are particularly important because Marcou was the first professional geologist to view Arizona's petrified forests and also the first to publish a description of Triassic plant fossils in the Southwest. He recognized that the petrified wood in Lithodendron Wash was coniferous and noted that tree ferns and *Calamodendron* (fossil stems) also occurred. Finally, Marcou correlated the rocks in Lithodendron Wash with the Triassic Keuper Formation in Germany, and that correlation proved essentially correct. "We are in the middle part of the Trias," he recorded in his notes. "No Jurassic." [12]

Although W. P. Blake had not accompanied the expedition, he relied on its reports, illustrations, and specimens to write his own review of the geology of Whipple's route. In it he denied that Marcou had conclusively established the age of the rocks that encased the petrified trees in Lithodendron Wash. Further, he questioned the correlation with the Triassic formation in Europe. Marcou did not identify the terrain as Triassic on the basis of fossils found in Arizona. He simply recognized the similarity of the landscape around Petrified Forest to that in Germany with which he was familiar. Blake was correct in noting that Marcou had not offered any fossil evidence for his contention. [13]

Like the other Pacific railroad surveys, Whipple's examination of the thirty-fifth parallel route was confined to rapid reconnaissance. Consequently, the information it acquired was limited and sometimes lacking in detail. Mid-nineteenth-century paleontologists primarily were stratigraphers, intent upon placing formations in their proper order and correlating sequences with formations elsewhere. Their goal was to use strata to better understand the history of the earth. [14] Möllhausen, in his capacity as topographer and artist, proved a valuable asset, providing many of the illustrations for Whipple's report and for his own diary. His drawings of the topography around Lithodendron Wash and his sketches of petrified trees and stumps were among the first published illustrations of Triassic plant fossils in the Southwest.

The railroad surveys informed Americans more fully about the scenery of the West. More than that, the reports represented a compendium of information about this new region. Members of the various expeditions shared common antebellum assumptions about the landscape and naively anticipated finding magnificent mountains, extensive forests, and sublime views, all of which fit within the context of nineteenth-century romanticism. From studying accounts of earlier explorers, they also knew that they could expect deserts and arid plains. From time to time, at places in the Rocky Mountains and the Cascades, the monumental scenery was overwhelming—just what artists and illustrators hoped for. In other instances the absence of greenery and the stark terrain came as a shock. Oftentimes, historian Anne Farrar Hyde has noted, "stranger kinds of scenery proved more difficult to describe," and sometimes deserts and mountain formations "stunned survey parties into descriptive silence." Whatever their experience with earlier eastern scenery and European aesthetic standards, describing some aspects of the West proved difficult. Since many expedition members were scientists, they understandably retreated to the language of science and simply produced listings of plants, animals, and geographical features.[15]

This was in fact the tendency of Whipple's contingent at Petrified Forest. The lieutenant's comments invariably were terse and factual. Marcou spoke almost exclusively as a scientist, and even the romantic Möllhausen was restrained in his commentary. His illustrations are comparatively simple, unembellished portrayals of petrified logs and stumps. Earlier writers often compared American scenes to those in Europe, but in northeastern Arizona, there was no basis for comparison of landscapes. Petrified forests, the Painted Desert, and surrounding areas had no counterpart elsewhere. The single connection with Europe's geography was Marcou's correlation of the terrain with the Triassic Keuper Formation of Germany.

Möllhausen returned to Germany late in 1854, bringing along a number of specimens of petrified wood for the German paleobotanist H. R.

Goeppert, who identified them as belonging to the coniferous species. One he named *Araucarites möllhausianus* after its discoverer, but he neglected to publish the requisite scientific description. Consequently Möllhausen's name is not linked with the specimen.[16] Möllhausen returned to the American Southwest briefly in 1858 as a member of an expedition led by Lieutenant Joseph C. Ives and paid a last, brief visit to the petrified forests. The trek across northern Arizona provided an opportunity for Ives and geologist John Strong Newberry to examine the terrain north of the Little Colorado, and on May 7 they came across an extensive deposit of petrified wood. These fossil trees exhibited a broad spectrum of colors, ranging from brilliant red jasper to more subtle agate and opalescent chalcedony. Although the location was some sixty miles north of the Black Forest, Newberry was certain that they came from the same rock unit that encased the Lithodendron Wash fossils.[17]

From time to time, other reports of discoveries of petrified wood appeared in print. François X. Aubrey, the enterprising and well-known Santa Fe merchant, mentioned finding a number of very large petrified trees near the Little Colorado in August of 1854. Four years later, Lieutenant Edward F. Beale, in his report *Wagon Road from Fort Defiance to the Colorado River*, described several petrified trees just west of Carisso Creek, thirteen miles from Navajo Springs. Beale's expedition had occasionally followed the indistinct route left by the Whipple survey, and Beale most likely was describing fossil trees that earlier parties had observed. Similarly, in *Seven Years' Residence in the Great Deserts of North America* (1860), Abbé Emmanuel Henri Dieubonné Domenach described "a little forest of petrified trees" on the banks of Lithodendron Wash. His observation that the logs were brown and black in color, as if they had been burnt, suggests that he, too, had wandered into the Black Forest.[18]

The Civil War interrupted scientific explorations and surveys in the Southwest. Following that conflict, the Atlantic and Pacific Railroad Company (which evolved into the Atchison, Topeka, and Santa Fe) was chartered to build along the thirty-fifth parallel, and by the 1880s crews were laying track across northern Arizona. The little towns of Winslow, Holbrook, Adamana, and a few others grew up along the right-of-way. In the 1870s and 1880s, Mormon emigrants settled in the Little Colorado Valley, and ranching emerged as an important economic endeavor. As a consequence of the influx of population, the petrified trees became increasingly well known, and articles about the area appeared in regional and national magazines.

General William Tecumseh Sherman reawakened scientific interest in Arizona's Petrified Forest in 1878. During the course of a cross-country tour, the general stopped at Fort Wingate in western New Mexico Territory. In conversations with the post commander, Lt. Colonel P. T. Swaine, he asked Swaine to procure two specimens of petrified wood "sufficiently large to be worthy of a place in the Smithsonian Institution." That duty fell to Lieutenant J. T. C. Hegewald, who found suitable fossil logs in Lithodendron Wash and forwarded them to Washington.[19]

Professor Frank Knowlton of the National Museum later examined the fossil trees and concluded that they all belonged to the genus *Araucarioxylon* and were probably of the same species. He added that the Smithsonian specimens might be the *Araucarites möllhausianus* that E. H. Goeppert had named in 1854. Since Knowlton could find no description of that specimen and was unable to examine the one Goeppert had deposited at the University of Berlin, he described the specimens under the name *Araucarioxylon arizonicum*.[20]

The soldiers and scientists who had discovered and examined the petrified trees in Lithodendron Wash saw only a small part of a much larger and varied expanse of silicified wood in northeastern Arizona. The discovery of that deposit itself had been accidental, and subsequent visits to the site were generally incidental to other endeavors, such as the Whipple railroad survey. Nevertheless, the early work was significant. Jules Marcou had correctly placed Petrified Forest in the Triassic period, an important first step in identifying the region's ancient environment.

Neither Marcou nor his detractors then realized the implications of his bold assertion. Today's scientists view the 30 million years of Triassic history as a critical time of transition—a geologic period that intervenes between an old and a new world. Some amphibians typical of Permian faunas disappeared before or during the transition from Permian to Triassic. Others, such as labyrinthodonts and therapsids, survived to become prominent Triassic faunas. Appearing at the beginning of the Triassic and continuing on to their extinction at the end of the period were the newcomers—the thecodont reptiles, "harbingers of the future," one authority has called them, whose descendants would inherit the earth during the late Triassic and the next two geologic periods.[21]

For the last decade of the nineteenth century, Petrified Forest was on the fringes of scientific investigation in the Southwest. Archaeologists—and in some cases untutored pothunters—actively dug into prehistoric sites in the region, and geologists similarly continued their research into the earth's history. But for the time being, that activity occurred beyond the boundaries of the present park. New discoveries of petrified wood in those years were due to the meanderings of curious travelers and enterprising businessmen.

Although a number of parties had visited Lithodendron Wash, it was not the only location in the area that contained extensive deposits of petrified wood. By the latter part of the nineteenth century, it was not even the best known. About twenty miles south of the Black Forest and only eight miles south of Adamana station on the Santa Fe line, a broad expanse of petrified wood already was being heralded as "Chalcedony Park" by residents of Holbrook and other small towns in the vicinity. Because of its close proximity to the railroad, the so-called park attracted a growing number of visitors. In contrast to the expedition scientists who examined the petrified trees in Lithodendron Wash, few of the tourists who visited Chalcedony Park had any framework for understanding these sites. Some were awestruck, others simply puzzled by the scene.

Once tourists reached such isolated places as Holbrook, Carrizo, or Adamana, they had to depend on their own resourcefulness to reach Chalcedony Park. One of the first to publish his impressions was the Reverend H. C. Hovey, who interrupted his eastward journey aboard the California Express in 1892 to visit the site. Fearing that he might miss Petrified Forest entirely, Hovey appealed to the conductor, who arranged to stop the train briefly at whistling point 233. The conductor pointed across the desolate terrain to a windmill visible on the far horizon, identifying it as Adam Hanna's ranch, the only house within ten miles. "Maybe you can get a horse there," he told Hovey. "If not you can foot it in the morning." Moments later the California Express disappeared in the distance, leaving the clergyman and his Kodak alone in the desolate high desert.[22]

Hovey successfully reached Hanna's ranch and rented a horse for the ride to the petrified forest. There he spent several days exploring the scattered deposits of fossil wood. Later he warned readers of *Scientific American* that no actual forest existed there, despite the tendency of local residents to boast of their Petrified Forest. Nor was there anything resembling a park, though everyone freely described the place as Chalcedony Park. Instead, the scene reminded Hovey of a logging camp, where lumberjacks had tossed the huge trees at random, leaving them to become rain soaked and moss covered. Hovey nonetheless delighted in the brilliant petrified logs and gathered plenty of specimens to take home. "Each crystal or moss agate, or amethyst, or onyx, seems most desirable till it lies in your pocket or saddle pouch," he wrote, "and then others assert their superiority."[23]

Hovey departed the forest reluctantly, made his way back to Hanna's to return the horse, then flagged down an approaching train to resume his journey. Content with his pouch of glistening treasures, Hovey was convinced that "whatever marvels may have existed in the days of Arabian Nights' entertainment, none in these more modern times could rival, in its way, the petrified forests of Arizona." Like many subsequent visitors, the Reverend Mr. Hovey advocated establishing a national park there, both to protect the deposits and to improve access to them.[24]

Few visitors experienced as many difficulties as did Hovey, and most easily arranged transportation from Holbrook or Adamana. But like him, they tended to interpret the words "forest" and "park" literally. Both terms evoked precise images in the nineteenth century, and writers were determined to disabuse their readers of any images of well-groomed parklands or tall pine forests. S. A. Miller, for example, in 1894 warned members of the Cincinnati Society of Natural History to "cast out of mind the idea of a forest, for there is none." Instead, he prepared his readers to find petrified logs broken into short pieces, some even shattered, and strewn across the landscape. The phrase "Chalcedony Park," he pointed out, was simply erroneous.[25]

The leading nineteenth-century authority on precious stones and gems was George Frederick Kunz. He discussed Arizona's Petrified Forest in a brief article in the *Popular Science Monthly*, and in his well-known *Gems and Precious Stones of North America* he speculated about the uses and value of the chalcedony, jasper, and agate that abounded in the area. He estimated that the deposits contained a million tons of fossil wood, but only a small portion of it was suitable for decorative purposes. At that time, petrified wood had been used in only one major work—the base of a silver centerpiece that was presented to the sculptor F. A. Bartholdi. Joseph Pulitzer had selected the wood, and the Tiffany Company of New York had cut and polished it into a low, truncated pyramid that measured eleven inches square at the base and was ten inches high. It was, according to Kunz, the largest piece of petrified wood that had been cut into a definite shape in this country. He was convinced that the hard, lustrous material would be useful for various interior decorations in exclusive American homes, including floor tiles, mantles, clock cases, table tops, and similar items.[26]

Popular scientific magazines invariably carried illustrations of the more dramatic features of Petrified Forest. The *Scientific American Supplement* of September 1889 included pictures of places that it identified as "Jasper Hill" and "Chalcedony Canyon" along with an illustration of the "Natural Bridge," now called Agate Bridge, which it described as "an entire tree converted to silex."[27] Photographers never tired of shooting it, particularly when a small crowd of tourists could be induced to pose on top.

If popular writers acquainted people with the petrified forests, they also supplied varying amounts of information that was simply wrong, albeit interesting. The writer of a column for young people in the *Cambrian* explained that "the great forest was petrified, not fallen as we now find it, but standing in hot or warm waters." Ages later, this imaginative writer continued, earthquakes caused the lakes to drain and also threw down the fossil trees, leaving them broken and strewn across the high desert.[28] Writing in *Frank Leslie's Popular Monthly* in 1887, C. F. Holder suggested that nearby volcanoes suddenly spewed millions of tons of ash and lava into the forest. "The weight of the shower may have broken many trees down," he suggested, "or an earthquake felled them to the ground."[29] Foremost among the proponents of the earthquake theory was the exuberant author of *Some Strange Corners of Our Country* and editor of *Land of Sunshine*, Charles F. Lummis. "I can conceive of but one power that can have mowed them down so marshalled—an earthquake of the first dimension, traveling from the crest of the continent southerly." Later, he theorized, the trees were "embalmed to perennial gems."[30] In the late nineteenth century, such explanations seemed reasonable, and ash from volcanoes, of course, did play an important role in the process of petrification. But neither volcanoes nor earthquakes were responsible for toppling the ancient trees.

By 1891, when *Some Strange Corners of Our Country* appeared, Lummis already had traveled extensively in the Southwest and had written sensitively about its people and culture. The volume is subtitled *The Wonderland of the Southwest*, and Lummis included descriptions of the Grand Canyon, Montezuma Castle, Canyon de Chelly, Petrified Forest, and other unique places. In a brief article, "A Forest of Agate," he explained that the petrified trees revealed much about the history "uncounted millenniums" earlier, when the region had been inundated by the sea. The erosion that had exposed the fossil trees was a comparatively recent phenomenon, he wrote. A close observer of nature, Lummis recognized that Petrified Forest was an important link with the past. Whatever the geological implications, Lummis was more concerned to place the petrified trees within his book's theme of "strange corners," and he wrote enthusiastically about "this great natural curiosity—the huge Petrified Forest of Arizona." It was, he boasted, "an enchanted spot" where one seemed "to stand on the glass of a gigantic kaleidoscope, over whose sparkling surface the sun breaks in infinite rainbows." The rainbow forests were remarkable to look at—great curiosities, like many other novel places in the region. As was often the case among popular writers, scientific importance was overwhelmed by the tendency to describe natural phenomena as wonders, oddities, and curiosities.[31]

Neither scientists nor popular writers had yet given educated Americans any precise reasons to preserve the petrified forests, beyond the simple plea to save the colorful deposits for future generations. Not many Americans in the late nineteenth century thought in terms of geologic time, and no one had fashioned any critical link between contemporary life and the continent's ancient landscape. While Americans might describe Petrified Forest as a natural wonder, clearly this reserve fell short of the monumental scenery at Yellowstone or Grand Canyon. The petrified trees, consequently, often were relegated to the status of curiosities that attracted tourists and perhaps businessmen who might find a market for the commodity.

By the last decade of the century, Petrified Forest was easily accessible. The little settlement at Adamana never developed beyond the few buildings clustered along the Santa Fe right-of-way, but it quickly became the most important gathering point for visitors to the petrified forests. Santa Fe Railroad officials arbitrarily named the place by combining the names of Adam and Anna Hanna to produce Adamana. For several years, Hanna had run stock in the area, but he recognized early the benefits of meeting tourists at the station and conducting them to his ranch, from which they could easily visit the forests.

Late in the summer of 1895, Hanna greeted a group of Californians at the station. Leading the contingent was Pasadena bookstore operator Adam Clark Vroman, who later would gain fame for his photographs of southwestern Indians. With him were Mrs. Thaddeus Lowe, Horatio Nelson Rust, and C. J. Crandall. Hanna loaded them into his lumber wagon, and he and a nephew guided them through the collections of petrified trees nearest the ranch. "The team was slow beyond measure," Vroman complained, "and the road nearly as smooth as no road at all. Simply a trail." [32] He was equally disappointed when he found no standing trees but "simply broken pieces of petrified wood lying about." He recognized, too, the limits of black and white photography. "To capture the intensity and variety of colors in this wonderful freak of nature is difficult," he acknowledged; "the one thing lacking, Color, is so important." Nevertheless, Vroman took a number of pictures and could not resist lining up his friends on the agate bridge for the customary photograph. Jotted on the back of the picture is Vroman's telling comment: "Some heathen will lay a pound of dynamite on it some day, just to see it fall and thus removes [sic] the most interesting part of the forest." [33]

Vroman may have been simply predicting the future, but his statement more likely was a comment on the destruction of the fossil logs. Vandals and souvenir hunters had carried off untold amounts of petrified wood already. Even more destructive were crews of men, some hired by eastern jewelers, who dynamited the logs in search of the quartz and amethyst crystals often found on the inside. Since the mid-1880s, the semiprecious fossil wood had been the object of occasional business ventures. Because of its extreme hardness and myriad colors, petrified wood had the potential for numerous uses, particularly in decorating homes, as George Kunz had predicted. When cut and polished, it exhibited a lustrous finish that was nearly impossible to mar. Even smaller pieces, when carefully cut and polished, could be fashioned into cane and umbrella handles, paperweights, jewelry, and similar items.

The late nineteenth century was a time of sustained economic growth in the United States. The industrialization and urbanization of the East

Coast and upper Midwest had its counterpart in the exploitation of western resources from forests and grazing land to mineral deposits. Entrepreneurs in the West had little appreciation for scenery and were determined to develop resources, regardless of an area's designation as national park or forest reserve. The country's few national parks already bore the marks of visitors and developers. Fences, haphazard construction, and extensive grazing had marred the Yosemite Valley, and before Yosemite National Park was established in 1890 thousands of acres of pristine forest lands fell to private operators. At Yellowstone, game was slaughtered and geysers and craters defaced. As early as 1882, Yellowstone's historian Richard Bartlett has written, the park was "already under siege." Both parks eventually passed under temporary administration by the U.S. Army. Others were not so fortunate. Redwoods in Santa Clara and Santa Cruz Counties, California, as well as the East Bay, were cut during the gold rush years and used to build Oakland, Berkeley, and the towns in Santa Clara County. At Arizona's Grand Canyon, prospectors filed mining claims, and when Congress established Mount Rainier National Park at the end of the century, the legislators allowed mining and mineral exploration to continue. In short, exploitation of resources was common in the various federal reserves in the West. The deposits of petrified wood inspired the same kind of economic interest. Mineralized wood was potentially valuable, and optimistic businessmen understandably envisioned these deposits as the core of future wealth.[34]

To take advantage of the seemingly endless supply of petrified wood in the region, a group of San Francisco businessmen organized the Chalcedony Manufacturing Company in 1884, filed several mining claims in the deposits of petrified wood, and within a short time shipped about fifteen hundred pounds back to San Francisco. Their crude lapidary equipment proved incapable of cutting and polishing the wood, and the partners soon became disillusioned. When William Adams Jr. offered to buy out their operation for two thousand dollars a year later, the Californians were happy to turn the enterprise over to him.[35]

The new owner, "Petrified Adams" to local residents, would never realize his dreams of wealth, although he reorganized his Jasperized Wood and Mineral Company several times in the 1880s. To secure a constant supply of petrified wood he hit upon the novel idea of filing placer claims, reasoning that these stone trees were, after all, mineralized. In all, his company tied up more than eighteen hundred acres that included extensive deposits of petrified logs. Still the operation did not prosper.[36]

In the meantime, the U.S General Land Office became suspicious of Adams's activities, despite his pleas that his workers had caused little damage to the petrified trees and had removed nothing that would injure the value of the site. Still, Adams had shipped out some eighteen tons of petrified wood by the summer of 1888, and the General Land Office wanted his operations curtailed. Tom M. Bowers, an agent on the scene, advised that petrified logs be designated specifically as wood, not minerals, and therefore not subject to the Mining Law of 1872. Adams's claims therefore could be canceled or declared vacant. Concerned by this federal threat to his enterprise, Adams quickly secured a lease to operate on Santa Fe Railroad land.[37]

Most of the petrified wood from this area was shipped to Sioux Falls, South Dakota, where the Drake Company had established a business to cut, polish, and market petrified wood. In addition to Col. James H. Drake, associates included the Arizonans Francis Hatch and Frederick Tritle. Drake spent years experimenting with various methods of cutting and polishing silicified wood before he ever succeeded. Even then, he later admitted to John Muir, the enterprise had not been a financial success. "I fancy that we threw into the waste heap material which represented $25,000 in expenditures," he complained. The major problem was not only the hardness of the petrified wood but the fact that it also was extremely brittle. After virtually days of careful, monotonous sawing, Drake explained, the pieces often cracked and then broke. By 1906, he simply had stopped working with the material.[38]

What success the company enjoyed had been limited to its exhibition and sales at the Chicago World's Fair. Drake displayed polished slabs of petrified wood both in the Arizona Building and in the Manufacturers' Building, and thousands of visitors admired the specimens. But even at that early date, it was evident that Arizona's petrified forests contained few logs that were sufficiently perfect for the production of large flawless slabs. Any large objects fashioned from petrified wood were destined to be costly luxuries.[39] At best, smaller segments might suffice for such items as cane handles and paperweights. The single exception remained the base for the Tiffany centerpiece that had been presented to Bartholdi.

Despite the dreams of wealth held by people like Adams and his partners, the cutting, polishing, and sale of petrified wood never proved profitable. The Jasperized Wood Company must have exercised a near monopoly on the supply of the commodity, but the business never amassed the wealth its owners anticipated. In the 1892 edition of *Gems and Precious Stones of North America*, George Frederick Kunz provided estimates of the value of silicified wood produced and sold in the United States. The total for 1883 was only $5,000; in 1884, $10,500; and in 1885, $6,500. The last years of the decade showed some improvement, particularly 1887, when $35,000 worth of silicified wood was sold as specimens and curiosities and another $1,000 worth sold for cutting into gems.[40] A year later, though, the annual total was down to $16,500—well above the figure for the early 1880s but hardly enough to sustain businesses of any size. Moreover, Kunz's figures reflected national sales of petrified wood, not just the commodities produced in northeastern Arizona.

Because of the expense and difficulty of cutting and polishing petrified wood, Adams found the demand for his wood gradually tapering off. But theft and vandalism at the hands of visitors continued unabated, and a new threat emerged when a Chicago company made plans to erect a stamp mill to crush petrified wood for industrial abrasives. By then, Arizonans living in the vicinity of Chalcedony Park already were concerned about the depredations. Territorial Representative Will C. Barnes and several Holbrook residents took the initiative in a movement to preserve the area's scenic and scientific wonders. On February 1, 1895, Barnes introduced in the Eighteenth Territorial Legislature House Memorial No. 4, which called on the General Land Office to withdraw from settlement all public lands covered by the petrified forests until an investigation was undertaken to determine whether the sites deserved federal protection as a national park or reserve.[41]

The threat posed by the abrasives company had repercussions far from Arizona. The firm had announced its intentions in the *Albuquerque Democrat*, and before long word had filtered back to the Interior Department in Washington. Secretary David R. Francis, alarmed that Armstrong Abrasives of Chicago was "appropriating the petrified forest and shipping it back to Chicago where it will be converted into grindstones and emerywheels," asked the GLO to dispatch an inspector to the site immediately. On December 15, he followed up with a proclamation formally withdrawing from settlement two townships containing deposits of petrified wood.[42] By his quick action, Secretary Francis had satisfied the first part of the Arizona memorial—withdrawal of the land from settlement. A similar proclamation four years later doubled the amount of land closed to public entry. Such actions obviously were temporary expedients, but they were the only measures the federal government could employ to protect valuable sites at that time.

The memorial itself was critically important in the lengthy procedure that culminated eleven years later in a presidential proclamation that established Petrified Forest National Monument. It put Arizona's politicians squarely behind the effort to preserve the valuable deposits, and in the intervening years, scientists, local residents, bureaucrats, and political leaders laid the foundations for preserving the Petrified Forest. Though little would be done immediately to prevent thefts and vandalism, settlers were directed elsewhere, and the forests gained a temporary reprieve from commercial development.

3

PETRIFIED FOREST
NATIONAL MONUMENT

The dog poisoner, the library mutilator and thief, the despoiler of our
monuments—these three should be boiled in oil (beginning at zero).

Charles F. Lummis

Closing the petrified forests to settlement was one thing; offering the sites real protection was another. Establishment of a Petrified Forest
National Park was a possibility, presuming that the collections of fossil
logs could meet the ill-defined requirements for a national park. Failing
that, new legislation was needed to extend federal protection to natural
sites like Petrified Forest. In fact, these ancient forests were not unique
in suffering at the hands of thieves and vandals. Throughout the Southwest, hundreds of prehistoric ruins—America's antiquities—faced similar
threats. Within the next decade, archaeological sites, along with historical
places and objects of scientific interest, all fell under the protection of the
federal government when Congress passed the 1906 Act for the Preservation of American Antiquities.[1]

In the meantime, local residents remained concerned about theft and
vandalism in the forests, and the stamp mill, though not operating, repre-

sented an overwhelming threat to the integrity of any future national park.[2] The owners never started the mill, and the reason has never been fully explained. If Congressman John F. Lacey of Iowa is correct, this "commercial vandalism" was averted only because another suitable stone was found in Canada.[3] At the same time, jewelry and lapidary companies were losing interest in petrified wood as a semiprecious commodity, primarily because it was so difficult to cut.

S. J. Holsinger, special agent for the General Land Office, conducted a thorough examination of Petrified Forest in 1899 and was grateful to learn that comparatively little fossil wood was then being shipped out. More important, he found enthusiastic support among local residents for establishing a federal reserve to protect the petrified wood, the only opponent being Adam Hanna. Holsinger's own examination of the sites convinced him that the region deserved such protection, and he suggested the name of Chalcedonia National Park—the first official notice that the area deserved protection.[4] The budding national park movement caught the attention of Charles Lummis, who praised the effort in Land of Sunshine. Protecting the petrified forests would represent an important step in preserving numerous sites in Arizona and New Mexico from the "relic-seekers and money grabbers," he proclaimed. The Arizona Graphic agreed, adding that the next generation would not find a pound of petrified wood if the government did not protect it.[5]

Holsinger was not the only federal agent roaming around Chalcedony Park in 1899. In response to the Arizona Legislature's memorial, GLO Commissioner Binger Hermann went to the Smithsonian Institution for information about the site's potential as a national park. The Smithsonian called on Lester Frank Ward, a paleobotanist with the U.S. Geological Survey and associate curator of the National Museum, to visit the forest and determine whether it should be designated as a national park.

Ward arrived in Holbrook on November 9, 1899, and on the following day proceeded to the petrified forests to begin his work. His subsequent report was precisely what Arizona park proponents wanted, for Ward stated that the earlier descriptions by Möllhausen, Marcou, Newberry, and other early explorers had understated both the scientific importance and the popular appeal of petrified forests. The fossil trees truly were among the country's natural wonders, and Ward recommended that the government not only preserve them but advertise the sites for American tourists.[6]

The petrified trees in northeastern Arizona were millions of years older than those found in Yellowstone and in California. Ward placed them in Mesozoic time and probably of Triassic age, as compared to the Tertiary age (66 million to 1.6 million years old) of the others. Blocks of petrified wood of Triassic age occur in other locations, but the Arizona deposits were much more extensive and were the only ones, according to Ward, that deserved the designation of forest. Ward also was impressed by the unique forms and varied colors exhibited in Chalcedony Park and the nearby deposits. These, he noted, were the major attractions for visitors. The state of mineralization placed some of these specimens in the category of gems and precious stones. Chalcedony and agates were common, many approaching the characteristics of jasper and onyx.[7]

Ward added an additional important argument in support of protecting the ancient forests. The stone trees were a source of wonder for visitors. Already mere curiosity had attracted thousands of people to Petrified Forest, and however aimless it might appear, Ward was convinced that curiosity formed the "true foundation of all discovery and progress" and should be carefully nurtured. Here was a natural site that might stimulate the imagination of visitors and expand their perception of the country's ancient natural environment.

The number of visitors and relic hunters naturally would increase, necessitating measures to reduce vandalism and theft. He realized what local residents had known for years—that visitors would take as many specimens as they could carry, although these would likely be only smaller fragments. Ward's report identified the crucial dilemma that would always confront personnel at Petrified Forest: how to facilitate public access to the remarkable collection of fossilized logs while at the same time protecting them from those very visitors. (See also chapter 4 on Ward.)

Ward's observations identified both the scientific value and the popular appeal of Petrified Forest, and he also suggested a framework for interpretive programs to stimulate and guide the natural curiosity of visitors. Yet a critical ingredient of national parks did not figure in his writings on Petrified Forest, or in any of the commentaries of nineteenth-century visitors. Monumental scenery (or variations of that theme), perhaps the feature that most clearly identified the existing six national parks, never appeared in

descriptions of Petrified Forest. The fossil forests were remarkable and exhibited their own beauty—but not on the scale of the other parks. Consequently, early arguments for a Petrified Forest National Park would have to
rest on other considerations—namely the need to protect this resource
from vandals, thieves, and entrepreneurs. Lack of magnificent scenery did
not always preclude the park designation. The definition of what constituted a national park remained fluid in the early twentieth century, and a
number of small reserves in fact acquired park status.

Because he spoke with the disinterested voice of science, Ward provided
critical support for the establishment of a national park to embrace Chalcedony Park and the deposits of petrified wood in the vicinity. Promoters
naturally relied on his report as they sought to advance their cause over the
next few years. Even before the Smithsonian Institution published Ward's
report, "The Petrified Forests of Arizona," Congressman John F. Lacey of
Iowa introduced a bill in the Fifty-sixth Congress in 1900 to establish Petrified Forest National Park. A veteran supporter of measures to support
wildlife and forests, Lacey also became interested in the preservation of
prehistoric ruins in the Southwest and actively promoted legislation to
protect these American antiquities. He was a natural advocate for Petrified
Forest, which he praised in Congress as "a more wonderful scene than
even the Grand Canyon itself." But the focus of his comments was on its
vulnerability. "The Grand Canyon of the Colorado and the sunny climate
of Arizona can take care of themselves," he told members of the House of
Representatives, "but the Petrified Forest will be destroyed unless it is protected by law."[8]

Lacey's comments convinced House members, but the bill failed in the
Senate. Two years later, in 1902, the Iowan was back in the House of Representatives with essentially the same bill. This time he defended the measure on the basis of the future park's location adjacent to the Santa Fe line,
emphasizing that increasing numbers of tourists would visit the place if
decent facilities were available. Further, the forest was located in an "at-
mosphere of the purest and cleanest air ever breathed." The surrounding
land was of practically no value, he added, therefore, preserving it would
not interfere with any settlement in the area. Lacey's bill embraced about
two townships and included an important provision authorizing the secretary of the interior to acquire private holdings within the proposed park

through land exchanges. The Santa Fe Railroad owned alternate sections in the area, but Lacey again assured his colleagues that there were no settlers and that the land was "utterly worthless for any agricultural purposes." In so defending park status for Petrified Forest, Lacey employed a theme that consistently has been used in behalf of national parks—the useless scenery argument. Parks were fashioned only from terrain that held no value for miners, lumbermen, ranchers, or farmers, even though the scenery itself might be spectacular. The requirement of uselessness was an unwritten policy, but no other qualification outweighed it.[9]

The bill engendered no debate and little questioning from Lacey's colleagues in the House. It passed easily and was forwarded to the Senate, where it died in the Committee on Public Lands, as had its predecessor. Another measure failed in 1904. Lacey introduced a similar version in 1906, noting that the House had passed bills to establish Petrified Forest National Park in the Fifty-sixth, Fifty-seventh, and Fifty-eighth Congresses. "For some reason I have never been able to learn why," he complained, "the bill has not received favorable action at the other end of the capitol." It had the support of the Interior Department and the General Land Office, and the House Committee on Public Lands also strongly recommended its passage.[10] But this measure, too, died in the Senate Committee on Public Lands.

In the course of debates on Lacey's Petrified Forest bills, congressmen had raised few questions. Only in 1902 did his colleagues press Lacey for any major revision, and then their concern focused only on that bill's land exchange provision. Serano E. Payne of New York, along with a few others, worried that private landowners within the proposed park's boundaries might trade their worthless land for more extensive or more valuable acreage elsewhere. But Lacey included restrictions that virtually eliminated that prospect. That same issue might have arisen in the Senate Public Lands Committee and may explain why the bill never made it out of committee. Arizona then was still a territory, represented in Congress by a single nonvoting delegate. With no effective representation in either house, Arizonans who favored the measures simply lacked the political influence to push the measure through Congress.

The Petrified Forest bills likely were casualties of the still loosely defined guidelines for establishing national parks. At that early date, a full decade before the establishment of the National Park Service, the federal government had not evolved a coherent set of guidelines for national parks. In the late nineteenth and early twentieth centuries, Congress had authorized a number of new parks that ranged from Yosemite, Crater Lake, and Mount Rainier to the "inferior parks" at Platt, Wind River, and Sully's Hill. The latter small, "unworthy" parks, historian John Ise complained, simply did not meet the standards embodied in the other "superlative" national parks. In 1906 Congress established Mesa Verde National Park to protect the cliff dwellings in southwestern Colorado, but carefully restricted its acreage to include only the prehistoric sites. The diversity of those national parks underscores the vague requirements that Congress applied to expansion of the country's park system. "If the government had a plan for the parks it was establishing," Joseph Sax has observed, "it certainly was casual about it." [11]

For its part, Congress could exhibit a reluctance bordering on stubbornness when considering new parks; at other times it greeted new park proposals with apathy. An earlier bill for Crater Lake National Park engendered no serious opposition when proponents first introduced it, historian H. Duane Hampton has pointed out. Yet sixteen years elapsed before the legislation received approval in 1902. Similarly, the proposed Mesa Verde National Park encountered no opposition in 1891, but its adherents petitioned Congress until 1906 before the new park was finally authorized. Had the 1906 Act for the Preservation of American Antiquities been on the books earlier, Robert W. Righter has speculated, Crater Lake and Mesa Verde would have been designated national monuments and then quickly "upgraded" to national parks. This "monument-to-park" device represented a handy way to circumvent a belligerent, reluctant, or merely apathetic Congress. Petrified Forest lost its last bid for national park status just after Congress passed the Antiquities Act. Consequently it was an obvious candidate for preservation under the new law. [12]

The energetic Congressman Lacey was among the key figures in shaping that legislation. During the same years when he had shepherded the park measure through the House, he also actively supported bills to protect American antiquities. Throughout the Southwest, theft and vandalism were common occurrences in the isolated prehistoric ruins that dotted the region. Such depredations eventually stimulated a movement to protect all places that contained archaeological sites. That endeavor, if broadened to include scientific and natural sites, might also contribute to the preservation of the Petrified Forest. Although Lacey and others had always praised the valuable deposits of fossil wood there, the site also included a number of important ruins.

Scientists and academics from eastern universities and museums increasingly added their powerful support to the antiquities movement, and they could count on assistance from the Bureau of Ethnology and the Archaeological Institute of America, among other professional organizations. Similarly, the Office of Indian Affairs and the Geological Survey both were concerned about such vandalism on federal lands. Secretary of the Interior Ethan Allen Hitchcock was sympathetic to the movement, as were GLO Commissioners Binger Hermann and W. A. Richards. But the federal government could provide no real protection for archaeological sites, any more than it could safeguard the deposits of petrified wood. Commissioner Richards withdrew some sites from settlement and appointed temporary custodians to look after them, charging these new officials to post notices against trespassing. The General Land Office could punish trespassers, if they were caught. But the agency lacked the personnel to make arrests.

Nor did Congress provide much immediate assistance. Four bills to protect American antiquities were introduced in 1900, but none were successful. Measures proposed in 1904 and 1905 fared no better.[13] Despite setbacks in Congress, proponents of a vigorous federal policy of protecting cultural and natural sites persevered. Edgar L. Hewett of the Bureau of Ethnology, in particular, worked closely with federal officials and Congressman Lacey. In 1902, Hewett guided Lacey on a visit to Santa Fe and to the cliff dweller sites in the Pajarito region, providing the congressman with a firsthand introduction to archaeological sites in the Southwest.[14] The knowledge Lacey gained proved valuable in drafting legislation to protect antiquities.

In 1904, Hewett provided an assessment of the archaeological sites in the Southwest; by that date the very abundance of ruins had attracted numerous dealers, souvenir hunters, and vandals. Thousands of pieces of excavated pottery had been shipped from Holbrook alone, he observed, and dealers in the vicinity had extensive collections for sale.[15] Any person familiar with Petrified Forest might have added a similar statement about specimens of fossil wood.

To halt the trade and the damage it caused, Hewett recommended that the Department of the Interior employ inspectors or custodians to protect all ruins in the public domain. Further, he cited the need for legislation to create national parks and monuments and to restrict excavations of ruins, solely in the interest of science. When Hewett introduced the designation of monument, he actually added a new category of federal reserve. The precise origins of the phrase are uncertain, although Hewett obviously was thinking of a federal site that was smaller and more restricted than the familiar national parks. "If a single cliff dwelling, pueblo ruin, shrine, etc., could be declared a 'national monument' and its protection provided for," he argued, "it would cover many important cases and obviate the objections made to large reservations."[16] Like his colleagues in the antiquities movement, Hewett realized that Congress was not anxious to expand the country's neophyte park system by adding numerous small parks. The new national monument category, then, represented an alternative means to preserve and protect smaller sites. Further, the very title of national monument reflected the country's enduring quest to further buttress its cultural identity. Alfred Runte has speculated that Americans substituted the dwellings of prehistoric Indians for Greek and Roman ruins in the New World.[17]

When the American Anthropological Association and the Archaeological Institute of America met jointly in 1905, Hewett had ready a draft of his bill for the protection of American antiquities and presented it to the gathering. He had wisely drawn the measure to appeal to a broad spectrum of interested parties—not only to scientists and academics but to bureaucrats and concerned citizens as well. It required the various federal departments to watch over the ruins they administered and included objects of historic and scientific interest in addition to prehistoric structures. Hewett's proposed law gave the president the power to establish national monuments by proclamation, subject only to the provision that such sites be no larger than necessary for their proper care and management.[18]

On January 9, 1906, Lacey introduced Hewett's bill in the House, and Colorado's Thomas Patterson proposed the same measure in the Senate. It cleared both houses, and on June 8, Theodore Roosevelt signed the measure, known officially as An Act for the Preservation of American

Antiquities. It included the essential provision that Hewett had earlier presented to his colleagues—presidential authority to proclaim national monuments, defined as "historic landmarks, historic and prehistoric structures, and other objects of historic or scientific interest." These new monuments were to be confined to "the smallest area compatible with the proper care and management of the objects to be protected."[19]

The Antiquities Act not only opened a broad range of sites for designation as national monuments; it also granted the president considerable discretion. Since congressional approval was not required, the only legal restriction was the stipulation that monuments be selected from unappropriated public domain or from land acquired as a gift from a private donor. Inclusion of sites considered to be "of scientific interest" clearly expanded the scope of the law, and in Theodore Roosevelt preservationists had a president who was inclined to interpret his authority liberally and to implement it immediately. On September 24, he established Devil's Tower in Wyoming as the country's first national monument, and on December 8, he expanded the list to include Petrified Forest, Montezuma Castle, and El Morro.

The Chalcedony Park of northeastern Arizona now became Petrified Forest National Monument, having met the requirements of a scientific site, at least to the satisfaction of the president. The new monument included the deposits described by Lester Frank Ward, embracing ninety-five square miles (60,776 acres) between the Puerco River and the Little Colorado.[20] For Arizonans, the monument designation represented the culmination of a quest begun eleven years earlier with the Territorial Legislature's Memorial No. 4. True, there would be no Petrified Forest National Park, but the Antiquities Act at least extended federal protection to a vulnerable natural site that Congress consistently had refused to consider for park status. There always was the possibility that, at a more favorable time, the monument might be raised to a national park.[21]

Proponents recognized that designation as a monument afforded Petrified Forest and other sites only minimal protection. Congress had not bothered to allocate any money for the administration of the new reserves; indeed, no funds were forthcoming until after passage of the National Park Service Act a decade later. Consequently the newly created monuments languished under ad hoc administration and supervision. Often, custodians appointed by the GLO could do little more than cover the terrain with warning signs in the hope of deterring vandals and thieves.

The new law had been shaped by the desperate need to protect archaeological, historic, and scientific sites, and its authors consequently had not elaborated on the role that these monuments might play in the country's expanding park system. National parks, following precedents at Yosemite and Yellowstone, not only protected scenery and wildlife but also served as places of resort and recreation for Americans. The Antiquities Act prescribed no similar function for national monuments, although most of them attracted at least some tourists. A number of monuments, such as Zion, Bryce Canyon, and Grand Canyon, possessed sufficient scenic resources to warrant elevation to national parks in a comparatively short time.

Where this left Petrified Forest is not clear. The Santa Fe Railroad guaranteed a substantial number of visitors, and after World War I automobiles vastly expanded the number of tourists at the reserve. Because of excellent rail and highway access, Petrified Forest often attracted more people than did some of the national parks. Yet no one had considered how to convey the significance of the reserve's ancient environment to American tourists. Lacking such an interpretive plan, Petrified Forest always faced the prospect of becoming little more than a tourist attraction along the Santa Fe line and the National Old Trails Highway and its successor, Route 66.

While Congress was considering the Petrified Forest National Park bills and the various antiquities measures, the General Land Office looked for ways to protect the deposits of petrified wood. In 1900 the commissioner appointed special agent Holsinger as temporary custodian there and ordered him to place notices warning against trespassing. On a brief visit in the spring of 1903, Holsinger talked with Al Stevenson, proprietor of the recently built Forest Hotel at Adamana, hoping to determine the extent of theft from the various forests. He learned that each visitor carried off about ten to fifteen pounds of specimens. The 1902 guest register at the hotel indicated that 823 people had visited the Petrified Forest from Adamana and perhaps another hundred came from Holbrook. Based on these figures, the custodian calculated that visitors had carried away more than four and a half tons of specimens and chips that year. The figure represented only a small part of the damage, Holsinger told the commissioner.

Visitors picked up specimens from the most accessible sites in the forest and thereby seriously marred its beauty. "Photography and vandalism appear here to stalk hand in hand," he lamented. "The visitor first secures a photograph and then must have a specimen from the object of the photograph."[22]

Instead of hiring a resident custodian for Petrified Forest, the General Land Office resorted to appointing volunteers to serve as assistant custodians. Eventually a permanent official would take over, but in the meantime the volunteers could be given badges similar to those issued to personnel at Yellowstone and Yosemite. The solution was hardly ideal, but it was better than nothing. Otherwise, Holsinger warned, there would be no official "to stay the hand of the vandal or the greed of the specimen hunter." In the end, the combination of volunteer custodians and the agent's visits might be sufficient to reduce vandalism and theft.[23]

Predictably, the arrangement failed to prevent vandalism. In fact, there was no easy solution to the GLO's dilemma in the early years of the century. The country possessed a number of parks and monuments, but the Interior Department had neither a bureaucracy to oversee the reserves nor a ranger force capable of patrolling them. The national parks offered no administrative model for implementation at the monuments. When civilian officials at Yosemite and Yellowstone proved unsuccessful, for example, Washington resorted to administration by the army. But the theft and vandalism at Petrified Forest—or any other monument—did not warrant such dramatic measures.

Commissioner W. A. Richards recognized the shortcomings of the volunteer custodians; still the GLO could not spare one or two of its agents to police Petrified Forest. For the commissioner, like many others, designation of the reserve as a national park seemed to be the "only salvation," and Richards urged the Secretary of the Interior to support any legislation that would accomplish the goal.[24] National parks, after all, received annual appropriations to cover the costs of administration and protection. But this remote site in northeastern Arizona seemed destined to remain a national monument, continuing from year to year under the ad hoc supervision of unpaid, untrained custodians.

By 1907, Al Stevenson was nominally in charge of Petrified Forest. When George P. Merrill of the United States Museum visited the forest, he was dismayed to find no regulations posted and visitors from Holbrook removing specimens at will. Stevenson was not to blame for the conditions, Merrill acknowledged, for he was a well-meaning individual who knew the forests thoroughly. But he had no appointment, no authority, and no salary.[25] C. W. Hayes of the USGS was equally distressed by conditions a year later. Only the "more or less disinterested action of Al Stevenson" was responsible for preservation of the monument, he reported. Petrified Forest was easily accessible from the Santa Fe's stations at Adamana and Holbrook, and the railroad now was advertising the reserve extensively. Increased numbers of visitors meant more theft and damage, since the custodian could do little to prevent such activities.[26]

Federal officials who visited Petrified Forest National Monument invariably praised Stevenson, recognizing that he operated with little support or authority. Hayes suggested that Stevenson be given the position of "curator," and credited his "wholesome supervision" with minimizing depredations.[27] Knowing that his hotel and tours of the Petrified Forest depended on the condition of the roads, Stevenson undertook repairs and constructed two small bridges at his own expense. But these improvements brought him no favors from Washington. He received no compensation for his expenditures on roads and bridges, and when he asked for a grazing lease in 1910, the Secretary of the Interior flatly refused him.[28]

Merrill returned to Petrified Forest in March of 1911 to examine the condition of the various forests and to advise the government on policy concerning excavations and collection of specimens. His visit had an additional, and more important, purpose—to determine whether the monument should be reduced in size in keeping with the restrictions of the Antiquities Act. Accompanied by Al Stevenson, Merrill spent several days going over the reserve and locating the major deposits of petrified wood. His survey convinced him that Petrified Forest ought to be reduced from its original ninety-five square miles to only about forty and a half square miles. The restricted boundaries did not exclude any major deposits, though some collections of logs were scattered about the terrain outside the monument. These were not particularly unique or likely to attract tourists, Merrill felt. And since the government was not out to corner the market on fossil logs, these inferior deposits were best left outside the monument.[29]

Merrill was essentially correct, although his recommendations were narrowly focused on meeting the Antiquities Act's limitations on the size of monuments. Few scientists—and virtually no politicians or bureaucrats—then defined boundaries with reference to the environment, nor did they think in terms of ecosystems. The reduced boundaries therefore included the most easily accessible and well-known deposits. First Forest, just six miles south of Adamana, includes the Agate Bridge and such sites as the Eagles' Nest, the Snow Lady, and Dewey's Cannon. Second Forest, two and a half miles farther south, covers about two thousand acres and embraces some of the largest, most colorful intact trees in the monument. And Third Forest, at the southwestern edge of the reserve some thirteen miles from Adamana, is the location of the longest whole trees, ranging up to two hundred feet in length. The fossil logs there are particularly colorful, and visitors described the area as Rainbow Forest. A smaller collection of logs called Blue Forest (now Blue Mesa) remained outside Merrill's boundary lines, as did the famous Black Forest in the Painted Desert.[30]

In reducing the monument's size the Interior Department was simply adhering to the specification in the 1906 Antiquities Act that the limits of national monuments should not extend beyond the smallest area necessary for proper care and management. When Roosevelt proclaimed Petrified Forest National Monument five years earlier, the Interior Department had no idea of how much land was required to ensure the protection of the petrified wood. Initially, the government erred on the side of generosity, assuming that ninety-five square miles would be sufficient to protect the various deposits until a thorough geological survey could be made. Merrill contributed the requisite information, and on July 31, 1911, President William Howard Taft signed a proclamation reducing the monument's size to conform to his recommendations. Some of the land withdrawn from entry in 1896 and 1899 fell within the acreage now excluded by Taft, so the earlier withdrawal orders were revoked and the land opened to settlement.[31]

Reducing the size of Petrified Forest did nothing to stem vandalism and theft. Al Stevenson, now officially custodian, received one dollar per month for his efforts in behalf of the monument, but his real interest, understandably, was operating his Forest Hotel and tours of the forests. In 1907, an estimated 1,500 to 2,000 people visited Petrified Forest, and

1889 photograph of Petrified Forest by William Henry Jackson (Courtesy of the Cline Library, Special Collections and Archives, Northern Arizona University)

Stevenson allowed each person to carry away about eight pounds of specimens as souvenirs. Given the limited supervision, both Stevenson and the General Land Office acknowledged the futility of any prohibition against removing specimens, since such a ruling never could be enforced. The Santa Fe Railroad also contributed to the problem through its advertising, distributing a brochure that actually invited visitors to help themselves to specimens. The General Land Office objected, and the Santa Fe changed the pamphlet to include a notice about penalties—fines or imprisonment—for injuring, destroying, or appropriating petrified wood or objects of antiquity.[32]

Western railroads like the Santa Fe had supported the establishment of

Agate Bridge. Note the concrete support that was put in place in the 1930s. (Photograph from the J. C. Clarke collection, courtesy of the Museum of Northern Arizona)

national parks, realizing that transporting tourists to these reserves would enhance corporate profits. The relationship between the railroads and the national parks was clearly pragmatic. Tourism was profitable in itself, and there was always the possibility that onetime visitors might return as settlers. In turn, the western lines promoted western scenery and brought the region's national parks to the attention of more Americans. The development of national parks had coincided with the marketing strategy of the railroads, Alfred Runte points out in Trains of Discovery. Following completion of the first transcontinentals, the lines worked hard to stimulate interest in the spectacular scenery of the West. As early as 1903, the Santa Fe began acquiring paintings of the Grand Canyon, Petrified Forest, and other southwestern sites to adorn its stations and executive suites. National parks and monuments that were easily accessible to the main line were the primary attractions in promotional literature.[33]

Railroads made no secret of their economic motivation, but preservationists, including John Muir, acknowledged the value of their support. Corporate leaders may not have shared Muir's aesthetic ideals, but they nevertheless acknowledged a common goal of preservation. Railroad tourism provided parks with their economic justification, which was a vital argument in sustaining funding. The railroads' attention to parks reflected major social changes in the years around the turn of the nineteenth century. From the 1880s on, more American families enjoyed more leisure time and had more money to spend on it. This emerging mass market competed with the new rich of the East Coast and Midwest for the attention of railways and the tourist industry. Both realized that profits could accrue from serving the middle class along with their traditional, wealthier clientele.[34]

By 1912 the Santa Fe was advertising "stop-overs" at Petrified Forest National Monument. Since the General Land Office provided little information about the monument, the railroad's brochure and a short article by Charles Lummis in the company's *Santa Fe Magazine* were among the few sources of information about the monument available to tourists. Indeed, the Santa Fe's pamphlet contained one of the few accessible, early maps of the area. The stopover at Adamana was particularly convenient; the six-hour journey was a leisurely one that left the Forest Hotel late in the morning and returned at dusk, after tourists had taken in most of the nearby sites. Those with more time could arrange to see the Second and Third Forests further south, or even journey beyond the monument boundaries to the Blue Forest or the *Sigillaria* Grove, both of which were recent discoveries by the naturalist John Muir.

"Today this is all yours," Lummis proclaimed. "You can sleep on a Santa Fe Pullman til time to get up. You transfer to a comfy hotel, and Stevenson shows you these pages of the past."[35] Visitors were conveyed through the forests aboard a twelve-passenger coach pulled by four horses. The route followed a natural highway, packed hard by frequent travel and blown free of sand. Tourists who took advantage of the Santa Fe stopovers at Adamana and Holbrook were assured "the unfailing joy of a wide horizon, the bluest of blue skies, and an air whose breathing is like a draught of wine."[36]

Whatever the condition of the monument's "natural highway," the General Land Office could claim no credit. Although Stevenson had performed some maintenance in the monument, the GLO did not think "serious road building operations" were necessary to make the reserve accessible to most wheeled vehicles. Given Petrified Forest's location in arid northeastern Arizona, Washington officials were convinced that the land was dry and stony for most of the year and required little maintenance beyond minor grading and bridging washes.[37] Local residents knew better, and as automobiles led to greater visitation, the matter of road maintenance became nearly as aggravating as the chores of preventing vandalism and theft.

Chester B. Campbell accepted the one-dollar-a-month custodian's job in January of 1913 and also took over operation of the Forest Hotel. About 1,500 tourists had visited the First and Second Forests between July 1 and October 1, 1913, according to the hotel's guest register. Campbell wanted roads repaired and suggested that the government drill a well in Dry Creek between the two forests. But when he raised these points with Roy G. Mead of the General Land Office, his notions were brushed aside abruptly.[38]

Lacking federal support, Campbell initiated his own construction projects, improving the old trail between First and Second Forests into an adequate wagon road and building a parallel automobile road. Over the years he installed culverts, filled sandy washes, hauled brush, and built bridges, all at his own expense. "If I have spent $1.00 on the roads," he informed Horace Albright, then assistant to Stephen Mather at the Interior Department, "I have spent to date $2000." In return, Campbell wanted to lease the roads from the government, with the option for annual renewal. Primarily, he wanted to protect himself against competitors. Anyone with an automobile could convey tourists along Campbell's roads and across his bridges, benefiting from his work and expenses, and then simply abandon the endeavor when business fell off.[39]

Campbell also intended to build two "sightly houses" as shelters for visitors and to pipe water from a spring near Agate Bridge. The Interior

Department had no objections to the projects, so long as the spring and rest areas remained free and unrestricted to all visitors. But the department could not lease the roads to Campbell or to anyone else. A complaint to Stephen Mather at the Interior Department brought no results, so Campbell acquiesced and contented himself with the growing number of visitors who stayed at his hotel and booked tours in his vehicles. About 5,700 people visited the monument in 1915, and he anticipated a substantial increase the following year.[40]

While Campbell battled with the Interior Department over roads, bridges, and repairs to the Agate Bridge, substantial administrative changes were occurring in Washington as a result of the passage of the National Park Service Act of 1916. The law created a new agency, the Park Service, which acquired title to all national parks and monuments administered by the Department of the Interior. More important, it was empowered to promote and regulate the use of these diverse reserves.

What this new agency promised for Petrified Forest was not at all clear, though Campbell could hope for improvements over the limited attention his monument had received in past. By 1916 Petrified Forest was one of twenty-one national monuments administered by the Interior Department (another dozen fell under the authority of the Forest Service, and two were run by the War Department), and even after President Taft had reduced its size to forty and a half square miles, it remained among the largest of such reserves. Further, its close proximity to the Santa Fe line at Adamana guaranteed it a growing number of visitors, and Campbell could only guess how many more visitors would be arriving by automobile. Measured by the conditions in 1916, the future could only be better. In that year, each monument had only $166 to cover its costs. The entire National Park Service budget was only $30,000. In the words of one writer, "the Park Service was barely operational."[41]

4

SCIENTISTS AND THE PETRIFIED FOREST IN THE EARLY TWENTIETH CENTURY

The hours go on neither long or short, glorious for imagination . . . but tough for an old paleontological body nearing 70.

John Muir

When Edgar Hewett broadened the concept of national monuments to include scientific sites, he created a special niche for Petrified Forest. The new monument contained a few important ruins, but the extensive deposits of petrified wood shaped the reserve's essential identity. Its boundaries in 1906 enclosed only a small portion of the fossil-rich Chinle Formation that is exposed throughout much of the Plateau Province. Petrified Forest therefore shares in the geological history of an extensive ancient environment; and as scientists and naturalists found and described additional fossils, they revealed the unique character of this future national park.

Long before President Roosevelt had set aside Petrified Forest National Monument, scientists already were searching the terrain for fossils. The petrified logs were well known, of course, but they represented only the most obvious and spectacular features that had eroded out of the Chinle.

In 1889, Frank Knowlton of the National Museum had described these giant fossil trees as *Araucarioxylon arizonicum*. Knowlton and John Wesley Powell both collected leaf fossils from the Chinle Formation in northern New Mexico in the late 1880s and early 1890s, and George F. Kunz published descriptions of the deposits in the area known as Chalcedony Park. These efforts represented only the beginning, for a wealth of plant and animal remains lay entombed in the colorful rocks of the Chinle.

Since early in the nineteenth century, geologists had known that sedimentary rock units could be identified by the distinctive fossils they contained. This discovery, known as the law of faunal succession, made possible the erection of a stratigraphic classification based on time relations rather than on rock types. As a result, scientists could define major sedimentary rock units and, by using their distinctive fossils, distinguish time counterparts at various localities—even on opposite sides of an ocean. Stratigraphic units, each representing a segment of the geologic time scale, became known as geologic systems—the now familiar names of Cambrian, Ordovician, Silurian, Devonian, Carboniferous (Mississippian and Pennsylvanian in North America), Permian, Triassic, Jurassic, Cretaceous, Tertiary, and Quaternary. The Triassic (or Trias), important for Petrified Forest, was introduced in 1834, based on observations in western Germany and in Italy. On this side of the Atlantic years later, scientists identified additional fossil remains in the Triassic. Their endeavors continue into the present.

Awed by the size and brilliant colors of the petrified trees, few early visitors bothered to look for vertebrate fossils, but at nearby locations in northern Arizona, Utah, and New Mexico scientists had found in the Chinle Formation enough bones to identify phytosaurs and *Typothorax*.[1] Both are thecodont reptiles, ancient ancestors of the dinosaurs that developed when the Triassic was still young; they gradually became extinct at the close of that geologic period.

At the very end of the century, Lester Frank Ward arrived at Petrified Forest and undertook an extensive survey of the terrain. Ward recommended that the federal government protect the place as a national park, but his work there extended well beyond justifying a new federal reserve. In his report, Ward referred consistently to Arizona's petrified "forests," specifically employing the plural to describe several distinct deposits in the area south of Adamana. He identified the now familiar Chalcedony Park as the principal location, noting that petrified logs there were literally countless and lay scattered on knolls, spurs, and buttes and in ravines and ditches. The ground everywhere seemed "studded with gems"—mostly broken fragments of all shapes, exhibiting all the colors of the rainbow. An additional forest, much smaller in extent, was situated north of Chalcedony Park, not far from the Puerco River. A third accumulation, which Ward simply called "middle forest," lay about two miles to the east.

These three forests, Ward wrote, were "geographically speaking, entirely out of place." He believed that the fossil trunks at Chalcedony Park had been washed out of their location atop a plateau that bounded the area and rose some seven hundred feet above it. Ward noted that, directly to the west, the plateau exhibited a series of petrified trunks, many of which had weathered out on the slope or rolled down to the valley below. Just below the summit, in a bed of coarse, gray sandstone, the geologist found a number of places where logs and branches of petrified wood were embedded. "This, then, is the true source of the fossil wood," he declared.[2]

Ward's observations naturally raised questions about Möllhausen's earlier descriptions of the standing stumps in Black Forest in Lithodendron Wash. Ward could find no evidence in Chalcedony Park to confirm Möllhausen's contention that at least some trees had grown in place and been buried and petrified; nor did interviews with local residents provide any support for that view. "The only trunk I saw standing," he wrote, "was one that was inverted and had its roots in the air." There was no point in searching for standing stumps in Chalcedony Park and its neighbors, he asserted, since all of the logs in that area lay several hundred feet below their point of origin. The very abundance of these fossil trees ruled out their having grown in the same place. "Even if every tree had been preserved, there are places where it would have been impossible for them to stand as thickly as they now lie on the surface," he pointed out, "not to speak of the space that trees in a forest need to survive." The fossil logs not only were prostrate, but they lay in "little collections and huddles quite differently from what would be expected if they were precisely where they grew."[3]

The great accumulations of silicified trunks resembled the collections of logs and debris in the eddies of modern river deltas, convincing Ward that the logs had floated into the area some time before being petrified. The coarse sand and gravel beds in which the fossils occurred were highly favorable for silicification, he added, and the crossbedding indicated the existence of rapid and changing currents. According to Ward, the beds containing the petrified wood had probably sunk, and finer deposits had ultimately buried them at the bottom of the sea that covered the region at one time in the Mesozoic era. There they remained until the entire country was raised some five to six thousand feet during the episodes of mountain building that created the Sierra Nevada and Rocky Mountain ranges.[4]

Ward was the first paleontologist to examine thoroughly the area around Chalcedony Park, and his report generally expanded on the observations of earlier scientists and naturalists. Ward's descriptions were detailed and accurate, providing a reasoned, scientific basis for extending federal protection to the petrified forests. Perhaps most significant, he established that the extensive collections of fossil trees were of scientific interest. They were not simple "curiosities" or "freaks of nature"; nor were they mere commodities suitable for decorative or even industrial purposes.

While in Arizona in the fall of 1899, Ward ventured well beyond Chalcedony Park and investigated much of the Little Colorado Valley. His discovery of phytosaur bones at Tanner's Crossing, near the present Cameron, Arizona, quickened his interest, and he determined to return to the site later. In 1901, accompanied by Barnum Brown of the American Museum of Natural History, Ward was back at the location—now known as "Ward's bone bed." Here the two men collected two new kinds of animals from the Chinle Formation—*Metoposaurus fraasi*, a giant amphibian; and *Placerias hesterus*, a huge reptile known only by its humerus. The *Placerias*, scientists later determined, was the first record in North America of mammal-like reptiles called dicynodonts. The boneyard proved over the years to be a valuable and productive site for paleontologists. In 1936, Ward and Brown returned to the site and excavated the largest known phytosaur skull, which measured four feet, eight inches in length.[5]

Ward also searched doggedly for remains of leaves but had only limited success. Some poorly preserved imprints were found in a sandstone bed near Tanner's Crossing, and Ward thought they were remnants of coniferous twigs and branches. He also found the remains of a small petrified cone northwest of the present park. Like most geologists, Ward was generally convinced that the petrified trees throughout that region had floated to their locations from some other site. In 1901, though, he and Barnum Brown discovered north of Cameron twenty stumps that apparently stood exactly where they had originally grown.[6] The location was some distance from Petrified Forest, but it rested in the same geological formation and confirmed that some trees had been growing in that area when the Chinle Formation was deposited. Among the chips and blocks of wood surrounding the stumps, Ward found a large number of "fruit-like objects," which he thought to be resin or pitch. Several decades later, investigations by Lyman Daugherty disproved Ward's assertion; the "fruit-like objects" proved to be the remains of pecky-heart rot caused by a fungus that attacked *Araucarioxylon arizonicum*.[7]

Ward's research had taken him well beyond Petrified Forest, and his work indicated that the fossil trees now embraced by the national park are part of a much larger ancient environment. The extensive Chinle Formation yielded fossils that dated back more than 200 million years and provided a glimpse of the earth's early history. In their research, Ward and his associates added a few more components to the region's Triassic landscape, though the picture still was far from complete.

Those same rocks also yielded the secrets of the early human inhabitants who first lived among the scattered trunks of petrified logs. In 1901, archaeologist Walter Hough of the National Museum guided members of the Museum-Gates Expedition through Petrified Forest. Like many of the early archaeological activities in the Southwest, the primary goal of this one was the simple collection of artifacts. But, in the course of their fieldwork, expedition members excavated portions of numerous sites (usually focusing on burial grounds), compiled ethnological information on the Hopi and myths of clan migrations from the south, and located and mapped some of the larger ruins in the area. Hough also provided a unique perspective on prehistoric human activity in the petrified forests. In an article for *Harper's Monthly Magazine*, "Ancient Peoples of the Petrified Forest of Arizona," he remarked on how the brightly colored fossil trees "expanded the fifth sense of wonder." But that was not all, for his research revealed that "a touch of human interest" was involved in the region's prehistory. Petrified Forest and the surrounding countryside had been home to tribes of ancient pueblo dwellers, he explained, people who "lived and loved, builded, fought, starved, and perhaps dined on one another."[8]

Within the present park boundaries, Hough examined the Puerco Indian Ruin and the nearby petroglyphs as well as the Twin Buttes site. Milky Hollow, Canyon Butte, and Stone Axe ruins, all in the immediate vicinity, also were investigated. Canyon Butte proved particularly intriguing, for the site had no access to water whatsoever and bore no evidence of vegetation. Yet it yielded considerable pottery, shell beads, prayer sticks, and other objects. Hough described one of the structures as the "pueblo of the cannibals." Among the orderly burials, workers uncovered a heap of broken human bones, apparently the remains of three people. The shattered bones had been clean when placed in the ground, Hough wrote, and some clearly had been scorched by fire. A few bore the marks of whatever tools had been used to break them. "Without a doubt, this ossuary is the record of a cannibal feast," he commented. But since this was the only such find in the area, Hough described it as "probably anthropophagy from necessity." The same pueblo ruin yielded the skeleton of a priest, Hough believed, and a extensive collection of implements of that profession. These artifacts and the pottery found at the site suggested its connection with the Zuni.[9]

In all, his investigations in and around Petrified Forest convinced the archaeologist that four different "stocks" of Indians had lived there—a substantial number for a locality without permanent springs. He was certain that one of the groups was Hopi, possibly a clan on its northward migration to Tusayan. Another seemed to be related to the Zuni, although Hough was less certain about this group. The remainder he categorized as enigmas, people in a low state of advancement in comparison to the others.[10]

Hough's work in Petrified Forest and its vicinity was part of the larger Museum-Gates Expedition, which undertook excavations and surveys from the White Mountains northward through Petrified Forest and on to the Hopi Mesas. In all, some fifty-five ruins were visited and eighteen sites excavated in a region roughly two hundred miles by seventy miles. A recent archaeologist describes these early endeavors as "pioneer regional archaeology" but cautions that such early surveys and excavations are not to be dismissed. People like Hough made astute observations, and the hypotheses advanced early in the century are today being tested and sometimes justified.[11] Hough was the first professional archaeologist to conduct major investigations in Petrified Forest and its immediate environs, and his work provided the first glimpse of the region's prehistoric inhabitants. In addition, he sought to describe them within the context of the prehistoric cultures of the Southwest. Modern archaeologists know that Petrified Forest rests in an area where several cultures mingled, and Hough's early observations anticipated these later findings.

While Hough had made Holbrook the base for the Museum-Gates Expedition, other investigators preferred to operate out of tiny Adamana because of its proximity to the deposits of petrified wood. The Santa Fe Railroad also found it a convenient spot to deposit tourists, particularly after the Forest Hotel was constructed just before the turn of the century. Even then, Adamana consisted only of four buildings—the other three being a nondescript station, a coal bunker, and a water tower. The hotel, a ranch-style structure set back a short distance from the tracks, included a number of comfortable guest rooms, all of which opened onto a veranda that ran the length of the structure. A Santa Fe Railroad brochure published in 1912 assured travelers that they would be "nicely cared for." Board and room were a modest $2.50 per day, and the hotel could accommodate twenty guests. The dining room served thirty. Despite its remote location, the owners of the Forest Hotel offered travelers good food and clean rooms. Young Alice Cotton, visiting the petrified forests with her father in January of 1906, was impressed with its charming living room and comfortable guest quarters.[12]

If its proprietor, Al Stevenson, never grew wealthy, he and his family apparently earned an adequate living. The owners maintained a garden that yielded radishes, green onions, and a few other vegetables. In the spring of 1906, the steady stream of guests at the Forest Hotel had given the Stevensons a taste of real prosperity, and they purchased a camera and made plans to seed a lawn. In the meantime, though, one guest admitted, "there are the usual tin cans and grubs much the same."[13]

When the Cottons visited the establishment in January 1906, they were the only guests registered. Temperatures in northeastern Arizona often drop below freezing at that time of the year, and the desolate, windswept

The Forest Hotel, gateway to Petrified Forest from the late nineteenth century until the 1930s (Photograph from the Willard Drake collection, courtesy of the Coconino National Forest)

terrain along the Santa Fe line seldom induced passengers to abandon their warm coaches or Pullman cars to endure a frigid tour of Petrified Forest. But, for the Cottons, this was the last stop on an extended western tour. At dinner the first evening were the Stevensons, the local schoolteacher, a few employees, and a couple of young hoboes who were enjoying the Stevensons' hospitality. Seated next to Miss Cotton were a young woman and her father—a thin, bearded man who appeared to be about sixty years old. "His serious and scholarly countenance was lighted by a gay twinkle in his eyes," she still recalled years later. Throughout the meal, she tried to place him, finally realizing that her dinner companion was the writer and naturalist John Muir.[14]

Muir undoubtedly entertained the small group at the hotel. A natural storyteller, he loved to talk, and his Scottish brogue enhanced his tales. He explained that *Cosmopolitan* magazine had engaged him to do a series of articles on the petrified forests.[15] In reality, Muir's visit to Petrified Forest had comparatively little to do with writing; rather, it was the poor health of his daughter Helen that brought Muir to Arizona in 1905. Muir's wife, Louie, had died suddenly that summer, and shortly afterward he moved to Adamana with Helen and her older sister Wanda. Helen's lingering pneumonia was a source of constant worry for Muir, and he hoped that the dry desert air might restore her health. At Adamana the trio became "permanent guests" at Al Stevenson's establishment. Actually, they only took their meals at the hotel, since Muir had arranged for a comfortable, two-room cabin with a fireplace. On many occasions, they preferred to sleep in a tent.[16]

Helen responded quickly to the desert climate, and Muir was delighted with her improvement. The sojourn at Adamana also helped him to recover, for the trying events of the 1905 summer had left him "stunned and decidedly tired," he told a friend.[17] But for some time Muir lacked the concentration and discipline necessary to write. Instead, he found a new avocation in exploring the nearby deposits of petrified wood. To Robert Underwood Johnson of Century magazine he wrote enthusiastically about "a half dozen or more thousand acres . . . strewn thickly with huge agate trunks millions of years old." Johnson hoped that Muir might eventually contribute an article for Century, and he often gently prodded the naturalist to write. But Muir's responses typically began with allusions to his inability to concentrate, followed by exuberant descriptions of the petrified logs.[18] Clearly, study of the fossil trees was now the focus of Muir's intellectual interests, but that was no guarantee of an article or essay.

As a student at the University of Wisconsin in the early 1860s, Muir had enrolled in geology courses taught by Ezra Slocum Carr, a protégé of Louis Agassiz, and he never lost interest in the subject. He was also a precise observer of nature, and earlier, in Yosemite, he had ascertained the role of glaciers in shaping the steep canyon walls and cliffs of that park. Northern Arizona presented a markedly different environment, but the petrified trees near Adamana captured his imagination immediately. He identified *Araucaria, Sigillaria, Lipidodendrons,* and tree ferns that he believed "flourished gloriously millions of years ago in the bogs and woods of the Carboniferous period." By early in 1906, Muir's excavations among the deposits near Adamana had improved his spirits considerably. To a friend he wrote that "this hard work and hard enjoyment I find good for all sor-

John Muir at Petrified Forest, 1906 (Photograph from the Helen Muir Collection, courtesy of Petrified Forest National Park)

row and care," and to another he announced that "hard work in the petrified forests hereabouts has brought back something of the old free life with Mother Nature." [19]

Muir was an enthusiastic geologist, but he was not particularly well grounded in the discipline. He correctly identified *Araucaria* and *Calamites*, but other observations were wrong, particularly his placing of the fossil forests in the Carboniferous period (360 million to 250 million years ago) rather than the Triassic. Once convinced that the deposits dated back to the much older Carboniferous, he unavoidably made mistakes in his identification of some fossils. Muir placed nearly all his faith in experiencing and carefully observing nature and consequently deprecated the value of books. They were, he once remarked, "at best signal smokes to call attention." But from time to time on his visits to the family home at Martinez, California, Muir continued on to Berkeley to consult sources in the University of California library. His sketchbooks for 1905 and 1906 contain numerous pencil drawings of *Sigillaria* and *Lipidodendron* fossils, all of them apparently copied from standard texts of the period. Presumably, Muir used the sketches made at Berkeley to identify the actual fossils he found near Adamana. In his enthusiasm, he named those deposits the "*Sigillaria* Grove" and on a rough map he located them about six miles north of Adamana.[20]

Neither *Sigillaria* nor *Lipidodendron* exist in Arizona's petrified forests, which date back only to the Triassic—information that was well established by the early twentieth century and easily accessible as well. Judging by Muir's correspondence, notebooks, and sketchbooks, he did not consult any of the material relating to exploration of the region, nor was he aware of descriptions and reports by such scientists as Marcou, Knowlton, and Ward. Not knowing the Triassic origins of the area and unaware of recent scientific literature, he may have mistaken two other fossil trees, *Schilderia adamanica* and *Woodworthia arizonica*, for *Sigillaria*. Neither of those two had been described back then, and surface markings might have led Muir to identify *Woodworthia* as *Sigillaria*. A second possibility remains. Fungus found on some *Araucaria* fossils might have convinced him that they were *Lipidodendron*. The fungus had not yet been identified either, which helps to explain Muir's erroneous descriptions of it.[21]

In his wanderings about the area, Muir came across extensive deposits of petrified logs about six miles southeast of Adamana. He named the new site Blue Forest (now Blue Mesa), a name prompted by the blue-gray tint of the terrain. Between this new find and the *Sigillaria* Grove, Muir kept busy excavating among these stone trees, occasionally interrupting his work to travel back to his California home and, when possible, to Berkeley. By the spring of 1906, he was convinced that few scientists knew more about the "carboniferous forests" than did he and his daughters, and he was confident that they could "make a grand picture of those which flourished about the hills and dales and grazing lands." From Berkeley, he instructed Helen and Wanda to "gather up everything old and queer and see if I can't name them when I get back later with Greek and Dog-Latin."[22]

Muir published very little about his findings at Petrified Forest. On one of his trips back to California by train, he talked briefly to a correspondent from *The World's Work*, lightheartedly discussing the novelty of the stone trees. Although the Santa Fe Railroad had advertised stopovers at Adamana and the Petrified Forest for years, Muir pointed out, "those fellows had waited all that time for me to come down there and find three more forests that not even the people in that country knew about—and one of them is the biggest one there."[23] Santa Fe officials eventually heard about the newly discovered Blue Forest and Sigillaria Grove and included a description of the sites in their advertising.[24]

Muir's digging and collecting at Petrified Forest coincided with Congressman Lacey's endeavors to establish Petrified Forest National Park. Muir knew about the 1906 park bill and naturally hoped that the legislation would pass, but he did nothing to help the measure along.[25] Lacey relied extensively on Lester Frank Ward's recommendations, among those of several others, but he never called on Muir—the country's most widely known naturalist and proponent of national parks, not to mention something of an expert on the very petrified forests that Lacey hoped to preserve. By 1906, when Lacey introduced his fourth bill to establish Petrified Forest National Park, the testimony from "John of the Mountains" would have strengthened his arguments, not to mention the publicity that Muir and such colleagues as Robert Underwood Johnson might have stimulated.[26]

Although Lacey ignored Muir, the Interior Department looked to him for advice concerning the area's suitability as a national park. In particular, the General Land Office wanted his recommendations about which deposits of petrified wood ought to be included. Further, because no current, official map of deposits of petrified wood existed, Washington needed from Muir a sketch of the area. Muir was glad to comply and recommended inclusion of the well-known First, Second, and Third Forests, along with his own recently discovered Blue Forest. These, he felt, would be most attractive to tourists because of the profusion of colors and the inherent beauty of the stone trees. He also recommended the inclusion of the Sigillaria Grove, which students of geology would find important. In that area, he noted, some of the stumps remained rooted where they had grown. Lacey's bill of 1906, of course, did not include these Sigillaria Grove. Although Muir favored a larger reserve (about three and one-half townships), he suggested that those deposits might initially be omitted to facilitate passage of the bill. The critical task was to secure the national park designation. Increasing the new reserve's size would be "a comparatively easy matter after it is better known and appreciated," he advised the GLO.[27]

With that advice, Muir was content to return to his Sigillaria Grove, leaving the preservation of the petrified trees in the hands of Congress and

President Roosevelt. The summer of 1906 was the family's last one at Adamana. Helen had recovered completely, Wanda was making wedding plans, and Muir had been thoroughly rejuvenated by his lengthy excursions in "God's Auld Lang Syne," as he described Petrified Forest to a friend. For much of a year, he had worked in the deposits near Adamana, and he acknowledged that his "only great gain from these troubled times is the views I've gained from these grand forests of the world which flourished uncounted millions of years ago."[28] But for all his digging and research, Muir had not written so much as a page for publication. "How does your pen work these days?" Robert Underwood Johnson inquired in June 1906, adding a plea that Muir write his long-delayed piece for the Century.[29]

The Muirs left the Forest Hotel in August 1906 and returned to the family home in Martinez. Muir eventually made a halfhearted commitment to begin writing a piece for Robert Underwood Johnson, but he was much more interested in identifying the fossils he had retrieved from Petrified Forest. He lost no time in contacting paleontologist John C. Merriam of the University of California, who examined the small collection of vertebrate fossils and identified them as the remains of phytosaurs.[30] Muir eventually presented the fossils to the university, and they became part of its paleontology collection.

The article for Century magazine never appeared, nor did Muir ever write anything on Petrified Forest. For all his fond references to "God's Auld Lang Syne," he never placed his experiences in Petrified Forest within the framework of his other writings on nature. No "grand picture" of that ancient environment ever emerged. The omission is unfortunate, for Muir had long been convinced of the interdependence in nature. "When we try to pick out anything by itself," he had written earlier, "we find it hitched to everything else in the universe." To what were these fossil trees hitched? And where did they fit in the scheme of nature? Muir's serious excavation and his determined study of fossils suggests that he was anxious to learn about the origins of Petrified Forest. And after months of intensive work, he obviously had moved toward some conclusions, as implied by his comment to Johnson that his "great gain" in 1905 and 1906 had been "the views I've gained of these first grand forests of the world." Whatever perceptions Muir had developed, he kept them to himself, leaving others to puzzle out the importance of these ancient forests and the creatures that dwelled within them.

For Muir, the year at Petrified Forest had been a time of rest and renewal following the death of his wife. His daughter's subsequent recovery in the high desert air naturally relieved him, too. And there can be no doubt about his enthusiasm for excavating and studying the area's fossil trees. The year of relatively intense fieldwork, combined with the excitement of making seemingly new discoveries, had contributed to his recovery and provided him with a sense of accomplishment. It had been a needed respite— a time to regain strength and nurture his daughters.[31]

Muir contributed only in a small way to the preservation of Petrified Forest. And he did not broaden our understanding of geology or paleontology, because many of the fossils he discovered were identified incorrectly. For a while thereafter, both the Santa Fe Railroad and local newspapers touted his discoveries of the *Sigillaria* Grove and Blue Forest. But eventually they dropped references to the former. The nature of Muir's contribution to science at Petrified Forest is difficult to assess. He in fact discovered the unique Blue Forest, but beyond that the renowned naturalist made no seminal discoveries, despite the expenditure of considerable effort.

Muir observed Petrified Forest as a naturalist and scientist, seeking to place the fossil trees in the context of the earth's history. He recognized them as ancient forests (too ancient, since he identified them as Carboniferous), and he understood that they had grown in a landscape obviously different from that of the twentieth century. Like glacial valleys, geysers, and eroded canyons, Muir recognized Petrified Forest as a geological creation that helped define America's cultural identity and also captured the interest of tourists.[32] By the early twentieth century, Americans were learning more about the West—its landscape, inhabitants, and climate. The remains of these ancient forests suggested that the region's past was more extensive, and perhaps more significant, than people had realized.

For the next decade, little scientific activity occurred precisely within the new monument, but scientists were busy at a number of places in the Chinle Formation of the Plateau Province. S. W. Williston and his assistant, Paul Phillips of the University of Chicago, gathered a small collection, including phytosaur bones, in the Zuni Mountains in 1912. The party returned a year later and discovered a complete phytosaur skull. A few years later, Maurice G. Mehl and his student G. M. Schwarz of the University of Wisconsin, worked both at Cameron in the Little Colorado Valley and at the Zuni uplift, where additional phytosaur remains were unearthed.[33]

From time to time, even local residents around Petrified Forest uncovered remains of these crocodile-like animals. Robert R. Alton, proprietor of a small store near Adamana, found a portion of a phytosaur skull just a few miles south of the town. Eventually, that fossil ended up in the geology collection of Case Western Reserve University in Cleveland. Then, in 1919 at Muir's Blue Forest, Ynez Mexia made an important discovery of vertebrate fossils, including the first phytosaur skull from Petrified Forest, which she sent on to the University of California.[34]

Mexia's find also caught the attention of Berkeley's Annie Alexander, who was familiar with Muir's fossil collection. With her friend Louise Kellogg, she retraced Mexia's steps and made important discoveries of phytosaurs and *Placerias*. The two women not only excavated beds near Blue Forest but also discovered a rich new site at Devil's Playground above Lithodendron Wash. Neither Alexander nor Kellogg was a scientist, but Annie Alexander, in particular, had a long-standing interest in paleontology that had begun when she and friends attended lectures by John C. Merriam, then an assistant professor at the University of California. Not long after she and Kellogg had found the fossils in Petrified Forest, she established the Museum of Paleontology at the university and later provided it with an endowment for scholarships.[35] The excavations by Alexander and Kellogg marked the beginning of intensive work by the University of California at Petrified Forest.

So promising were the discoveries by Alexander and Kellogg that Charles L. Camp, a new Columbia University Ph.D., traveled by train to meet the two women at Adamana. Fieldwork at the sites began in earnest that summer and yielded some two thousand pounds of fossils, which were shipped back to Berkeley. The intense summer fieldwork at Petrified Forest largely shaped Camp's early career. His interest in the Chinle Formation and its fossil vertebrates drew him back to northeastern Arizona and northern New Mexico again and again. Two years later he discovered a rich zone of fossil deposits in the Blue Forest area. The site, named "crocodile hill," yielded numerous skulls of phytosaurs and metoposaurs. During that same season, Camp's field assistant found a new fossil location at Billings Gap, about four miles to the southeast. In 1927 Camp spent a week at Petrified Forest, concentrating his work at Devil's Playground. He met a local resident named Dick Grigsby during his stay there, and the latter led him to a concentration of fossils in a tributary of Lithodendron Wash. "Almost every specimen is a phytosaur skull," Camp wrote. "I saw six of them including the one already collected by Grigsby." This discovery was particularly significant because the skulls exhibited a series of growth stages and sexual differences in a single phytosaur species.[36]

Camp excavated a number of sites in New Mexico and Arizona in the 1930s. He made his last visit to the Chinle Formation in northern Arizona in 1934, when he and Samuel Welles continued excavation at the "Placerias Quarry" near St. Johns. Over the years this single site yielded some 815 skull bones that came from at least thirty-nine of the animals, along with the remains of phytosaurs and other ancient creatures. Camp's work was important beyond the sheer wealth of fossil amphibians and reptiles that he and his associates collected. His real success, as his colleague Samuel Welles pointed out years later, was his ability to stimulate his students to undertake investigations on other horizons of the extensive Colorado Plateau.[37]

In a broader context, Camp, like Annie Alexander and John Muir, exhibited that sense of curiosity that Lester Frank Ward had eloquently described decades earlier. The fossils they discovered went back to Berkeley, and these early naturalists and scientists contributed to the expanding discipline of geology. Gradually, such research shaped the identity of Petrified Forest National Monument. The deposits of petrified logs would always attract visitors, but by the first decades of the twentieth century, scientists had revealed that the primeval swamps that buried these great logs also were home to phytosaurs, Placerias, and a variety of other creatures—residents of an ancient wilderness that awaited further exploration.

Phytosaurs are perhaps the best representatives of the Triassic faunas of the region. They were thecodont reptiles from which later dinosaurs evolved, but they differed from bipedal members of the order that walked on powerful, birdlike hind legs (such as *Hesperosuchus*). More advanced thecodonts, phytosaurs became increasingly larger until some of them grew to almost giant stature. The bipedal pose was left behind, and phytosaurs developed into long quadrupedal reptiles inhabiting the shores of streams and lakes. As they evolved, they retained the armor plates characteristic of primitive reptiles. Some grew into heavily armored animals—what one expert calls "veritable Triassic tanks."[38]

Phytosaurs seemingly abounded in and around Petrified Forest, and their presence suggests that the ancient ecosystem depended on the existence of numerous streams and lakes—the habitat of these aggressive animals that fed on a variety of smaller creatures. Similarly, the residence there of the large herbivore *Placerias* indicates considerable vegetation to sustain the foragers. Such discoveries incrementally added to the overall understanding of the Triassic period in the earth's history. The evidence still was sketchy, but scientists later would identify this as a crucial time of transition, when the planet's ancient life was giving way to evolutionary pressures exerted by new and vigorous plants and animals that would dominate the earth for the next 100 million years.[39] Scientists in the first third of the century had found at the reserve an immense laboratory that promised to expand our understanding of the Triassic. And this suggested, too, that in the future Petrified Forest would play a broader interpretive role among the country's parks and monuments.

None of these discoveries had fully registered with Stephen Mather and Horace Albright, or with any other officials at the National Park Service or Interior Department. Although the Antiquities Act specifically identified sites of scientific interest as worthy of monument status, the measure did not commit the federal government to supporting scientific research or establishing educational programs. Mather and Albright probably were not fully aware of the extent and significance of research under way at Petrified Forest. Local administration there was in the hands of volunteer custodians, whose correspondence with the Interior Department tended to be infrequent and often dwelled only on matters of theft and damage.

By the 1920s, Petrified Forest was the destination of growing numbers of travelers, thanks to the popularity of the automobile. These new visitors, far surpassing the numbers that had come aboard the Santa Fe before

World War I, were a cause for concern at Petrified Forest. Not only did they secrete away uncounted tons of souvenirs over the years, but they also defaced and vandalized natural features. Consequently, park policy focused narrowly on protecting the petrified logs, while little time or money was set aside for educational endeavors and displays to exhibit the discoveries that researchers made. Decades later, when expanded ranger forces and modern facilities helped monitor visitors, the Park Service could turn its attention fully to science and interpretive displays at Petrified Forest.

5

CUSTODIANS AND PROPRIETORS

The souvenir hunters seem to think that no harm is being done because "there is so much of it."

William Nelson, 1923

The handful of scientists who visited Petrified Forest National Monument were overshadowed by the hundreds of tourists who found their way to the reserve. Most arrived on the Santa Fe, but after World War I an increasing number traveled there by automobile. Railroads had largely handled the country's transportation needs for decades, so no real highway system yet existed. Across the country roads were poor and typically served only local areas. The lack of through connections frustrated any motorist who had the temerity to undertake long distance excursions. Few highways had even been built in the West, and drivers were inclined to take off cross-country or to use railroad rights-of-way. Some gave up and shipped their automobiles by rail, as did young Emily Post when her touring car disintegrated on Arizona's primitive roads near Winslow. The vehicle was in "a seriously crippled condition," she remarked; "any more arroyos and there really would be no more motoring on the trip."[1]

At the major national parks, the Army Corps of Engineers took care of road building, and automobiles were admitted to Mount Rainier, Crater Lake, Glacier, and Yellowstone before the United States entered World War I. Stephen Mather, who in 1916 became the first director of the National Park Service, understood that automobiles would bring more tourists to the parks and that growing numbers of visitors would naturally impress Congress, which had to approve appropriations and expansion. Once encouraged, the automobile traffic quickly became a flood. In 1926, more than 400,000 cars and trucks entered the various national parks, up substantially from 55,296 in 1917.[2]

National park proponents embraced the automobile as enthusiastically as did middle-class Americans, realizing that these new mechanical marvels could increase the popularity of parks immensely. Most of the reserves were some distance from the country's cities, and automobiles were a convenient and comparatively speedy means of reaching them. Moreover, the American public was not likely to support the preservation of natural areas—no matter how monumental and scenic—unless such places were readily accessible. No one in the 1920s envisioned congested roads, crowded campgrounds, and hazy air as the eventual price for such convenience. As Enos Mills, the "father of Rocky Mountain National Park," put it: "The traveler wants the automobile with which to see America."[3]

Mather effectively expanded the prewar "See America First" campaign as a way to attract more visitors to the parks. America's early motorists did not require much coaxing, particularly after the war when Detroit began to manufacture larger and more comfortable automobiles. These vehicles ceased to be playthings and became serious means of transportation that offered considerable freedom of action.[4] Still, touring by automobile inevitably was slow. Poor roads, low speed limits, interminable mechanical breakdowns, and flat tires all meant that motorists typically averaged less than twenty miles per hour. The slow pace offered a degree of compensation, though, allowing time for some attention to detail and appreciation of regional variation. Like the nineteenth-century stagecoach, the automobile offered a more "natural" schedule, emancipating travelers from fixed railroad timetables. Trains, once acclaimed as the most efficient and comfortable means to reach the national parks, now were decried as too fast and too scheduled. The view from the train, motorists knew, was simply a blur.[5]

While the National Park Service promoted the great national parks and maintained their facilities, the national monuments seldom received much attention. At Petrified Forest, the administration could not keep pace with the growing number of tourists, and the situation was further complicated in 1918 when Chester Campbell abruptly sold the Forest Hotel and also resigned his position as custodian. The new proprietor and caretaker for the reserve was William Nelson, a former employee.

In these early years of the National Park Service, no clear policy toward concessionaires had yet been developed. Director Stephen Mather and his assistant Horace Albright were resigned to the fact that Congress would not appropriate enough money to develop fully the various parks, so they compromised by allowing each reserve to become a thoroughly regulated business preserve for a single franchise holder.[6] In the case of Petrified Forest, Nelson's dual positions as federal custodian for the monument and private hotel owner and tour operator continued a precedent that went back to Al Stevenson's time. The system had never worked very well. Custodians could not effectively police the monument, even after its dimensions were reduced in 1911, and the minuscule federal funds did not allow for much improvement to roads and other facilities. Under such circumstances, custodians naturally focused their energies first on their own enterprises and looked after the monument as time allowed.

By the time Nelson purchased the hotel, renaming it the Adamana Hotel and Auto Livery, it had served as the unofficial headquarters for Petrified Forest for nearly two decades. The place had been improved over the years and now boasted sanitary plumbing and electric lights. The hotel could accommodate thirty-five guests, and additional visitors were lodged in tent-houses and other buildings. In addition, Nelson had assembled a small fleet of vehicles to transport guests to the various Petrified Forest sites. As identified in the establishment's advertising, he was not only proprietor but also "Government Custodian of the Petrified Forest."[7]

The contrast with park administration is revealing. By the 1920s, the national parks received bids from private entrepreneurs who hoped to build hotels and to operate transportation services. Often these companies, such as those at Yellowstone, Grand Canyon, and Yosemite, were subsidiaries of railroads. At Petrified Forest, though, the current owner of the local hotel in Adamana still doubled as the federal custodian. Responsibilities focused on protecting the petrified logs, although custodians might take on any number of projects at their own expense.

William Nelson was an old-timer in northeastern Arizona. Like many of the area's earlier settlers, he had engaged in some ranching, but little is known about him before he went to work for Campbell. At some point he had met the governess who had cared for children of Rudolph Spreckles, the wealthy California banker and sugar baron. Nelson and the erstwhile governess soon married and in 1918 took over the tasks of managing the Adamana Hotel and guiding tourists through Petrified Forest.

The Nelsons' venture was typical of early tourist camps, cabins, modest hotels, and other facilities that catered to motorists after World War I. For both practical and aesthetic reasons, a married couple was essential to running such an establishment. Husbands normally took care of maintenance and also screened clientele for deadbeats; wives actually managed the daily business. Unlike commercial hotels that catered to men, chiefly salesmen, tourist facilities exhibited a woman's touch—chintz curtains, doilies on dressers, rocking chairs, and flower boxes.[8]

Even as automobile travelers were outnumbering those who arrived at Adamana on the Santa Fe, Lucy Nelson found it difficult to tolerate this new assortment of visitors. Guests who arrived aboard the Santa Fe had proven to be good sources of income for the Nelsons, but those who drove their automobiles to Adamana spent much less money. Lucy Nelson despised them as "auto trash" and sometimes refused them service. The Park Service was powerless to intervene in the hotel's operation, since the establishment was five miles outside the monument and was not operated as a concession. Yet its operation could not be divorced from Petrified Forest, given Nelson's dual positions. The situation represented the obvious weakness of the Park Service's reliance on dollar-a-month custodians who derived their main income from other endeavors.[9]

Personal traits aside, the Nelsons had much in common with other small business operators along the stretch of highway that in 1926 was officially designated as U.S. Route 66. The road passed through country "where life was rough and poverty was the norm," Susan Kelly writes in

Route 66. Proponents of the highway expected it to generate business in the Southwest, but few realized that it would actually keep towns and people alive in the 1920s and 1930s. The Roaring Twenties meant hard times for much of rural America, and that decade's poverty induced people to search out new sources of income. In the Southwest, numerous residents tried to capitalize on local curiosities and tourist attractions like Petrified Forest. For the Nelsons, income from the hotel, tours, and garage, along with Bill Nelson's minuscule salary as custodian, enabled them to get by financially. In all likelihood, their income was modest and their lifestyle rather insecure until the Park Service later hired Nelson full-time.[10]

By the time Nelson took over as custodian, the automobile already promised to increase substantially the number of visitors to the country's national parks and monuments. The Chevrolets, Fords, and Overlands that stimulated travel after World War I all needed reasonably well maintained roads, and in this respect Petrified Forest suffered particularly. U.S. 66 passed just north of Adamana, but the road between the main highway and the monument often was impassable. Within Petrified Forest itself, roads were virtually nonexistent.

The major obstacles were the Puerco River and a tributary called Dry Creek, which separated the monument from Adamana. For most of the year the streambeds were dry, but even then the sandy bottoms often caused automobiles to bog down. After heavy rains, both were impassable, and quicksand remained a hazard for days after the water subsided. Since Nelson derived a good share of his income from his tour business, he assiduously guided visitors through Petrified Forest as long as the Puerco could be crossed. When automobiles stalled in the sand or mud, he resorted to teams and light rigs. But few travelers cared to risk their automobiles and lives in any reckless attempt to negotiate the Puerco or Dry Creek. They typically avoided Petrified Forest altogether, sometimes complaining bitterly about the inaccessibility of the place. A modern bridge across the Puerco was essential.[11]

Nelson found a strong supporter in Frank Pinkley, a fellow custodian at Casa Grande Ruin and Tumacacori Mission in southern Arizona. Pinkley had nearly two decades of experience at Casa Grande, and his extensive understanding of the problems of national monuments made him an important asset to the National Park Service. He already had earned the confidence of Mather and Albright when Nelson met him in 1918. Pinkley verified Nelson's assessment of the Adamana road. "It is in bad condition," he told Mather, noting that there was no satisfactory material available to resurface it. Nelson simply dragged and packed the surface, filled the holes and ruts after storms, and dragged it again.[12]

Nelson's requests for funds to build and maintain roads did not seem excessive to Pinkley, and he was anxious to keep the custodian at his post. His long residence in the area had given him a deep appreciation for the petrified forests, and he was an enthusiastic student of the region's geology. Nelson, though, simply did not seem much interested in Park Service matters beyond his own monument, and he exhibited none of the team spirit that Pinkley and Mather liked to see among superintendents and custodians.[13] While Nelson's attitude concerned Pinkley, it actually revealed nothing more than the Park Service's inattention to the monuments and also the problems inherent in hiring part-time custodians.

Nelson's first year and a half at Petrified Forest were discouraging. The Park Service had neglected to pay even his meager salary of one dollar a month, and extended periods of rain had thoroughly disrupted his tours. When the number of visitors occasionally tapered off, he also suspected that the Santa Fe Railroad conductors and station agents were demeaning the accommodations at the Adamana Hotel and discouraging stopovers at Adamana. By the early spring of 1919, Nelson was thinking about abandoning the hotel and the custodianship to return to cattle ranching.[14]

Nelson had reason for complaint, as did his fellow custodians. During the 1920s, the Park Service funded developments at the national parks but generally neglected the monuments. In 1923, the Park Service had only $12,500 to expend on the entire system of twenty-nine national monuments across the country. That year, Frank Pinkley had been appointed superintendent of the Southwestern National Monuments, and a year later he administered his fourteen sites on a budget of less than $15,000. Though this represented a degree of improvement, Pinkley remained perturbed by the disparity between parks and monuments and undertook his own analysis of the Park Service's funding. At the thirteen national parks, he discovered, the appropriation per visitor averaged 68.4 cents. But for the national monuments around the country, the Park Service expended only a nickel per visitor. The fourteen southwestern monuments under Pinkley's supervision fared a little better at 9.2 cents per visitor.[15]

Pinkley hoped that the Nelsons could be induced to take advantage of postwar highway construction and the immense popularity of automobiles.[16] In addition to U.S. 66 just north of Adamana, another important route skirted the southern boundary of Petrified Forest, connecting the Apache County seat of St. Johns with Holbrook, where it joined Route 66 and proceeded westward across northern Arizona toward California. Rather than tap this lucrative automobile traffic, the Nelsons seemingly clung to a romantic vision of their hotel as a western resort fed by the transcontinental Santa Fe Railroad.

Nearly all visitors—both auto tourists and Santa Fe patrons—entered the monument via Adamana; few of them ever journeyed southward beyond the Second Forest to Third Forest (increasingly now identified as Rainbow Forest), a distance of about thirteen miles from Adamana. When Nelson became custodian, the stretch of road leading to Rainbow Forest had been abandoned, and over the years storms had washed out numerous sections. Yet the new St. Johns–Holbrook highway presented a strong argument for repairing and opening that part of the monument road. A south entrance from St. Johns impressed Pinkley as a reasonable way to increase the number of motorists visiting Petrified Forest.[17] The real task was to convince Nelson of the benefits.

If Nelson had any doubts that the future belonged to the automobile, his own observations should have convinced him otherwise. His reports to the Park Service identified a growing number of automobile tourists, who in 1920 contributed to a 100-percent increase in travel over the previous year. "During the last six months of the season the sight of up to 100 cars daily on the PFNM road was not by any means uncommon," he reported in October 1920. The numbers impressed Assistant Park Service Director Arno Cammerer, who was concerned that Petrified Forest was not receiving the attention from Washington that it deserved. In fact, he wondered whether Pinkley ought to take on the duties of custodian there and allow the Nelsons to devote all their energies to operating the hotel and tours as Park Service concessionaires. Instead, he provided funds to hire a part-time ranger.[18]

Neither Nelson nor his ranger were prepared for the influx of motorists and the theft and vandalism that came in their wake in 1922. Nelson already harbored a simmering resentment toward auto tourists, and now their tendency to help themselves to specimens of petrified wood further exasperated him. The landscape in the monument was dotted with warning signs, but few motorists ever stopped to read them. "It shows the general attitude of the traveling public," Nelson complained to Mather. Instead, motorists blithely helped themselves to colorful souvenirs of petrified wood, sometimes chipping pieces from easily accessible logs. Nelson observed that visitors to the monument carried hammers and did not hesitate to use them. He had surprised a number of people who were casually pounding on petrified trees in the hope of breaking off a special specimen. Even a visitors' shelter constructed earlier by Chester Campbell was not spared; determined souvenir hunters stole the blocks of petrified wood that formed the foundation, leaving the structure tilting precariously.[19]

From Nelson's viewpoint, such behavior was simply malicious. He resented the attitudes of America's new auto tourists as they visited the monuments in the Southwest. By the 1920s, national parks were well known to Americans, and the Park Service actively promoted tourism. But monuments lacked precise meaning for most people. If scenic national parks were the destinations for vacationing tourists, the various monuments scattered across the Southwest seemed to be little more than interesting rest stops. Indeed, this was a function that Mather advocated for them.[20] But that characterization had the deleterious effect of defining some national monuments as tourist attractions with little regard for their essential historical, cultural, or scientific merit.

Consequently, when they stopped for a short time at a national monument, tourists may not have regarded their behavior as inappropriate, much less malicious, when they picked up a piece of petrified wood or broke off a specimen from a prostrate log. Surely, no visitor thought twice about adding another name or drawing to the pictographs in the monument or otherwise defacing the site. Monuments, after all, were relatively small, and typically only a small sign explained their significance. In short, many people did not think that monuments were all that special.[21]

A recent study by anthropologist Dean MacCannell provides additional perspective on tourist behavior. He has observed that "the act of sightseeing culminates with tourists linking a sight with markers of their own making." Photographs are one kind of marker, as are comments (verbal markers) that describe and perhaps assess whether a sight has lived up to its expectations. Graffiti represents the most blatantly obvious and most destructive kind of "tourist marking."[22] The practice was extensive, even in the early years of the century. When Irvin Cobb visited the Grand Canyon in 1913, he noticed that Bright Angel Trail bore the autographs of uncounted tourists who came armed with pencils, chalk, paints and brushes, and even stencils.[23] Throughout the Southwest, as in other parts of the country, the story was much the same.

America's early motorists were causing irreparable damage to Petrified Forest, and Nelson used the theft and depredations to advance his argument for appointment of a full-time, resident custodian. He fully expected to fill the opening himself. To his credit, he understood the monument's vulnerability and also was familiar with its natural history. He proposed to sell the Adamana Hotel and move on to the monument. Nelson's personal automobile would suffice, at least temporarily, for patrol work. As for living quarters, he told Mather, "I can get along with most anything." He was equally accommodating about the salary—$900 or $1000 would be perfectly suitable.[24]

Cammerer accepted his offer, and "Petrified Bill" Nelson, as he occasionally signed his letters to the Park Service, became Petrified Forest's first salaried, resident custodian. In addition, the Park Service made plans to allot $1500 for construction of a cottage to serve both as a residence and as headquarters for the monument. Another $25 was allocated immediately for more warning signs to proclaim that destruction or removal of petrified wood was prohibited by law.[25]

Secure in his new position, Nelson went after thieves and vandals with the determination of a frontier marshal. Even before his appointment was confirmed, he stopped an automobile and uncovered a 150-pound block of petrified wood secreted in the tonneau. When the party refused to part with its prize, Nelson strode back to his automobile, retrieved his Winchester, and forced the group to unload the block. Still suspicious, he unpacked their camping supplies and bedding, which yielded another 100 pounds of various specimens. Only then did he escort the humbled motorists to the monument boundary.[26]

Both Nelson and Cammerer realized that the theft of specimens could never be halted completely, and the custodian grudgingly acquiesced in the decision to allow tourists to help themselves to a few small pieces of petrified wood, not to exceed half a pound. Already on edge about the continuing theft, Nelson preferred to halt all specimen collecting but had to go along with NPS policy. In the meantime, he occupied himself by placing more warning signs throughout the monument while awaiting the arrival of his custodian's badge. "I hope I can get one that is visible 1/4 mile away," he told Mather. Too many drivers, unable to see his small ranger's badge, ignored his frantic gestures to stop, and Nelson feared being run down by the very people who were plundering his reserve.[27]

Although funds had been appropriated for construction of a combination custodian's residence and monument headquarters, Nelson could not wait for the project's completion. Instead, he quickly fixed up the old rest house in Second Forest as a temporary accommodation. He moved in with such alacrity that Cammerer wondered if his real motive might have been to get away from Mrs. Nelson.[28] When Frank Pinkley paid a visit in September, he found Nelson "as much in love with his monument as ever," remarking to Mather that "he always thought of Petrified Forest first and his wife and the rest of the world afterward." At that time, Nelson had two men feverishly working on the monument's main road, hoping to complete the project before cold weather set in. He, of course, persistently patrolled his domain, ever vigilant against the transgressions of vandals and thieves. Custodians had authority to make arrests, and both Cammerer and Pinkley cautioned Nelson to exercise that power only as a last resort. Pinkley still admitted to a few lingering doubts about Nelson, particularly concerning his antagonism toward motorists. But he departed from Petrified Forest in September 1922, convinced that the reserve was better administered than ever, though certainly not yet perfect.[29]

Petrified Forest was hardly a Park Service showplace in the 1920s. Like other monuments, it had not received any thorough attention from officials in Washington. Mather and Albright were much more concerned with the monumental, scenic national parks, and their devotion to these great federal vacationlands had relegated the monuments to a distinctly second-class status.[30] Confident of Pinkley's ability, in 1923 they handed him fourteen sites scattered across Arizona, Utah, Colorado, and New Mexico, officially designating him Superintendent of the Southwestern National Monuments. The appointment of the dedicated, experienced, and knowledgeable "Boss" Pinkley was a fortunate one for the ragged collection of archaeological ruins and natural sites. But Pinkley's talents could carry the monuments only so far; they needed funding even more desperately than did the national parks.[31]

Because of its size (then 25,625 acres, the largest of the southwestern sites) and rapidly increasing number of visitors, Petrified Forest was destined to occupy a large share of Pinkley's time. In 1923, it was the second busiest of the southwestern national monuments, and vandalism there exceeded that at all others. About 8,500 tourists drove through the monument that year, and Nelson, now equipped with a motorcycle, relentlessly pursued anyone he suspected of violating Park Service regulations. In all, he personally confiscated 1,605 pounds of petrified wood that motorists had hidden in their vehicles.[32]

When the number of visitors tapered off in the fall, Nelson had time to gather specimens and prepare them for exhibits in a rustic "specimen building" he had constructed near the headquarters. Using a homemade electric saw, he patiently cut thin slices of petrified wood and mounted them on glass slides. He next photographed them through a microscope and then converted the photographs to lantern slides to display to tourists during the next season. He also produced a series of rough sketches portraying Petrified Forest's geological history, and these too were added to the collection of lantern slides. At odd moments, he made plans to improve the electrical service and to expand the monument's campgrounds. "Some might think that Mr. Nelson had a lonesome proposition, housed up in a one-room cabin with no neighbors and only a blizzard for company," Pinkley remarked in his December 1923 report. But such conditions rarely depressed Nelson, who found any number of projects to occupy his time. If he needed anything, it was another ranger to relieve him of some of the burden of patrol work while he developed more displays and slides to enhance the educational programs he envisioned for his monument.[33]

While Nelson and Pinkley could derive some satisfaction from the progress of the monument, businessmen in Holbrook and other towns remained disappointed that the reserve never stimulated as much tourism as they expected. Rural northern Arizona could generate few good jobs, and Petrified Forest was closely tied to the local economy. Its expansion promised more employment at the monument and also meant more tourists for motels, campgrounds, and restaurants at towns in the vicinity. Local pride also was involved. Petrified Forest paled in comparison to Grand Canyon, which was elevated to a national park in 1919. Certainly, local merchants and residents reasoned, Petrified Forest deserved to be a national park, too. As the secretary of Holbrook's chamber of commerce pointed out to Congressman Carl Hayden of Arizona, only then could the reserve acquire a fair portion of national park appropriations to facilitate building good roads, campgrounds, water systems, and "imposing petrified wood arches." [34]

Nelson fully supported the park movement and eventually confessed that he was among the originators of the scheme. But the endeavor received no support in Washington, primarily because half of the land within the monument was privately owned. That precluded any consideration of Petrified Forest for national park status. Pinkley objected to the park designation, too, arguing that Petrified Forest simply was not a national park. "Parks are not higher than National Monuments in status but simply in another field," he explained patiently to Nelson, "and it wouldn't elevate your monument to make a park out of it." [35]

Finding no support for the park plan, Nelson turned his attention to the educational programs he had developed during the winter. A friend in Cleveland, Ohio, had sent him a 110-volt dynamo, and Nelson hooked it up to an old Cadillac motor to provide electricity to his small combination museum and specimen building. The same benefactor also had sent him a Bausch and Lomb stereopticon, which Nelson installed in the museum to display his lantern slides. Illustrated lectures soon became a regular feature during the summer tourist season, and Pinkley was delighted to see that Nelson had outgrown his obsession with apprehending thieves to focus on the educational aspects of his job. The superintendent knew that Americans were only vaguely familiar with the region's natural history and its prehistoric inhabitants, and he viewed the monuments as excellent tools to expand their appreciation of this diverse heritage.[36]

Park Service interpretive programs were in their infancy at that time. Joseph Grinnell of the University of California persistently advocated public education at the larger parks as a way to inform visitors about wildlife and conservation, and in 1920 Yosemite inaugurated the Park Service's first official program of field interpretation—an endeavor that received the support of Grinnell and his Berkeley students. The situation at remote Petrified Forest could not compare with the more sophisticated programs at Yosemite, yet Nelson and Pinkley were acutely aware of the educational value of such programs at the smaller reserves like Petrified Forest. Nelson's educational background was limited, but it did not prevent him from becoming a perceptive and imaginative custodian. Overseeing the monument was a complicated task, and Nelson mastered it gradually by trial and error.

On several occasions in the early 1920s, Holbrook residents were the source of vague rumors about Nelson. A few harbored an ill-defined suspicion that the custodian somehow favored Adamana businessmen over their competitors in Holbrook, but they never substantiated the charges. Others claimed that Nelson bestowed certain favors on his friends. Nelson generally managed to avoid direct confrontations and directed his energies toward improving conditions at the monument. Over the years he had treated vandals and thieves harshly, and he may have injured the feelings of visitors from Holbrook, particularly if he suspected them of stealing petrified wood. Indeed, Nelson was certain that Holbrook citizens were responsible for a good share of the pilfering of petrified wood that occurred in his domain.[37]

In 1924, another wave of complaints about Nelson emanated from Holbrook and eventually reached the Park Service in Washington. For several months, Cammerer had been concerned about persistent rumors that Nelson was selling petrified wood at his little museum and at a refreshment stand that Lucy Nelson had opened in Rainbow Forest. Though the practice was not precisely illegal, the sale of polished pendants and other items created a bad impression. Visitors were warned not to take pieces of petrified wood, yet they found the custodian selling souvenirs.[38] Nelson immediately halted the sale of pendants and other items, although he vowed that they had been fashioned from material collected well outside of the monument.

Allegations about the sale of petrified wood continued, resulting eventually in an Interior Department investigation. Although Nelson was cleared, he submitted his resignation in October 1925, and the Park Service accepted it without prejudice. Nelson's relationship with Pinkley and Cammerer had deteriorated badly during the year. Even though he had been cleared of any suspicion, the allegations had damaged his reputation and probably limited his effectiveness as custodian at the monument. Pinkley made no effort to induce him to remain; indeed, he may have been glad to see him go. Though he liked Nelson and appreciated his dedication to Petrified Forest, Pinkley invariably was disappointed that Nelson never exhibited any of the team spirit that he sought to inculcate in custodians at the southwestern monuments. Nor did Nelson pay any homage to Park Service ideals. He speaks of Washington "as though it were some distant organization," Pinkley had earlier complained to Mather.[39]

For seven years, Nelson had guided the development of Petrified Forest. He was particularly conscientious after he became the monument's full-time, resident custodian in 1922. Thieves and vandals were pursued relentlessly and sometimes arrested, roads were maintained, and a few jerry-built structures were put up within the reserve. More important, his collection of specimens and his magic lantern shows were innovative attempts to establish educational programs that enhanced the visitor's experience at the monument. In the 1930s, such educational endeavors would be developed further under the direction of the Park Service's naturalists.

Nelson was among the last of a unique breed of Park Service officials. Like his neighbors around Adamana, he tried to eke out a living on the high desert terrain of northeastern Arizona and found that catering to tourists provided a modest income. The last of the dollar-a-month custodians, he tenaciously nudged the Park Service toward making the position permanent and full-time. His willingness to abandon his Adamana business for a low-level Park Service salary suggests that serving motorists was not particularly remunerative. In any event, his full-time appointment finally terminated the ill-conceived practice of combining custodian and local entrepreneur.

As custodian, his administration had been a one-man operation, and he succeeded as well as could be hoped, given the agency's inattention. Pinkley was correct when he categorized Nelson's perception of the Park Service as "some distant organization." When Mather and his assistant Horace Albright were encouraging visitation to the national parks and improving roads and facilities, they paid scant attention to the monuments. In turn, Nelson barely acknowledged the agency's existence.

In 1906, the Antiquities Act had clearly defined the national monuments, but in the succeeding decade no one had developed a rationale for their management or identified a mission for them. As historic, prehistoric, and scientific sites, these reserves required considerable interpretive efforts, which in turn demanded a degree of expertise among custodians. Nelson was comparatively untutored, but like Pinkley he understood that tourists needed direction and education if they were ever to appreciate a place like Petrified Forest. His novel illustrated lectures sought to address that need, but the Park Service did little to sustain his interest. And the surge of auto tourists in the twenties meant that an inordinate amount of Nelson's time had to be devoted to chasing down thieves and vandals—a task that he seemingly relished as much as his magic lantern shows.

If Pinkley ever dreamed that Nelson's departure might usher in a period of stability at Petrified Forest, he soon learned differently. He quickly hired a temporary ranger, Henry Phillips, who transferred from Grand Canyon to become custodian in February 1926. Although he had been with the Park Service for three years, Phillips endured Petrified Forest for only sixty days. Its rustic accommodations depressed his wife, who missed the social life and lodging at Grand Canyon. In comparison, the forlorn monument must have appeared to be literally a second-class facility. A hard winter further discouraged the Phillips family. "I trust you don't blame me," a frustrated Pinkley wrote from his headquarters in Casa Grande, "for I never played it up as a soft place." Phillips and his wife soon departed, leaving Pinkley to wonder whether Petrified Forest and the other national monuments could ever induce experienced park rangers to give up their comfortable quarters for the poorly equipped, remote southwestern monuments.[40]

Several short-term appointments followed over the next several years. None of Nelson's successors exhibited his understanding or appreciation of Petrified Forest, and none engaged in such heroic efforts to protect and improve the place. The central issue for Petrified Forest was the inadequate funding from the Park Service, but this was a problem shared by all of the monuments in the Southwest. The impact of theft and vandalism was magnified at Petrified Forest, simply because it attracted so many visitors and petrified wood was so easy to take. Its location adjacent to the Santa Fe Railroad and the heavily traveled Route 66 guaranteed that the reserve would attract larger numbers of tourists every year.

In 1928, Congress increased the appropriations for the national monuments to $25,000, up several thousand dollars from the previous year. But when spread over a total of thirty-one national monuments across the country, not just the southwestern reserves, the individual allocations were slight. Actually, monuments in Arizona did better than most in 1928, sharing $10,000. Petrified Forest was awarded $3,575, second only to Casa Grande, Frank Pinkley's Southwestern National Monuments headquarters.[41]

If Petrified Forest was not a major concern for Mather and Albright, it frequently was on the agenda of Arno B. Cammerer, assistant director of the Park Service, who stepped in as Mather's acting director from time to time. Most often, it had been Cammerer who provided direction and encouragement to custodians and to Pinkley, and when tourists complained directly to the agency's director, invariably Cammerer replied. He was the only high-ranking Park Service official to stay at Petrified Forest. He paid a brief visit to the Forest Hotel in 1921, and undoubtedly he knew more about the monument and its unique problems than did any other official in Washington. Since 1920, he had complained that Petrified Forest was not receiving the attention it deserved. Conditions had improved by the end of the decade, but Cammerer still complained that the Park Service administered Petrified Forest in a "half-baked way." Living quarters for the custodian and ranger were substandard, and drinking water was scarce. "Before we can ever expect to have a satisfied and competent administration in that desert area," he warned, "we must supply both."[42]

Cammerer might have added that the agency needed to identify Petrified Forest's place in the park system. Mather and Albright sometimes viewed the establishment of monuments as a "holding action," placing a site in a convenient interim position prior to its designation as a national park. For Grand Canyon, Zion, and Bryce Canyon, all neighbors of Petrified Forest, the duration of that status had been short, and the practice was a convenient way to expand the system. Understandably, Nelson and residents of the area were anxious to see Petrified Forest similarly "elevated," to use Director Mather's term, and that was the impetus behind the brief park movement of 1923. Unlike these other sites, Petrified Forest was not entirely in the public domain, and the Santa Fe's private inholdings undermined its progress toward achieving park status. Moreover, the reserve did not share the scenic grandeur expected of national parks, and that characteristic weighed heavily in the selection of new parks.

The first dozen years of Park Service direction of Petrified Forest were not particularly productive ones. Custodians were not always trained or well equipped to administer the reserve. With the exception of Nelson's term, the only continuity of administration came from Frank Pinkley, whose headquarters were several hundred miles to the south at Casa Grande. His directives, admonitions, and encouragement sufficed to provide direction and even a sense of professionalism to custodians like Nelson and his colleagues scattered across more than a dozen other sites in the Southwest.

Although Cammerer was optimistic about the monument's future, he fully realized the extent of the problems there. He hoped that the USGS might determine the extent of the local water table and provide information about other sources. As it was, the only good spring in the monument was situated on private land. In addition, a survey was needed to identify precisely the government's land as well as the sections owned by the Arizona and New Mexico Land Company, a subsidiary of the Santa Fe Railway Company.[43] That information was essential before a new custodian's residence could be built and a rational system of roads designed.

At the time, prospects of resolving the land problem were not particularly bright, since the Arizona and New Mexico Land Company was not interested in exchanging Petrified Forest land for other sections of the public domain. It wanted cash. Although Congress earlier had authorized an appropriation to purchase such land, the federal money had to be matched by contributions from independent sources. Such prospects remained dim in northeastern Arizona.[44] Petrified Forest National Monument appeared to be relegated permanently to the backwater of the park system.

In late 1928, Park Service personnel learned that Director Stephen T.

Mather had suffered a stroke that incapacitated him, and on January 12, 1929, thirty-nine-year-old Horace Albright became his "reluctant successor" as director. Albright had spent part of the 1920s as superintendent at Yellowstone National Park, and during off-seasons typically returned to Washington to work with Mather or to carry out duties related to his position as the director's field assistant. Nothing in his career indicated that he had any deep interest in the national monuments.[45]

Among Albright's general goals when he assumed his new position was to improve the Park Service's administration. Perhaps that objective induced him in May 1929 to assign M. R. Tillotson, superintendent at Grand Canyon National Park, to undertake a comprehensive study of Petrified Forest National Monument. Cammerer, too, undoubtedly played some role in that decision. Tillotson agreed, requesting only that he be given sufficient time to investigate all phases of the reserve.[46]

That summer, Albright received a premonition of what might be expected from the Tillotson report when T. S. Palmer of the Bureau of Biological Survey described conditions at Petrified Forest. The monument, he pointed out, had attracted about 75,000 visitors in 1928—more than any monument other than Muir Woods near San Francisco. Ten of the prestigious national parks had drawn fewer visitors. But conditions at Petrified Forest were deplorable. The custodian lived in a "two-room shack"—obviously the structure that Nelson had remodeled when he took up residence in 1922. One of his successors had added a rough lean-to, making room for an office and living quarters for his wife, child, and mother-in-law. Nelson's so-called museum, Palmer feared, was likely to be destroyed by fire at any time, and water supplies were inadequate. Worse yet, none of the staff seemed to know much about the monument's natural history.[47]

The monument desperately needed appropriations to remedy at least the worst defects. Palmer correctly identified the reasons for most of the difficulties that hampered Petrified Forest in the 1920s. "Any reservation that has nearly 100,000 visitors annually without proper means of handling tourists becomes at once a center of trouble and complaint," he advised.[48]

Tillotson's lengthy and detailed report arrived on September 29, 1929. It comprised a catalog of decrepit buildings and shoddy facilities—a clear measure of Washington's neglect of Petrified Forest. Beginning with an assessment of the roads, Tillotson repeated the complaints leveled by every custodian since Al Stevenson had first raised the issue before World War I. The section between U.S. 66 and the northern border of the monument was in poor condition and sometimes impassable because of flooding. This Adamana road, he emphasized, was critical since most of the transcontinental travel was following Route 66. A bridge across the Puerco River was "absolutely necessary," he advised. Within the monument, the existing road was a disgrace, and a new one had to be constructed as soon as private land titles could be transferred to the federal government. Tillotson added that U.S. 70 (the St. Johns–Holbrook highway) might be directed across the southwestern corner of the monument. In this way, tourists would see the large deposits of petrified wood in Rainbow Forest from car windows and might be induced to proceed on to the museum and headquarters.[49]

As for buildings and equipment, Tillotson described them as "practically nil." The museum was nothing more than a small, dilapidated shack, as was the custodian's residence. A third shack served as bachelor's quarters for a ranger, and a last shack stood close to the spring at Agate Bridge and accommodated a ranger stationed there. "None of these buildings is fit for human habitation," he wrote, "and they are all of them a disgrace to the Service." The only decent water came from a spring about eight miles from the headquarters, but the flow was only fifty-five gallons every twenty-four hours. Well-drilling had been unsuccessful, and Tillotson warned that water would have to be hauled from Holbrook or the little settlement at Hunt.[50]

Only a single concessionaire operated within the monument's boundaries at that time. H. F. "Dick" Grigsby occupied the single decent building in the vicinity, "a not unattractive stone building" constructed near the headquarters. Grigsby also operated a store at Adamana, where he sold supplies, groceries, and gasoline, along with polished petrified wood, Navajo blankets, and similar items. Tillotson found Grigsby to be helpful and cooperative and suggested that the Park Service allow him to add a few tourist cabins and install a lunch counter at his Rainbow Forest enterprise.[51]

With respect to the enduring controversy over the theft of petrified wood, Tillotson argued for simply giving visitors a few small specimens gathered from remote places within the monument. Perhaps a concessionaire could be allowed to operate within the reserve, closely monitored, of course, to cut and polish specimens for visitors. Tillotson's proposal ran counter to existing policy, but he argued that the signs "posted all over the place" had not deterred theft, nor could an expanded ranger force thoroughly eliminate theft and vandalism.[52]

All such problems were minor ones in comparison to the matter of privately owned land within the monument. As long as the Arizona and New Mexico Land Company controlled alternate sections, the Park Service could not develop any consistent management plans. Even construction of a road was impossible, given the checkerboard pattern of private and public parcels, and consideration of the reserve for a national park was out of the question. The only hope for resolution of the problem was legislation to authorize an exchange of private land within the monument for public land elsewhere. And there was no guarantee, at the moment at least, that the land company could be induced to accept land in lieu of cash.

Tillotson's report concluded with a list of essential objectives, ranging from construction of various buildings, residences, and campgrounds to development of water and sewer systems. The total cost was substantial—about $47,000, according to his calculations. An estimated 80,000 visitors would drive through the monument by the end of 1929, and Tillotson argued persuasively that the public was entitled to decent services and accommodations. The Park Service could not afford to injure its reputation by tolerating conditions at Petrified Forest that were below the high standards of the national parks.[53]

Palmer and Tillotson had compiled a comprehensive summary of Petrified Forest's deficiencies, but without exception they identified only the obvious problems—those that related to accommodating tourists. Both men described the monument as if it had become merely a dilapidated tourist attraction. Tillotson, in particular, focused on the needs of tourists to the extent of facilitating their purchase of petrified wood souvenirs. But the more subtle issues of identifying Petrified Forest as a scientific national monument and introducing visitors to its ancient environment were never mentioned and probably never thought about. By the late 1920s the monument and its environs had been the site of considerable scientific investigation, ranging from John Muir's observations and collections to the more sophisticated excavations of Charles Camp and other university-trained scientists. Their fossil discoveries had filled in a few more of the components of the region's ancient past, and the Park Service might now have used this new information to inaugurate interpretive activities there.

Instead, officials opted only to repair and replace dilapidated structures and build roads. All national parks, they understood, were to some extent "roadside points of interest" that might hold a tourist's attention for a few hours or a few weeks. "Selling scenery," Peter J. Schmitt has observed in *Back to Nature*, "was a matter of making park features attractive to a transient, largely inexperienced audience."[54] Petrified Forest typically attracted precisely such visitors, and improvements there would follow the pattern established at the national parks. Facilities would take precedence over science, education, and interpretation until a later time.

Tillotson's work represented a substantial blueprint for development of the monument. But such plans were unlikely to be followed unless the Park Service hired a dedicated and capable individual to assume the duties of custodian. Albright was aware of the procession of custodians who served briefly at Petrified Forest, and he was determined to appoint a person with a Park Service background who could administer the monument efficiently and work successfully with local residents. His choice fell on Tillotson's chief ranger at Grand Canyon, Charles G. "White Mountain" Smith. The selection was an enlightened one. As an outsider to the region, Smith was not prone to entanglement in the quarrels of Holbrook and Adamana. And as a career Park Service official, he had a precise vision of the role of parks and monuments. The history of Petrified Forest National Monument in the decade to come was very much the story of White Mountain Smith.

6

THE IDEAL NATIONAL MONUMENT

There are neither snow-capped mountains nor abysmal canyons in
the monument, yet it is by no means devoid of scenic value on a
smaller scale.

NPS landscape architect C. E. Peterson, 1930

M. R. Tillotson's lengthy report prompted the Park Service to
make a crucial decision about Petrified Forest. With the number of visitors
approaching 100,000 annually, the agency no longer could face the embarrassment of the reserve's dilapidated facilities, nor could it rely any
longer on unprofessional, short-term custodians. In the future, Petrified
Forest's administration would reflect the Park Service's professional guidelines, and its buildings and roads would also meet standards. Attaining
these goals meant a major change for the reserve, and in veteran ranger
White Mountain Smith, Albright selected an individual capable of shep-
herding Petrified Forest through a major transition. Between 1929 and
1940, when Smith departed, the reserve was virtually transformed. Not
only were facilities improved, thanks to the money and labor provided
by Franklin D. Roosevelt's New Deal programs; but the monument itself
nearly doubled in size with the acquisition of the scenic Painted Desert. By

the end of the 1930s, Park Service promotions acknowledged the changes and often described Petrified Forest as the country's "ideal national monument."

White Mountain Smith was a Connecticut Yankee, but he had lived in the West for years and for much of that time had been associated with the National Park Service. Prior to his serving as chief ranger at Grand Canyon he had worked as a government scout at Yellowstone, his career there in the 1920s overlapping with a portion of Albright's superintendency. In fact, the Park Service chief personally chose Smith as Petrified Forest's custodian in 1929, intervening in a decision that typically had been left to Frank Pinkley.

If the appointment represented a promotion for Smith, his new domain—remote, neglected, and decidedly shabby—was an unquestionable challenge. Clearly it was not in the same class as the Grand Canyon or Yellowstone. Living quarters were, as Tillotson had described them, dilapidated shacks, shabby enough to have sent an earlier custodian and his wife scurrying for another job. Fortunately, by 1929 a modern three-room residence was under construction near Agate Bridge; it was the only truly habitable building evident that summer when Smith looked over the reserve. Overshadowing all other problems was the issue of private land within the monument. The checkerboard pattern of federal and private holdings dated back to the original railroad land grants in the region, but now those inholdings precluded all development. The north-south road across Petrified Forest was really more of a trail than a highway, but the Interior Department could not authorize expenditures to improve a road that crossed private holdings every other mile. For part of the year, Smith complained, this "trail road" was nearly impassable.[1] Beyond that, lack of a bridge across the Puerco River disrupted traffic between U.S. 66 and the monument—a particular frustration in the summer travel months, when Arizona's monsoon-like rains turned the Puerco and nearby Dry Creek into torrents.

The only solution, Albright realized, was elimination of the privately owned land.[2] With the support of the Park Service and Interior Department, Congress on May 14, 1930, passed a land exchange act authorizing the federal government to obtain title to privately owned land within Petrified Forest National Monument through exchanges for similar public land of equal value in Apache County, Arizona. Smith had held preliminary talks with a representative of the Arizona and New Mexico Land Company even before the measure passed, and the two soon worked out an agreement that allowed the company to select five acres of public domain for each one of its acres within Petrified Forest.[3]

As the Santa Fe relinquished its holdings in Petrified Forest, the federal government was also able to expand the monument by 11,010 acres and return some of the land that President Taft had retracted in 1911. President Herbert Hoover took care of the matter by proclamation in November 1930, adding Muir's Blue Forest and the Puerco Indian ruins and nearby petroglyphs. In addition to these sites, the small acquisition contained the only practical site for a bridge across the Puerco.[4]

In the meantime, the Park Service made plans to eliminate the unsightly shacks and provide new rangers' quarters. Dick Grigsby held the only concession in the monument, and his store was one of the few presentable buildings within its boundaries. Therefore the Park Service allowed him to build several housekeeping cabins and even provided an architect to draw up plans. To the blueprints the Park Service architect appended his opinion that Petrified Forest "will never become a vacation retreat such as the national parks are."[5] The remark identified a critical issue at Petrified Forest. Though there was no doubt about the importance of its geological and archaeological sites, the monument lacked the grand scenery that Park Service officials and tourists alike associated with national parks. Given such perceptions, White Mountain Smith's national monument seemed unlikely ever to become anything more.

At the same time that automobiles were bringing more visitors to Petrified Forest, the Santa Fe Railroad and the Fred Harvey Company initiated their Southwestern "Indian Detours." The Santa Fe had advertised stopovers at various points of interest for years, and the new detours expanded on these original side trips. Hunter Clarkson of the Harvey Company in 1925 designed the excursions, which embarked initially from Las Vegas and Albuquerque, New Mexico, to visit Santa Fe and various pueblos. When announcing the new tours on August 20, 1925, Clarkson aptly described them as "detours." The company inaugurated its Petrified Forest Detour on June 1, 1930, when a tan-and-brown Packard "Harveycar" delivered a single California tourist to Petrified Forest. For Smith, the arrival of this lone visitor marked the beginning of a new era for the monument. The Californian was the first of thousands, Smith predicted optimistically, who would take advantage of the Santa Fe–Fred Harvey experiment to visit the forest.[6]

The detours treated travelers to an exceptional view of the Painted Desert, along with a tour of the Petrified Forest and a lecture at the museum. Clarkson's seven-passenger, open touring cars featured leather upholstery, two jump seats, and a folding rear windshield. On the radiator of each, "Packard Harveycar" was spelled out in a special script. The larger sixteen- and twenty-six-passenger coaches had similar leather upholstery, swiveling seats, and large glass windows to enhance the travelers' view. Along the way through Petrified Forest, visitors enjoyed basket lunches, and on some tours they could anticipate dinner at Harvey's La Posada in Winslow or another of the Harvey inns.[7] During the 1930 travel season, despite the impact of the stock market crash and the early effects of the Great Depression, visitors arrived at Petrified Forest in record numbers. In September, Smith recorded 12,394 visitors, about 1,200 of whom took advantage of the detour service. The year's total reached 105,433.[8]

Tourists who reached Petrified Forest via U.S. 66 invariably were impressed by the views of the Painted Desert, which stretches off to the northwest of the monument and extends eventually some 150 miles along the Little Colorado River toward its junction with the Colorado. Lithodendron Wash crosses it, and the Black Forest rests on its floor. The desert varies in width from about fifteen to forty miles, and its eastern part exhibits a particularly striking example of badlands terrain. Its southern fringes are only a few miles north of Petrified Forest, and this colorful stretch of land was a natural scenic complement to the monument. Its subtle shades of reds to pinks dictated its name, a designation that recalled the *Desierto Pintado* of the sixteenth-century Spanish explorers.

In 1924 Herbert D. Lore built a trading post and hotel, appropriately called the Painted Desert Inn, on a bluff that offered a panoramic view of the colorful desert landscape below. By then the automobile's popularity already was undermining rail-oriented institutions like the Adamana Hotel. Whereas the Nelsons had resisted the obvious trend toward automobile tourism in the 1920s, Lore astutely took advantage of it. The inn, labeled the "stone-tree house" in brochures, was a more substantial operation that the roadside gas stations and other businesses strung out along the highway. But like the smaller operators, Lore and his wife recognized that money could be made from Route 66 travelers. To guarantee that no one missed the inn, Lore constructed a large, red, electrically lighted sign at the main entrance road to his establishment. The place was an oasis for travelers who endured the heat, dust, and isolation along the route, and it served as an outlet for Navajo and Hopi arts and crafts.[9]

By the 1930s, Lore was willing to dispose of his holdings, and he sounded out the General Land Office about exchanging Painted Desert acreage for public domain elsewhere. He also wanted to sell the inn and its improvements to the government. At the same time, the Santa Fe Railroad offered its land in the vicinity for exchange. The two proposals raised the possibility of substantially expanding the monument by adding the scenic desert terrain.

White Mountain Smith initially was not an active proponent of the acquisition, although he had long admired the Painted Desert's vivid colors and its quiet beauty. He was convinced that it would attract enough visitors to justify its acquisition, but he also had a pragmatic reason to support federal control over the area: Lore's Painted Desert Inn actually competed with Petrified Forest. "When one has paid admission to Lore's area and carried away free wood as a souvenir," Smith explained to Assistant Director Conrad Wirth, "that person does not care to visit Petrified Forest National Monument."[10] Incorporating the inn and surrounding desert would end this competition and also increase the number of visitors to Petrified Forest. That should translate into more funding to operate the monument, Smith realized.

By the summer of 1931, support for incorporating the Painted Desert into Petrified Forest National Monument was virtually unanimous. The principal landowners—Lore, the Santa Fe, and the state of Arizona—were ready to negotiate exchanges, indicating that the Park Service could acquire the land (but not Lore's improvements) at little cost. From Washington, Assistant Director Conrad Wirth added momentum to the cause when he stated that the addition of the Painted Desert to other scenic areas in Petrified Forest would qualify the expanded reserve for national park status.[11]

As a veteran official of the Park Service, Wirth knew that neither his agency nor Congress would be likely to support national park designation for any reserve that could not boast at least some extent of spectacular landscape.

The scenery of the Painted Desert was clearly a crucial argument in favor of expanding Petrified Forest, but there was also the issue of protecting the Black Forest. With thousands of visitors stopping at the Painted Desert every year, the potential for theft and damage was immense. Smith knew that nearby residents had carted off substantial amounts of petrified wood; he had seen it for sale at the shacks they constructed along Route 66.[12]

Roger Toll, superintendent at Yellowstone and a frequent advisor to Albright on park matters, also supported the addition. He verified that the Painted Desert had little land available for grazing or commercial development. Its striking scenery constituted its only real value.[13] He also identified the importance of the Painted Desert Inn as a symbol for the expanded monument. The inn rests on a peninsula that projects into the desert and commands an incomparable view of the terrain. It was, Toll pointed out, comparable to Grand Canyon's El Tovar Hotel and "the central key to the situation."[14]

By the end of the summer, Park Service officials had worked out land exchanges, but the purchase price of the inn and Lore's other improvements still had not been negotiated. The addition of the Painted Desert needed only the director's formal approval and the requisite proclamation from the president. Albright had maintained a good working relationship with President Hoover that dated back to his Yellowstone superintendency, and Hoover generally had favored the Park Service during his administration. He continued that relationship on September 23, 1932, when he signed a proclamation that added the Painted Desert to Petrified Forest National Monument. In extending federal control over 53,300 acres of the southern and eastern parts of the Painted Desert, Hoover relied on the 1906 Antiquities Act that Theodore Roosevelt had invoked to establish the monument. Smith's domain now embraced 90,218 acres, adding to the original Petrified Forest the scenic desert terrain, the Black Forest in Lithodendron Wash, and a narrow neck of land connecting the two parts.[15] U.S. 66 now virtually bisected the expanded monument, almost equidistant from the original Petrified Forest National Monument and the newly acquired Painted Desert.

Smith's monument was now more than twice its size when he had arrived two years earlier, and it promised a future more complex and varied than otherwise could have been anticipated. The expansion also marked a degree of maturity for Petrified Forest, in that the months preceding Hoover's proclamation were filled with important internal accomplishments. Congressional appropriations provided for construction in 1932 of a modern highway across the monument, including a bridge at the Puerco. To dedicate the structure, Horace Albright journeyed to Petrified Forest in July and joined Smith, Pinkley, Tillotson, and Arizona civic leaders for the ceremony. He also used the occasion to announce Smith's promotion to superintendent. With that, Petrified Forest became an independent reserve and was no longer subject to Frank Pinkley's direction from Casa Grande.

Pinkley had always emphasized the importance of educational exhibits and programs at the monuments, and in the spring of 1932 had arranged for Park Service naturalist R. W. Rose and field naturalist Dr. C. P. Russell to construct and arrange displays for Petrified Forest's new museum. The two assembled collections of petrified wood in glass cases and arranged other displays. The facility also acquired the skull of a phytosaur and that of an early amphibian, which the naturalists arranged for viewing by visitors. Another room was set aside for display panels that employed diagrams and sketches to explain the process of fossilization, the variations of colors in petrified wood, the formation of crystals, and similar topics. Russell added drawings of the Triassic landscape, portraying the lush semitropical terrain.[16]

"Petrified Bill" Nelson had long since departed, of course, and gone was his shabby little specimen room with its stereopticon and magic lantern shows. But the emphasis on public displays in the new museum—though now more sophisticated and elaborate—continued a precedent that Nelson had set in the 1920s. The Park Service finally had developed an interpretive program that defined, albeit briefly, the significance of the reserve and attempted to convey the message to tourists.

The expansion of Petrified Forest, the substantial construction projects, and Smith's elevation to the position of superintendent all took place against the backdrop of the Great Depression. As the number of visitors slowly declined, personnel at the monument were reminded that the country was caught up in a severe economic crisis. The monument remained popular with motorists, although the number of visitors tapered off in 1932. Harveycar arrivals declined, too, and by September, Clarkson had abandoned the Petrified Forest Detour.[17]

The dwindling number of tourists at the monument was symptomatic of the conditions in northeastern Arizona in the early years of the depression. Even in prosperous times the region offered few good jobs, and residents scrambled to earn a living. Many of them looked to Route 66, where paving was under way from 1930 to 1937. People built service stations, tourist courts, modest hotels, and camping facilities—anything that might attract passing motorists. In the Southwest, such small-time operators capitalized on local curiosities, and petrified wood was often an item of commerce. The ubiquitous "trading posts" and "Indian villages" that still are evident along Interstate Highway 40, the successor to Route 66, testify to the enduring trade in local crafts and curiosities.[18]

In the fall of 1932 Smith constructed a checking station at the point where the Painted Desert rim road connected with U.S. 66. Cross-country travelers could easily leave the highway and follow this road along the Painted Desert to the old inn, some six miles to the northwest.[19] He expected the new acquisition to attract additional tourists, but neither he, nor Pinkley, nor Albright had given much thought to the impact of the expanded national monument on local residents, particularly the small operators along the highway near Petrified Forest. The Park Service presumed that the expanded reserve would stimulate the local economy somewhat. After all, more tourists should translate into a demand for more goods and services from businesses in St. Johns, Springerville, Adamana, Holbrook, and Winslow. But local resentment exploded in mid-1933, when Julia Miller, owner of an establishment on U.S. 66 called the Lion Farm, complained to Interior Secretary Harold Ickes and Park Service Director Arno B. Cammerer.[20] Smith's checking station and Painted Desert road, she charged, were ruining local businesses in the vicinity. Miller's complaints were accompanied by a petition signed by sixty-three residents, who demanded Smith's removal or transfer.[21]

Smith's rangers at the checking station in fact sent motorists along the desert rim road and on south to Petrified Forest, if they so desired, the superintendent maintained. The practice, of course, had the effect of inflating the number of visitors at his monument. The superintendent knew about Julia Miller and her Lion Farm and made no effort to disguise his loathing for both the woman and her enterprise. Park rangers ignored the Lion Farm, which, according to Smith, "would offend the sensibilities of any refined person." Miller kept a variety of animals in coops and cages, feeding them horse meat from animals killed on the range. "Sometimes the stench was overpowering," Smith complained. When he visited the place on August 2, Miller had on display an antelope fawn, two eagles, a bobcat, a fox, a mountain lion, a dog and a cat, and a couple of kittens. As far as Smith was concerned, the Lion Farm was "an unsightly, unsanitary place." Secretary Ickes shared Smith's disdain. Though he had never visited the establishment, he told Cammerer, "I have passed it on a number of occasions and I have felt it to be a blot on the scenery." Ickes understandably supported his superintendent at Petrified Forest, noting that he could find nothing in Smith's report that might be termed discrimination against Miller or her neighbors.[22]

The Miller affair might have ended at that point had it not been for the petition signed by local residents. That forced Ickes to turn the complaint over to the Interior Department's Division of Investigations early in 1934. The inquiry by special agent Paul F. Cutter continued through the summer and eventually exonerated Smith, but Cutter was adamant about removing the checking station. Local residents derided it as a "nuisance station," and it clearly was a source of ill will toward the Park Service and Petrified Forest. "Tourists ought to be able to make up their own minds about visiting the monument," he pointed out.[23]

Cutter was correct. Smith, in fact, inflated the number of visitors at the monument by registering motorists at his checking station. Harold Sellers Colton, custodian at Walnut Canyon National Monument near Flagstaff, happened to drive past Smith's station on U.S. 66 in May of 1934, and he encountered a ranger stopping all cars on the highway and registering them as visiting the monument. As a custodian, Colton recognized the ploy, which was not an uncommon one among Pinkley's custodians in the Southwest. Pinkley hoped, often in vain, that increasing the number of visitors would lead to additional funding. Money was allocated, at least partially, on the basis of the number of visitors recorded, and Colton realized that Smith "was seeing that his attendance was increased." Colton's complaint to Cammerer undoubtedly contributed to the arguments against the checking station. Walnut Canyon's custodian later heard that the offending ranger had been assigned elsewhere and that the registering of motorists had ended. "I was not very popular with Superintendent White Mountain Smith," Colton admitted.[24]

Cutter recommended that Smith be transferred to another location without prejudice but left the decision to Albright.[25] Having found a competent superintendent for Petrified Forest, the Park Service director was willing to overlook the conflict with Julia Miller and her supporters. Smith stayed on at the monument. Mrs. Miller offered to sell her property to the government about a year later, but since it occupied land leased from the state of Arizona, the Park Service did not act. The state hesitated to cancel her lease and indeed renewed it the next year. The warring parties in northeastern Arizona continued to coexist after that—Julia Miller secure in her property with a new lease, and White Mountain Smith exonerated by the Interior Department but undoubtedly somewhat humbled by the encounter.

Julia Miller and her neighbors had much in common with similar small operators along Route 66 in the Southwest. Most simply sought to earn a living from the highway's traffic and resorted to the obvious kinds of establishments—gas stations, lunch counters, small stores, and motels. Miller's Lion Farm was a novel variation of the roadside "zoos" that often advertised rattlesnakes, pythons, and "reptile gardens"—anything to induce motorists to pull over. Once they stopped, travel-worn tourists would eat at the lunch counter and probably purchase a souvenir or two.[26] The Lion Farm, officially called the Painted Desert Park and Zoo of Native Animals, was particularly obtrusive, and Miller's use of "Painted Desert" in the name suggested a connection with the national monument. By today's standards Miller's operation would constitute an incompatible land use, not to mention a violation of state and federal laws. But in the 1930s, those restrictions were unknown and such establishments common.

The Lion Farm episode also represented a variation of the usual conflicts between national parks and concessionaires. At the major parks, superintendents often tangled with private companies like the Yellowstone Park Transportation Company and the Yosemite Park and Curry Company and their political allies. But few national monuments were large enough to require the services of entrepreneurs. Petrified Forest's only true concessionaire was Dick Grigsby, and his operation was small—a store and a few tourist cabins. But nearby businesses—the Nelsons' hotel in Adamana, the Painted Desert Inn, and the Lion Farm—could be similar sources of tension. Like formal concessions, they were dependent on the monument for their income, yet they remained independent of Park Service regulations. The conflict over the Lion Farm was not the last such encounter for Petrified Forest. Like a ghost from the past, the enterprise would reappear to frustrate several later superintendents.

The Interior Department investigation had distracted Smith at a critical time in the monument's development. Once free of the incubus of the investigation, he could turn his attention fully to the needs of Petrified Forest, where federal public works programs had made available generous funding and extensive workforces to undertake major improvements throughout this vastly expanded national monument.

For the drought-stricken, economically devastated American West of the 1930s, Franklin Roosevelt's New Deal held considerable promise. Depression, drought, and dust—the "formidable trio," as historian Richard Lowitt has described them—brought disaster to the country's arid regions. New Deal programs addressed soil erosion, range management, reclamation, and related conservation issues, and over the years the Roosevelt program presented the West with "an opportunity to transform itself." [27] While many such programs were utilitarian in their objectives, the New Deal, in fact, had its proponents of preservation. In much the same way that Secretary of the Interior Harold Ickes had dominated conservation and reclamation programs in the West, this progressive Republican turned New Dealer also shaped measures to administer the country's national parks and monuments.

The most obvious feature of the New Deal for the parks and monuments was the sudden influx of cash. The amount of money allocated to the national parks skyrocketed during the New Deal years. The regular appropriations for the Park Service increased only modestly, but the Public Works Administration channeled $40,242,691 into the agency, and the Civilian Conservation Corps camps in various parks added another $82,250,467. Between 1935 and 1937 the Works Progress Administration added $24,000,000. Emergency conservation work in various park service units peaked in 1937, when the National Park Service counted 13,900 employees. These men were spread across a much expanded system that in 1940 encompassed 161 units, including 26 national parks and 82 national monuments in addition to historical parks, military parks, national battlefields, and historic sites—more than twice the number of units in 1933.[28]

For the usually neglected national monuments like Petrified Forest, the New Deal years represented a watershed in their history. The domination of the national parks within the system finally was eclipsed, as officials recognized the significance of the monuments and other categories of reserves. As the Park Service extended its responsibilities to embrace such places, the value of the monuments became increasingly obvious, and administrators exerted more influence over them than ever before. In part, the new recognition of the national monuments reflected the expanded appropriations available through New Deal agencies. "The Park Service received so much money in the 1930s," historian Hal Rothman has written, "that it was able to spread its resources throughout the system."[29] Not only did the monuments receive generous funding, but the CCC workers provided much-needed labor, particularly in the natural, or scientific, reserves like Petrified Forest.

Initially, local administrators like Frank Pinkley and White Mountain Smith had no idea what to expect from the new Roosevelt administration, although it soon became apparent that additional funds would be forthcoming. Congress had established the Public Works Administration in June of 1933 with an appropriation of $3.3 billion under Title II of the National Industrial Recovery Act. The new agency could operate in a number of ways: by instituting its own programs, by allocating funds to other agencies to finance construction work, or by providing loans and grants to the states to initiate such work. The goal remained the same—to stimulate the country's lagging economy by employing idle workers. In the fall of 1933, PWA money trickled into Petrified Forest National Monument and was used to construct and pave footpaths in the various forests. Additional money was allocated for bridges and roadwork.

While various PWA projects were initiated around the country, New Deal officials made plans for an expanded federal works program. Harry Hopkins, head of the Federal Emergency Relief Administration, was particularly anxious to put idle men to work and proposed such a program to Franklin Roosevelt in the fall of 1933. The country then was drifting into the fourth winter of the Great Depression, and Roosevelt liked the idea of a federal works program that would help some of the unemployed through one more winter. Since the PWA was slow getting under way, the president suggested that Hopkins might tap that agency's money to fund the new project. Out of this brief meeting came the Civil Works Administration, an emergency unemployment relief program. With funding from the Federal Emergency Relief Administration and the PWA, the CWA would employ men in a variety of federal, state, and local projects. Hopkins set a truly ambitious objective, announcing in mid-November 1933 that the agency expected to employ 4 million men by December 15. The target proved unrealistic; still, more than 2.6 million men were on CWA rolls on that date, and by the middle of January 1934, the 4 million mark had been passed.

In rural northeastern Arizona, the CWA jobs were accepted as gratefully as they were in such industrial centers as Detroit and Pittsburgh. Petrified Forest received a CWA allocation of $29,890 in early December to cover thirteen projects. "On December 7, I made a requisition on the National Re-employment Office for 25 men," Smith reported, "and on December 11, Civil Works Projects were under way." By the end of the first week, Smith had 69 men working; the number grew to 105 the following week, and at the end of December, Petrified Forest was employing 129 men on a variety of projects. Though the wages were meager, the money quickly entered the local economy. "It made possible a happy Christmas for many times the number employed," Smith acknowledged, "and has caused a brighter outlook for the coming year."[30]

Most of the work performed at Petrified Forest involved trail and road construction, campground development, landscaping, and fencing—projects that otherwise would have been delayed for years. More important, the CWA authorized an archaeological survey of sites within the monument. H. P. Mera of the Laboratory of Anthropology in Santa Fe, New Mexico, and his associate C. B. Cosgrove directed the endeavor. Their resulting list included 109 sites in and around Petrified Forest and provided an outline of the region's prehistory. They also excavated and restored Agate House, a Pueblo III site (A.D. 1000–1250), and the Puerco Indian Ruin, a much larger Pueblo IV (A.D. 1250–1450) complex built around a plaza near the Puerco River. The restored sites gave Petrified Forest two sophisticated archaeological exhibits and substantially expanded the possibilities for interpretive endeavors at the reserve. At the Flattops, a remote site in the southern part of the monument, Mera and Cosgrove's crew also excavated two pithouses in this Basketmaker II (up to A.D. 500–700) village, which includes the earliest known sites in the monument.[31]

The Civil Works Administration came to an end in the spring of 1934; on April 19, Smith discharged the last seventeen CWA workers at Petrified Forest and totaled up his expenditures. If administering the programs had been frustrating from time to time, given the seemingly arbitrary dictates from Washington, Smith found some comfort in the fact that funds appropriated between December 1933 and April 1934 dwarfed the meager allocations that the monument typically received. Seldom had the Park Service ever allocated Petrified Forest more than a few thousand dollars. In the larger perspective of the Southwestern National Monuments, the contributions of the CWA were easily lost in the day-to-day frustrations of shifting supplies and men among scattered sites in remote monuments. Frank Pinkley, who supervised several hundred men scattered over fifteen projects, vowed that he would always remember the CWA with the same affection that the Navajo accorded their Long Walk to Bosque Redondo in 1864.[32]

The Civil Works Administration was just the beginning, not the end, of federal projects destined to benefit Petrified Forest and its sister reserves. Hardly a month after Smith had said his good-byes to the last CWA workers, Lieutenant E. F. David arrived to establish a "fly camp" of fifteen Civilian Conservation Corps workers near the Puerco River. An unemployment relief measure, the Civilian Conservation Corps Reforestation Relief Act of 1933, authorized the Civilian Conservation Corps to provide work for 250,000 men between the ages of eighteen and twenty-five. As the measure's title indicates, the Corps was involved largely in conservation work, ranging from reforestation and prevention of soil erosion to flood control projects and improvements in national parks and monuments. Enrollees were stationed at work camps under the direction of U.S. Army officers and received $30 per month, part of which went to dependents back home. At the various National Park Service reserves, that agency's superintendent was responsible for carrying out the emergency conservation work programs.[33]

Much of the Civilian Conservation Corps activity consisted of mundane trail and road building and landscaping. Like CCC workers across the country, those at Petrified Forest planted trees, beginning with five hundred cottonwood slips set in place along the Puerco River.[34] Improved roads and trails made ruins and pictographs accessible to more tourists, and Petrified Forest's first Park Service naturalist, Myrl V. Walker, trained a contingent of CCC workers as guides to conduct nature walks. He found that the young men were dependable assistants for his geological research, so he also employed them on excavations at Blue Mesa. (See chapter 8 for details on Walker's career.)

Only a few CCC men were involved in the excavation, and the nature walks and related activities involved a small number more. The corps' major contribution at Petrified Forest was to be the virtual rebuilding of the Painted Desert Inn. Lore had originally purchased the Painted Desert land from the Santa Fe Railroad. The inn, constructed of stone and adobe by local Navajo workers, initially operated as a trading post and lunch counter. Lore had made few essential improvements and even continued to haul water to the inn rather than install a water system. The structure also lacked electricity and a telephone system, and there was no sewer system. When the Park Service purchased it, officials had determined to develop the inn and the surrounding area to allow visitors to enjoy the Painted Desert with at least a degree of comfort and convenience.[35]

Smith and NPS architect Lorimer H. Skidmore inspected the inn thoroughly before renovation began. Their examination revealed structural weaknesses that had not been anticipated. Cracks had spread across the building's walls—not a surprising development in plastered walls. But a bit of scraping and probing beneath the plaster indicated why. The mortar that held the stone walls in place was not really mortar at all, but rather a sandy mud. The walls appeared relatively solid only because Lore's builder had covered the joints with sound mortar, apparently to prevent the dried mud from dissolving in the rain and sloughing off. The mud would have to be dug out and replaced with real mortar—an endeavor that would slow down renovation by several months. The inn rested on an equally shaky foundation, which necessitated construction of supports and underpinnings for the existing walls before they could be remodeled.[36]

Renovation began in May of 1937, and the work proved excessively

Painted Desert Inn, 1940, following the renovation by the Civilian Conservation Corps (Photograph courtesy of Petrified Forest National Park)

time-consuming. New construction undoubtedly would have proceeded much faster. By the end of the 1937–38 winter's work, much of the building's first floor had been completed. When moderate weather returned in the spring of 1938, the old roof was removed and the second-floor walls remodeled. Installation of the new roof beams followed, and masonry work began on both the inside and outside. Workers next installed structural columns with corbels, shaping them with an adze to provide a rustic finish. When commercial door and window frames were used, they were sandblasted to present aged surfaces.[37] Once the laborious work of rebuilding foundations and walls was completed, renovation went forward quickly, even though shortages of labor and supplies occasionally stalled the project.

By the end of the following year, renovation was nearly finished. In all, the two-story inn enclosed 7,520 square feet of space. Its stone and plaster walls were twenty-seven inches thick by the time renovation was com-

A tourist and a "Harvey Car" at Petrified Forest, early 1930s (Photograph from the Fred Harvey Collection, courtesy of the Museum of Northern Arizona)

plete. The building's architecture clearly reflected southwestern pueblo construction, though it was modified somewhat to incorporate Spanish colonial influences through the adzed beams and carved corbels and brackets. Skidmore's plans separated the building into two parts—one primarily a Park Service facility, the other an extensive area to be leased to a concessionaire.[38] The latter included a lunch counter, kitchen, dining rooms, and an enclosed dining porch with access to decks that overlooked the Painted Desert. In this respect, the Painted Desert Inn functioned much as did Grand Canyon's El Tovar, and indeed it became a landmark above the Painted Desert.

The process of putting the final touches on the inn dragged through 1939, as did work on employees' residences and other facilities. On July 1, 1940, Standard Concessions, Inc., of Chicago signed the first contract to operate the Painted Desert Inn for three years. The company paid the government $10 per year for its concession to operate the inn, with net profits set at 6 percent.[39] On July 4, 1940, after almost three full years of work, the Painted Desert Inn opened its doors to tourists again. This time, travelers encountered a large, modern, efficiently operated facility, drastically different from the humble trading post and lunch counter that H. D. Lore had maintained.

Because of construction projects like the Painted Desert Inn and even the more prosaic work of reforestation and trail building, the Civilian Conservation Corps has left an enduring aura of goodwill. Indeed, its popularity has insulated it from much criticism, even though its construction projects in some parks and monuments adversely affected the environment. The corps proved adept at building facilities like those at Petrified Forest; all were labor intensive and employed young men idled by the depression—Washington's basic goal in the 1930s. Those projects, of course, encouraged tourists to visit the national parks and made their stay more pleasant.

Because facilities at Petrified Forest were so shabby, the CCC construction resulted in dramatic improvements from one end of the reserve to the other. The depression-era Civilian Conservation Corps offered a precedent for later federally sponsored improvements in such reserves. Slightly more than a decade elapsed between the end of the CCC and the initiation of another national park improvement plan—this one designated Mission 66. In its commitment to adding amenities for tourists, Mission 66 recalled its New Deal predecessor.

Completion of the inn coincided with another attempt by local businessmen and politicians to gain national park designation for Petrified Forest. The new movement was predictable, for during the 1930s Petrified Forest more than doubled its size through acquisition of the Painted Desert. Moreover, its facilities—once the source of embarrassment and derision—had improved immensely thanks to the PWA, CCC, and CWA. By the end of the depression decade, the monument in fact rather resembled a national park. Back in 1906, the expanses of petrified wood had provided sufficient justification to warrant its establishment as a national monument. But subsequent expansion, particularly the incorporation of Blue Forest and the Painted Desert, added to the original scientific site an expanse of scenic landscape—the ingredient that identified national parks and separated them from the monuments. If Petrified Forest's scenery did not quite match the monumental grandeur of Yellowstone or the Grand Canyon, it nonetheless possessed its own inherent, high-desert beauty and brilliant color.

The new park campaign began, as had others, in Holbrook. In the fall of 1937, members of the chamber of commerce and other leading citizens met with Arizona's Senator Henry Fountain Ashurst to discuss the project. White Mountain Smith, too, was invited, though his support was less than enthusiastic.[40] In contrast, Senator Ashurst was a vigorous and vocal supporter. He had earlier supported a bill to establish Grand Canyon as a national park and was anxious to do the same for Petrified Forest. He introduced such a resolution in the Senate in June 1938, and the measure was sent on to the Committee on Public Lands and Surveys with instructions to investigate all matters relating to the feasibility of establishing Petrified Forest National Park. In turn, the details of the investigation were assigned to a subcommittee chaired by Ashurst and including Senators Carl Hatch of New Mexico and A. E. Reames of Oregon, which held hearings in northern Arizona in August.

The "suave and splendid Henry Fountain Ashurst" delighted his constituents in Holbrook when he chaired hearings to elicit public response to the projected name change for Petrified Forest. Testimony from local boosters stressed the need to expand tourism as a means to stimulate the economy of northeastern Arizona. E. V. McEvoy was representative of the people in attendance as he explained to the committee that cattle ranching had virtually disappeared in the Little Colorado River Valley. Expanded tourism, he maintained, might take up the slack in the economy, and designation of Petrified Forest as a national park would likely have a positive effect. Others reinforced his argument, indicating that a good share of the residents of Navajo and Apache Counties supported the change in designation and expected to benefit economically from it.[41]

The story was much the same when the hearings moved to La Posada in Winslow. A. B. Cammerer, now director of the National Park Service, attended both meetings and was one of the few people to question the park designation. He argued that Petrified Forest was the country's leading national monument, but that as a park it would not enjoy such high status. Indeed, ranking well behind Yellowstone, Grand Canyon, and Yosemite,

Petrified Forest would find it difficult to compete for federal funds. He hinted, too, that in the future some federal money for the projected Petrified Forest National Park might be allocated to build hotels and restaurants within the park, and these would compete with businesses in Holbrook and Winslow.[42]

On January 23, 1939, Ashurst nevertheless introduced legislation to change Petrified Forest's name. By early spring, the bill was in trouble. Acting Interior Secretary Harry Slattery advised against it. "Petrified Forest is one of the oldest and most outstanding national monuments," he explained, "and is cited constantly in our public relations as an example of an ideal national monument." Its designation as a national park would lessen its prestige in comparison to Yellowstone, Grand Canyon, and "other large scenic parks." Secretary Harold Ickes later dashed the hopes of park proponents when he bluntly reminded them that "park designation was reserved for areas of scenic beauty; Monuments were objects or regions of peculiar scientific or historic interest."[43]

Secretary Ickes read the Antiquities Act literally, and Petrified Forest fit precisely within the law's definition of a place of scientific interest. The addition of the Painted Desert was not sufficient to redefine the monument as an area of scenic beauty—at least not in the secretary's eyes. Petrified Forest's case was similar to that of Bandelier National Monument. In the early 1930s the National Park Service considered establishing Cliff Cities National Park in northern New Mexico. After an inspection of the Bandelier area, Roger Toll advised against a national park there because the scenery was not "sufficiently unusual and outstanding." He explained to Albright that the choice was "between having a large and important national monument and a rather small and unimportant national park." Monumentalism, it is evident, still shaped Washington's definition of national parks, even at the end of the 1930s. Petrified Forest in 1939 was in essentially the same situation as the Bandelier area eight years earlier. And like Bandelier it remained a monument, its proponents accommodating themselves to the designation of "outstanding national monument."[44]

The perennial quest for a Petrified Forest National Park is understandable. Local residents and proponents perhaps did not understand the nuances between parks and monuments, but they clearly perceived that national parks were higher in status and more generously supported. Those characteristics easily translated into more federal expenditures on facilities and more tourists, too. The Park Service had fostered such impressions from the time of Mather and Albright. The agency's first director liked to employ such terms as "elevated" to park status, and he coined the phrase "national parkhood." The tendency of some monuments to move on to become national parks particularly irritated Frank Pinkley, who resented the practice. But National Park Service policy in the 1920s and 1930s seemingly encouraged the upgrading of at least certain scenic monuments to parks.[45]

Although people in Holbrook and Winslow would have much preferred a national park in their vicinity, Petrified Forest actually would have been better served by a policy that encouraged development and interpretation of unique resources. Important paleontological and archaeological work had occurred in Petrified Forest in the previous decades, but those scientific discoveries were only slowly integrated into interpretive programs, which usually consisted of displays and exhibits. Too often, visitors still missed the importance of the ancient environment in Petrified Forest and regarded the monument as a roadside attraction.

Whatever the Interior Department's rationale, local proponents were disappointed. Senator Ashurst was crushed; he described the defeat of the park measure as "the worst parliamentary defeat in 27 years as a senator." He had grown up in northern Arizona and had often referred to Petrified Forest in his speeches. But Secretary Ickes, he lamented, says "it is worthy of being nothing more than a national monument. No longer shall I be known as the gay and blithesome Henry Fountain, but as the sad and dolorous Henry Fountain."[46]

The defeat came in the spring of 1939, less than a year before completion of the Painted Desert Inn. And while Arizona's senior senator was deeply disappointed in the outcome, Smith and his staff at Petrified Forest had much to be thankful for. The Great Depression had not yet ended, but visitors were arriving in greatly increased numbers. After visitation plummeted in the early 1930s, the numbers gradually crept upward, reaching 105,396 at the end of the 1937 travel year, slightly more than in the record year of 1929. As of June 30, 1938, the figure was 109,331, with several

months of heavy travel still to be recorded for the year. In mid-July of the
following year, park officials noted that the number of visitors was close
to 175,000.[47]

Moreover, the national monument designation was hardly a curse. Petrified Forest, by the Interior Department's estimation, was the country's
leading monument, and at the end of the 1930s, it was not the forlorn
collection of dilapidated shacks and bad roads that had greeted White
Mountain Smith in 1929. Now augmented in size and facilities, it was a
modern, efficient reserve, complete with museum, sophisticated archaeological displays, and a professional staff. For the Park Service, these added
up to an ideal monument—not a national park. PWA funds and CCC workers clearly contributed to the monument's successful growth, and Smith
had largely determined its course of development and quietly guided its
steady improvement. When he moved on in 1940 to Grand Teton National
Park, he left his successor a facility that was well equipped to handle the
growing number of tourists who stopped there. And when another national park movement inevitably blossomed, Petrified Forest and its personnel finally acquired the long-awaited national park designation.

7

AFTER THE WAR: MISSION 66 TO NATIONAL PARK AND BEYOND

I couldn't see the forest and I never did find the monument, but you sure do have some mighty pretty rocks around here!

American tourist, ca. 1955

The national parks and monuments, which had enjoyed generous federal support during the New Deal, were nearly abandoned during World War II. Shortly after Pearl Harbor, Congress reduced Park Service appropriations by 50 percent, and in 1942 the agency's headquarters were moved to Chicago to make room in Washington, D.C., for the military. The Park Service naturally terminated its travel promotion efforts, and by August of 1942 the Civilian Conservation Corps had largely departed from the parks and monuments. Appropriations fell off to only $5 million in 1943 and remained at that meager figure until 1947.

During the war, various commercial interests—ranchers, lumbermen, miners, and others—sought to exploit resources in the parks in behalf of the war effort. The military, too, expected to use these reserves, and in some instances their activities were extensive and detrimental. Much more damaging was the general neglect over nearly five years, for immediately after the war these deteriorating federal reserves were engulfed by a new generation of automobile tourists. In record numbers they traveled to parks and monuments that had lacked maintenance for years and now were reopening with reduced numbers of rangers, naturalists, and other key personnel. By the late 1940s, the national parks faced nearly insurmountable threats to their integrity.

Repairing and refurbishing older structures and adding modern facilities were immediate needs, and the Park Service had a useful precedent in the Civilian Conservation Corps. Its new program, Mission 66, was the brainchild of Park Service Director Conrad Wirth. Authorized in 1956, it projected a major, ten-year agenda to improve thoroughly the various Park Service reserves. Like its CCC predecessor, Mission 66 was designed to renovate and expand facilities for tourists. Officials gave comparatively little thought to environmental issues in the parks, and their limited perspective had prompted considerable criticism by the 1960s.

A new series of concerns, loosely described as "external threats," emerged in the 1970s and 1980s and constituted an additional burden for the Park Service. Incompatible land uses on neighboring terrain, ranging from real estate development to mining, soon endangered the integrity of some parks, and before long both air and water pollution threatened even isolated reserves. Such external developments occurred almost imperceptibly, but by the 1980s many observers recognized that the country's parks faced a new kind of danger. The National Parks and Conservation Association testified to the extent of the threat in 1982 when it published its important study, *The National Parks in Crisis*.

None of these problems were even vaguely anticipated in 1940, when supervision of America's "ideal national monument" passed to Thomas E. Whitcraft. Petrified Forest then was in the best condition in its history, the result of government expenditures and Civilian Conservation Corps labor during the previous decade. It had more than doubled in size during those years to embrace 145 square miles, nearly all of it owned by the federal government. The exceptions were 7,963 acres of privately owned land and a small parcel of 637 acres that belonged to the state of Arizona. Part of that was leased to the proprietor of the Painted Desert Park, the descendant of Julia Miller's Lion Farm.

The new Painted Desert Inn was an immediate success. Easily accessible from U.S. 66, it became a popular stop for travelers, offering them an opportunity to relax, purchase a meal and drinks, and enjoy a panoramic view of the Painted Desert before continuing their journey across the high desert of northern Arizona. At the other end of the monument, Dick Grigsby retained his yearly Park Service permit to operate a general store and restaurant at the Rainbow Forest Lodge near the monument headquarters.[1]

The new facilities easily handled the record 230,427 tourists in 1941, the last year of peace before the United States entered World War II. The impact of that conflict on Petrified Forest became apparent the following year, as the number of tourists tapered off to 189,772 and then plummeted to less than 50,000 in 1943—a 74 percent decrease.[2] Employees at the reserve enlisted in the armed services or were drafted. The Painted Desert Inn closed for the next two years, and Petrified Forest, like the other monuments and parks, operated on a much restricted basis.

Within a year of the war's end, the number of visitors to the monument already approximated prewar statistics and in subsequent years far surpassed them, reflecting a pattern common throughout all Park Service sites. For the first time in years, Americans finally had the opportunity to enjoy their automobiles free of the restrictions of wartime rationing, and they flocked to the country's national parks.

Others went West planning to stay there. More than 8 million people moved to the western states after World War II, 3.5 million of them settling in California. Route 66 bore the burden of these new migrants, who shared common experiences along the "mother road," as John Steinbeck had named it in The Grapes of Wrath. Across the Southwest, desolate stretches of the highway were interrupted only by occasional motels, eating places, and roadside attractions. "We just drove, and then we'd stay in a motel," recalled one postwar migrant, Cynthia Troup. "We stopped at some caverns; then we did Will Rogers." At the Painted Desert they pulled over to take a few photographs but by then were exceedingly anxious to get to Los Angeles—a sentiment undoubtedly shared by millions of others in the late 1940s and 1950s.[3]

Only a small percentage of Route 66 travelers drove through Petrified Forest National Monument, but those visitors virtually overwhelmed the place and actually constituted a threat to its integrity as a scientific monument. They clearly attested to the popularity of Petrified Forest, and their numbers buttressed the arguments of those who still longed for the national park label. At the same time, though, officials were hard-pressed to maintain Petrified Forest as a unique natural wonder and not just another attraction along U.S. 66, which now blossomed with a variety of establishments catering to tourists.

With the burgeoning number of visitors came a resurgence of theft and vandalism, but Whitcraft lacked personnel to maintain effective patrols. His observations in the 1940s sound remarkably like those of William Nelson twenty years earlier, when automobiles were making their first appearances there. "The temptation for visitors to take small specimens of the fossil wood seems to be almost irresistible," the superintendent complained. Local residents, too, helped themselves to petrified wood and looted archaeological ruins, expecting to turn a profit by selling souvenirs to tourists.[4]

In June of 1947, the Fred Harvey Company took over the Painted Desert Inn concession. Shortly thereafter, the company called on Mary Elizabeth Jane Colter to oversee the decoration of the building's interior. Colter had been associated with Fred Harvey since 1902 as an architect and designer, and she had worked on nearly a dozen of the company's establishments in the Southwest, including Hopi House, El Tovar, Hermit's Rest, and the Watchtower at Grand Canyon. The Spanish-Pueblo style of the Painted Desert Inn was one that Colter liked, and she relied on that motif in designing the interior.[5]

Fifteen years earlier when Colter had decorated the Watchtower, she had hired a young Hopi artist, Fred Kabotie (then a guide and musician at Grand Canyon), to paint murals of his people's legends in the Watchtower's Hopi Room. In 1947, she again engaged Kabotie, who painted two murals in the Painted Desert Inn dining room. One displays the importance of the eagle in Hopi life; for the other Kabotie depicted the journey to a salt lake near Zuni, recalling that the Hopi once traveled from their mesas through the Painted Desert on their way to the lake to collect salt. "To get this salt of theirs," Kabotie explained, "the Hopi really make a big ceremony out of it." The murals effectively place Petrified Forest within the cultural context of the region and portray the complexity of local Indian traditions. Kabotie's murals became a central attraction at the inn, and in 1976 the room was officially dedicated as the Kabotie Room.[6]

The Painted Desert Inn had only a half-dozen small rooms for overnight guests, and it could not begin to meet the needs of the postwar automobile tourists. Superintendent Whitcraft resisted the inclination to build more accommodations within the reserve, maintaining instead that tourists should take advantage of motels, campgrounds, and restaurants in neighboring towns along Route 66.[7] In opposing construction of hotels and lodges, Whitcraft took an important step toward preserving Petrified Forest's essential integrity. Fewer guests staying overnight in the reserve would mean less theft and damage. Further, he anticipated recommendations that would be set forth in the 1960s by such organizations as the National Parks and Conservation Association, which criticized the road building and the accommodations that beckoned ever more visitors to the overcrowded national parks.

The number of visitors to Petrified Forest consistently set records. Once a source of pride and accomplishment, such statistics now engendered a degree of frustration. At the peak of the summer tourist season, Whitcraft had to acknowledge that "our service to visitors was considerably below par."[8] Even with the ranger force expanded by an additional ten seasonal rangers, the superintendent could not adequately protect the petrified trees and archaeological sites. The amount of wood confiscated at checking stations provided a broad measure of the extent of theft occurring within the monument. In 1948, rangers recovered about nine thousand pounds of purloined souvenirs, indicating that on a typical day, tourists tried to get away with twenty to twenty-five pounds. And what they could not remove, they often damaged. The necessary routine of ministering to tourists meant that plans for expanded interpretive programs had to be limited.[9]

At the same time, the Painted Desert Inn, so meticulously restored by the Civilian Conservation Corps, already showed signs of deterioration. New cracks appeared regularly in its masonry walls, and William E. Branch, who succeeded Whitcraft in 1950, wondered whether the structure could ever be stabilized. The inn rested on unstable bentonite, which expands and contracts in response to the climate. It seemed likely that the clay had gradually dried and contracted during the dry years of the early 1950s, causing the building to settle month after month. For the time being, the inn seemed safe, but extensive repairs would be needed soon. Branch rather expected to see the structure collapse with the next major storm. By the spring of 1951, both Branch and Lyle Bennett of the Park Service's regional office in Santa Fe generally agreed that the Painted Desert Inn would eventually face condemnation. In the interim, cracks could be filled and walls replastered; but the historic building's fate seemed sealed.[10]

The travelers who crowded into the snack bar and curio shop at the inn arrived via Route 66. While such interstate highways lured ever more tourists to the western parks and monuments, these routes often constituted indirect threats to the character of neighboring reserves by promoting incompatible land uses. As travel increased along U.S. 66, local businessmen naturally hoped to turn a profit by catering to motorists, continuing a practice that dated back to the 1920s. Postwar America was enjoying an economic boom, and the purchase of automobiles and subsequent cross-country travel was but one reflection of the country's affluence. All along Route 66, traffic invariably was heavy enough to support numerous roadside businesses. Combinations of gas stations and restaurants, usually operated by a husband and wife, were typical of such enterprises. Often a motel would be added, as business warranted, and in northern Arizona and New Mexico an "Indian trading post" could always attract motorists. The Jack Rabbit Trading Post, built in 1947 just west of Petrified Forest at Joseph City, has operated successfully ever since and has "made three or four owners rich," a local resident has remarked.[11] Often travelers themselves recognized the highway's potential for income and simply settled down and opened a gas station, motel, or restaurant. "Route 66 was a gold mine," one service station owner recalls.[12]

The Arizona Highway Department began planning the realignment and widening of U.S. 66 in the spring of 1951. Branch learned, to his pleasure, that the realigned highway would pass a mile and a half south of a roadside establishment called the Painted Desert Park. The place had been the nemesis of Petrified Forest superintendents ever since the 1930s when Julia Miller established it. Located on state land within the monument's boundaries, the old Lion Farm was now leased to Charles Jacobs and several partners, who preferred to call it the Painted Desert Park. Its shoddy appearance had

Painted Desert Park, 1957, on Route 66 near Petrified Forest (Photograph by F. Fagregren, courtesy of Petrified Forest National Park)

bothered Whitcraft, and Branch, too, despised the place. The name Painted Desert Park, unfortunately, easily misled tourists to believe that it was a Park Service operation. Whether intentionally or not, the owners profited from the travelers' mistakes.[13]

Jacobs hesitated to expand the operation, fearing that the new U.S. 66 would miss his land entirely. But he also owned additional nearby property along the highway and promptly built another roadside business—a trading post. Next to it he added a forty-foot-high observation tower from which tourists could view the Painted Desert. The place was "quite an eyesore," Branch complained to Washington, and since it was near Petrified Forest, visitors assumed that it was part of the monument. Jacobs had so constructed the trading post that it could be moved to a new location in the event that the realigned highway was too far from his property.[14]

An additional threat to the integrity of Petrified Forest National Monument also emerged in the early fifties, when northeastern Arizona was found to contain significant deposits of uranium. Prospectors filed claims on adjacent land and were eager to build access roads through the monument and even to prospect within its boundaries. Branch, of course, adamantly refused to consider such requests, aware that uranium mining represented the greatest threat ever to Petrified Forest.[15] It was not the mere mining of the radioactive ore that was dangerous, although that threat was substantial. Later accidents during uranium refining would pollute the ephemeral rivers that drain the area.

The overwhelming issue of the 1950s was neither uranium mining nor the Lion Farm, but the large number of tourists who drove through the monument. These hundreds of thousands of visitors attested to its popularity and prompted a resurgence of interest in gaining national park status for Petrified Forest. In Arizona Senator Carl Hayden, park proponents found a new champion for the cause; in 1955 Hayden introduced a measure to change the name of the reserve to Petrified Forest National Park.[16] That bill was unsuccessful, but with it the senator had initiated a process designed to achieve the coveted national park designation.

Revival of the park plan coincided with a major improvement program that was evolving within the National Park Service under the leadership of its new director, Conrad Wirth. The problems that frustrated personnel at Petrified Forest after World War II were only part of an extensive deterioration of all of America's parks and monuments. Although Park Service funding was once again above $30 million in 1950, Wirth realized that almost a decade of neglect had caused extensive deterioration to roads and facilities. Twenty-one new reserves had been added to the park system, and nearly twice as many people were visiting the parks and monuments as had done so in 1940. Appropriations consequently never kept pace with needs, and Wirth learned, too, that "Cold War costs left very little funding for the National Park Service."[17]

Popular magazines dramatized the deterioration of the parks and monuments, reflecting the complaints of American tourists. In January 1955, *Readers Digest* published "The Shocking Truth about our National Parks," in which Charles Stevenson warned tourists that a trip to a national park was likely to be "fraught with discomfort, disappointment, even danger." Park Service personnel could not provide essential services, and water, sewer, and electrical facilities were severely taxed. In an interview, Wirth conceded that "We actually get scared when we think about the bad health conditions." The *Saturday Evening Post* similarly editorialized about the deplorable conditions and urged improvements. Historian Bernard De Voto, in his *Harper's Monthly* column, described the conditions he found during the course of a trip that took him through fifteen national parks in 1953. Some of the housing for Park Service employees reminded him of the Hoovervilles of the depression era, and salaries were so low that rangers' wives often went to work for concessionaires—"a highly undesirable practice," he added. It raised the specter of conflict of interest, since the Park Service regulated those very companies. Until Congress appropriated more funds, De Voto argued, there was no alternative but to close some of the parks, beginning with Yellowstone, Yosemite, Rocky Mountain, and Grand Canyon. The army could guard them until funds were forthcoming.[18]

Such were the conditions that prompted the new Park Service director to initiate a massive, long-term program for the entire system. It was designated Mission 66; a special committee was charged to develop a ten-year plan to thoroughly improve America's parks and monuments by 1966— the fiftieth anniversary of the National Park Service. Specifically, the Mission 66 Committee had to address the somewhat contradictory objectives of providing Americans with the opportunity to enjoy their national parks while simultaneously protecting these scenic, historic, and prehistoric areas from overuse. President Dwight Eisenhower added his support to the program in January 1956, and Mission 66 formally began on July 1. Congress, too, favored the measure, increasing Park Service appropriations from $32.9 million in the 1955 fiscal year to $48.8 million in 1957. Wirth and his Mission 66 staff estimated the costs of the program at slightly more than $786.5 million, but over its decade-long existence, Mission 66 expenditures substantially exceeded $1 billion.[19]

Although Mission 66 was committed both to protecting scenic areas and to "providing optimum opportunity for public enjoyment," its planners favored projects that immediately benefited visitors. Roads, visitor centers, campgrounds, and similar facilities became the hallmarks of Mission 66 as the Park Service responded to the wants of the American tourist. Commitment to construction projects embodied at least implicit environmental threats. At worst, building hotels, restaurants, bridges, and roads could cause significant environmental damage and also affect wildlife habitat. Catering to the wishes of vacationers naturally made some observers uneasy. In an essay titled "Man and Nature in the National Parks," F. Fraser Darling and Noel D. Eichhorn sharply criticized policies that facilitated travel and accommodations but virtually ignored environmental matters. As the authors pointed out, "Mission 66 has done comparatively little for the plants and animals." Writing in the *Atlantic*, Devereux Butcher, then editor of the *National Parks Magazine*, offered a similarly harsh criticism. Still, such commentary came only after Mission 66 programs were well launched, and in contrast both tourists and the Park Service bureaucracy solidly supported the program. No one seriously considered limiting the number of visitors to the national parks; consequently, facilities had to be expanded.[20]

Unlike Grand Canyon National Park to the west, renowned for its magnificent scenery, extensive hiking trails, campgrounds, and structures like El Tovar, Petrified Forest remained a relatively small operation. It offered only limited facilities for extended visits, and its essential objectives focused on the protection of its major resource, the ancient fossil trees. Naturalists and rangers developed interpretive programs to describe the Triassic environment, and they also integrated the history of the Anasazi and Mogollon inhabitants. But tourists stayed only briefly—usually about two hours. Typically they exited from Route 66, drove through the monument, perhaps stopping briefly at the Painted Desert Inn or at Rainbow Forest, and then continued to Holbrook, Winslow, and Flagstaff to the west or to any number of small roadside establishments that dotted the highway east of Petrified Forest.

Because of the drive-through nature of the reserve, its real needs were limited to improved facilities and interpretive programs. No one advocated construction of hotels or even expansion of the monument's highways. The Painted Desert would remain free of excursions, and tourists would walk to the most important sites within the reserve. Initial Mission 66 plans for Petrified Forest projected only an expansion of facilities to accommodate visitors and construction of housing for employees. Along with those recommendations came the Park Service's acknowledgment that Petrified Forest now finally deserved to be a national park. The incorporation of that designation in Mission 66 plans was the crucial factor in the reserve's eventually successful transition to a national park.

Petrified Forest was the beneficiary of gradually evolving attitudes about national parks. By the 1960s, the definition of parks had broadened considerably to accommodate a diversity of reserves ranging from national seashores and lakeshores to urban recreation areas. Many park proponents still remained emotionally attached to monumentalism, but the political reality was that the park movement was changing.[21] A wider variety of sites would soon come under federal protection. The growing number of visitors at Petrified Forest attested to its popularity and importance in the park system and undoubtedly convinced Mission 66 planners of its national significance. A last factor buttressed the case for park status. The name change would cost very little, since nearly all of the land already was in federal possession, and no expansion was planned.[22]

Senator Hayden, in the meantime, continued his efforts in behalf of the national park designation, introducing a bill on June 21, 1957, to authorize the change. In the House of Representatives, Stewart Udall of Arizona introduced similar legislation. This new measure included a critical provision that would bestow the park title only after the Interior Department had acquired the remaining private lands within the boundaries of the monument. Land exchanges would take care of some of the transfers, but other acreage would have to be purchased. Mission 66 helped here, since funding had been included for that purpose. Congress went along with the legislation, and with Eisenhower's signature on March 28, 1958, it became law. Petrified Forest could become a national park, the new law decreed, but only after title to the private lands was vested in the federal government.[23]

The national park measure engendered only modest opposition, and virtually none came from Arizonans. But the National Parks and Conservation Association consistently opposed the name change. Petrified Forest, one brief editorial pointed out, was an exceptional national monument, though it clearly lacked the "outstanding scenic magnificence, varied natural features," and other characteristics that identified national parks. Devereux Butcher was more explicit. Congress had passed the measure with no opposition, he told Conrad Wirth, although he had done his best to prevent it. From Butcher's perspective, the national park designation for Petrified Forest was "the most flagrant violation of basic protective park principles to have occurred in recent years."[24]

Butcher's critique raised an important point about national parks in postwar America. By the 1960s, Butcher had gained notoriety as one of the more vocal critics of the overdevelopment of national parks and monuments through Mission 66. His essential aim was to "keep the national parks, as nearly as possible, as nature made them." Popularizing and commercializing these reserves, he maintained, is "to cheapen them to the level of ordinary playgrounds."[25]

As for designating Petrified Forest a national park, the National Parks and Conservation Association feared that the move was just another means to attract more visitors to the area and to secure private inholdings. At least on the first point, Butcher and the association were correct. Residents of sparsely settled northeastern Arizona had always pushed for the national park status precisely because they anticipated increased tourism and, with it, a stimulus to the local economy. Holbrook, a half hour's drive to the west, stood to benefit particularly, as did St. Johns and the small towns in the White Mountains south of the park. Arizonans were not looking for concessions within the new park; rather, they hoped to attract more visitors to their nearby towns and businesses. Park status therefore did not mean extensive commercialization of Petrified Forest; it projected only badly needed facilities and interpretive measures. More tourists could actually visit Petrified Forest National Park, but the Park Service would not have to cater to their needs with hotels, campgrounds, and other tourist attractions. Nearby towns, connected to Petrified Forests by modern highways, reduced the need for such facilities within the reserve.

Contrary to Butcher's contention, the park bill did not guarantee private holdings but rather provided a means to eliminate many of them. Throughout the monument's history, private lands had been a nuisance at best for the reserve's staff. Now these holdings—none of them compatible with park use—were scheduled for elimination. In the meantime, they threatened to delay, perhaps to prevent entirely, the long-awaited emergence of Petrified Forest National Park.

For the next several years, Petrified Forest's superintendents Fred Fagergren and Charles E. Humberger worked doggedly to extinguish private property titles, including that of the Painted Desert Park. That process ended only in April of 1962, when the last of the land was transferred to the Park Service. In the meantime, Mission 66 projects were under way, the most dramatic among them the reserve's visitor center near Route 66. The concept of visitor centers grew out of the realization that the small museums so characteristic of many parks and monuments were simply inadequate to meet the demands of postwar tourists. In response, Park Service architects designed open structures that included information about the park, interpretive displays, and other facilities.[26] The new Mission 66 visitor center at Petrified Forest included the park headquarters, housing for employees, and utility areas.

The new facility opened to the public in August of 1962. The Park Service scheduled an open house at this most recent Mission 66 creation on August 28 and also used the occasion to mark the forty-sixth anniversary of "Founders Day" in 1916, when the Park Service was established.[27] Two months later, Fagergren was promoted to the superintendency of Grand Teton National Park, and Petrified Forest, still a national monument, became the charge of Charles E. Humberger, formerly an assistant superintendent at Zion National Park in Utah.

In a general way, Fagergren's tenure at Petrified Forest had paralleled that of White Mountain Smith during the depression years, when federal funds had virtually created a modern national monument. Fagergren's task had been to supervise a second phase of modernization under Mission 66, and like Smith, he had taken on the responsibility for eliminating private lands within the reserve. Remarkably, the Lion Farm, albeit with a new name, had persisted beyond the tenure of both superintendents, although Fagergren acquired most of its holdings before he departed. Smith and Fagergren both witnessed the blossoming of national park movements during their superintendencies. The earlier endeavor had been dashed ingloriously by the Interior Department itself, but the recent quest succeeded.

Only two months after Fagergren's departure, his monument became a national park. On December 8, 1962, fifty-six years after Theodore Roosevelt had proclaimed it a national monument, Petrified Forest became the country's thirty-first national park.[28] Symbolically, Fred Harvey ended its operation at the historic but deteriorating Painted Desert Inn and took over as concessionaire at the new Petrified Forest Visitor Center, occupying a modern, efficient establishment called the Painted Desert Oasis.

Mission 66 and national park status resulted in one undeniable accomplishment: the Park Service now held title to all of the land within the boundaries of Petrified Forest. In the future there would be no incompatible land uses within the reserve—no lion farms, private "parks," trading posts, or similar enterprises. Extensive physical improvements had been added as well, and the new park derived some publicity benefits as a result of the name change. In the 1960s, the Park Service took an additional step to underwrite the reserve's integrity by proposing more than fifty thousand acres for wilderness designation. Congress responded favorably and in 1970 established Petrified Forest National Wilderness Area.[29]

In some of its structures, such as the Painted Desert Oasis and the visitor center, Petrified Forest clearly reflected the penchant among Mission 66 planners to cater to the wishes of visitors. At the new park, these activities were not particularly disruptive, and Mission 66 actually funded excavation and stabilization work at the Puerco Indian Ruin—an important expansion of interpretive activities. The real shortcoming at Petrified Forest was the fact that officials missed an opportunity to capitalize fully on the park's differences from its monumental, scenic sister institutions by developing further interpretive programs that reflected its ancient environment and the cultures of prehistoric inhabitants.

Although Mission 66 helped the staff at Petrified Forest to deal more efficiently with visitors, the program was of little assistance in meeting challenges that developed outside the park boundaries—"external threats," as the Park Service designated them. America's affluent society grew immensely after World War II, and so did its demands for energy, building materials, recreation, and living space. Nearly all of the parks and monuments faced some degree of danger from developments beyond their boundaries. But in the Southwest, with its ideal hydroelectric dam sites, extensive deposits of uranium, coal, and petroleum, and fast-growing population, the external threats became substantial. Upstream from Grand Canyon National Park, the Bureau of Reclamation had built the massive Glen Canyon Dam, and additional dams were proposed within the park itself. A smoky haze—traced to regional power plants among other sources—often obscures views at Grand Canyon, which also is plagued by noise generated by sightseeing helicopters and small airplanes.

Petrified Forest's very remoteness had given it a degree of protection throughout much of its history. Theft and vandalism were ever present, but the reserve had been spared some of the problems that plagued larger parks like Yosemite, Grand Canyon, and Yellowstone. It obviously contains no lucrative dam sites, and resort owners saw little potential in the area. Nor did that part of the Southwest appeal to developers seeking to sell vacation home sites.

Land ownership around Petrified Forest was in a state of flux in the decades after the reserve became a national park. The Arizona and New Mexico Land Company, as well as the state of Arizona, were anxious to consolidate their holdings in northeastern Arizona—much of it scattered in a checkerboard fashion along the Santa Fe's right-of-way. In particular, the land company wanted to sell out its holdings in the area and obtain land elsewhere that had more potential for profitable development. Historically, cattle ranches had bordered much of the reserve, and stock raising was generally compatible with its environment. Actually, ranches had served effectively as buffers to insulate Petrified Forest from incompatible outside incursions.

In the 1970s, local ranchers began to subdivide their ranges into forty-acre homesites, and that development led to an influx of people and to the construction of homes, garages, barns, and similar structures. On some of the homesites near the park boundaries, new landowners had put up a variety of shacks; others moved into trailers, and one was living in an abandoned school bus. Such structures detracted from the area's scenic vistas, but the Park Service was powerless to intervene on neighboring private land.[30] Naturally, the agency did not look forward to changes in ownership in the vicinity of the park, and it was clear that the unobstructed natural views in all directions were about to be modified. Gas and oil exploration posed another potential threat, as energy companies stepped up their activities in the aftermath of the oil shortages that grew out of the political turmoil in the Middle East. These enterprises would have an obvious visual impact, not to mention the potential for pollution.[31]

From a number of places in the park—Painted Desert, Blue Mesa, Twin Buttes, and others—visitors enjoy spectacular vistas of the surrounding high desert. More than a hundred miles to the west, the majestic San Francisco Peaks are visible, towering above the Colorado Plateau. Snow capped from fall to late spring, these sacred mountains of the Navajo and Hopi define the western horizon. To the south are the White Mountains—not so high or spectacular or snow capped—but nonetheless important visual assets. The Painted Desert itself embraces the northern part of the park and represents its greatest scenic attribute, challenging in its subtle tones the colors of the Grand Canyon if not its dimensions.

The clear air of Petrified Forest is also a major asset, and by the 1980s, park personnel worried that any deterioration in its quality would diminish the scenic vistas. The 1977 Clean Air Act Amendments designate Petrified Forest as a Class I area, and a program was established to monitor air quality and identify adverse developments. Only a few years earlier, the Arizona Public Service Company had constructed a new coal-fired power plant at Joseph City, just thirty miles west of the park. The installation, according to a 1981 resource management plan for Petrified Forest, had already had an adverse impact on long-distance vistas. More recent studies also have documented the existence of intermittent pollution at Petrified Forest.[32]

Much of the time, the park's air quality remains outstanding, and visitors still appreciate the colorful panoramas of the Painted Desert as well as the long-distance vistas. Personnel there also have been attentive to the importance of natural quietness within the reserve. Officials have worked with civilian pilots and the United States Air Force to ensure that low-flying aircraft do not degrade the natural quiet. The commitment stands in contrast to the approach taken at Grand Canyon, the site of numerous daily overflights. Small tourist planes from Las Vegas and other regional cities ferry tourists along the route of the canyon and, until recently, were allowed to fly below the rim.

Problems of noise and visual pollution were minor in comparison to the threat of contamination in the Puerco River. In 1979 tailings had spilled into the Puerco from the United Nuclear Corporation's dam at Gallup, New Mexico, 150 miles to the east. Park officials soon became concerned about the increased flow in this normally ephemeral stream, as erosion actually threatened Petrified Forest's main well and pump near the Puerco bridge. Radiation levels near the park remained within acceptable levels, but at Sanders, Arizona, only 30 miles away, measurements revealed increased radiation. Installation of pilings along the Puerco's north bank checked erosion and secured the park's water supply, but pollution still represented a threat. Again in 1986, United Nuclear discharged radioactive effluent into the river, causing a substantial increase in its flow. From Gallup westward into Arizona, the Puerco became a perennial stream. United Nuclear and other mines around Gallup closed before the end of the year, and the spread of surface radiation downstream ceased. No one knew what effect the effluent had had on shallow wells along the Puerco streambed, but the major threat had abated.[33]

The danger of such pollution at Petrified Forest was a measure of the complexity of maintaining the integrity of a national park in modern America. The history of the reserve in the decades after World War II illustrates that even a remote location cannot offer full protection from the intrusions of contemporary society. The park itself remained remarkably undisturbed, for it had experienced little development beyond the Painted Desert Inn and the Rainbow Forest complex. Even after the new construction at the Painted Desert Visitor Center and administrative headquarters, which are clearly separated from the deposits of petrified wood, archaeological sites, and important scenic places, the park retains much of its unspoiled character. It offers no overnight accommodations (except to a few backpackers), so the blight of hotels, campgrounds, and similar developments do not interfere with the visitor's park experience. The park actually operates in much the way that critics of the Park Service and Mission 66 advocated in the 1960s. The internal park highway has been widened and improved over the years, but Petrified Forest has been spared massive new road construction. Tourists can easily drive through it, spending as many hours as they wish, but they must find motels and campgrounds in neighboring towns.

While personnel can exercise considerable control over the internal environment, they are at the mercy of any outside developments, although federal offices such as the Environmental Protection Agency have the power to intervene in the park's behalf. The future of Petrified Forest depends on the federal government's ability to protect the reserve against intrusions from outside. The clean air, nearly pristine environment, and long-range vistas are all subject to whatever developments occur in northeastern Arizona—an area once thoroughly removed from the pressures of civilization.

8

RECENT SCIENCE AT PETRIFIED FOREST

[Research since 1981] has expanded resource information on the park to the extent that it is similar to a "new" park.

Statement for Management, 1988

Federal programs like the New Deal and Mission 66 had an immense impact on America's national parks and monuments. Most of the money and labor had gone to improve physical facilities, but some federal funds nevertheless were funneled into scientific and educational endeavors at a number of reserves, particularly in the Southwest. The same Civilian Conservation Corps labor that built roads and trails could also be directed toward archaeological work at monuments like Petrified Forest, Bandelier, and Chaco Canyon. And Civil Works Administration appropriations that funded landscaping and construction similarly could cover the costs of archaeological surveys as well as restoration and stabilization efforts.

The Park Service's commitment to research and education originated in the 1920s, but such programs did not become widespread for years. Some custodians, like Petrified Forest's William Nelson, exercised their own initiative and gave illustrated lectures, identified and described important sites within their reserves, and generally developed their own educational programs to meet the needs of visitors—endeavors that had the enthusiastic support of "Boss" Pinkley. In the 1930s, Horace Albright sought to enhance the professionalism of Park Service personnel, and one of the achievements of his reorganization of the agency was the establishment of a specific Division of Education to oversee interpretive programs in the parks and monuments. The new branch received its initial funding in 1930 and was headed by Dr. Harold Bryant, who had pioneered nature guide programs at Yosemite in the 1920s. Its focus was not simply education but also the promotion of scientific research. A number of naturalists were hired full-time at national parks, and Petrified Forest was one of the first monuments to employ a Park Service naturalist—geologist Myrl Walker. While such personnel were responsible for meeting the public demand for lectures, nature walks, exhibits, and similar activities, they also were expected to further research in their discipline as it related to their reserves.[1]

National parks and monuments, because they are set aside and protected, serve as excellent natural laboratories not only for Park Service naturalists but also for scientists associated with universities and museums.[2] These reserves consequently have been home to a variety of scientific endeavors over the past half-century, and Petrified Forest—whose origins were as a scientific monument under the Antiquities Act—has yielded important discoveries to geologists, paleontologists, archaeologists, and others.

Civil Works Administration money made it possible for H. P. Mera and C. B. Cosgrove to survey archaeological sites in Petrified Forest in 1933 and 1934. At that time, the extent of ruins there was virtually unknown. From the survey, Mera determined that Petrified Forest had been home to various peoples for almost a century after A.D. 500, from Basketmaker II to Pueblo IV in the Pecos Classification. The oldest ruins, pithouses situated on the Flattops, indicated cultural influences from the south, but by the seventh to ninth centuries, pottery exhibited cultural traits from both the Anasazi to the north and the Mogollon from the south. At a number of places, Mera found only Adamana brown pottery (A.D. 500)—the oldest known within the park's boundaries.[3] Early in the century, Walter Hough of the National Museum had concluded that several "stocks" of ancient peoples had occupied the terrain around the reserve. Mera's work was more elaborate and superseded Hough's, but it led to a similar generalization: different cultural groups had inhabited the area.

Mera and Cosgrove also stabilized and partially restored two ruins as part of the CWA project. The first, Agate House, was a small pueblo constructed of petrified wood; it had been occupied briefly during the twelfth and thirteenth centuries. Its eight rooms were small, only about six feet square. The archaeologists rebuilt and roofed over the largest, leaving its interior practically as they had found it. They also partially restored and stabilized the Puerco Indian Ruin, which overlooks the floodplain of the ephemeral Puerco River. The structure, occupied from late Pueblo III into Pueblo IV, contained 125 rooms and was only a single story in height, built around a plaza. Mera expected the excavation to yield an ancient village buried beneath the surface site, but workers found nothing of the kind. The last excavation was at the Flattops, where little was learned about the prehistoric inhabitants. The isolated dwellings were recognizable only by occasional wall slabs protruding slightly above the surface. Cosgrove could not even determine a floor level.[4]

Modern students of archaeology at Petrified Forest value Mera's survey as a valuable contribution for its time; his conclusions about temporal placement and his descriptions of pottery types still are valid. But Cosgrove's excavations tended to be incomplete and did not provide an adequate basis for comparisons and conclusions.[5] Nevertheless, the work was important for the emerging interpretive programs at Petrified Forest. Agate House soon developed into a popular attraction for tourists because of its petrified wood construction. Similarly, Puerco Ruin, as stabilized by Cosgrove's crews, is an easily accessible site for modern visitors, who have the opportunity to glimpse the environment of Pueblo IV people.

In 1941, the Park Service's regional archaeologist, Erik Reed, undertook another survey in Petrified Forest, intending only to relocate and stake the sites that Mera had found in the 1930s. But Reed's party frequently came across new, unrecorded sites, and he ultimately examined the entire area south of the Puerco River. In all, Reed and his assistants found 280 sites ranging from Basketmaker III to Pueblo IV. The new survey generally corroborated Mera's CWA work and indicated that occupation within Petrified Forest National Monument had been continuous from roughly A.D. 500 to 1400.[6]

At about the same time, researchers at the Museum of Northern Arizona found evidence that a prehistoric trade in pottery had existed between the present Flagstaff area and the Puerco River–Little Colorado drainage, which includes Petrified Forest. Museum personnel began studying the area, and the Park Service aided their efforts by making available the extensive sherd collection that had been assembled by Mera and expanded by Reed. A young Harvard graduate student, Fred Wendorf, analyzed a portion of the collection and confirmed some of Mera's and Reed's earlier findings. More important, his study of sherds in the laboratory naturally drew him into fieldwork. Hoping to learn more about the early sites in Petrified Forest, Wendorf spent the summer of 1949 at the monument, heading an expedition sponsored by the Museum of Northern Arizona. The young archaeologist was particularly interested in the period just after pottery was introduced around Petrified Forest. And since the present reserve is located near an area where different groups shared a common "frontier," he expected to record the effects that Mogollon and Anasazi culture had on one another.[7]

With a crew of students from various universities, Wendorf spent the summer of 1949 at the Flattops, sites that Mera and Cosgrove had examined briefly in the 1930s. Crew members identified some twenty-five structures strung out along the edge of the escarpment, but excavated only eight. They unearthed mostly Adamana brown pottery, and the site was identified as a Basketmaker II village. Wendorf believed that the inhabitants had sustained themselves by agriculture.[8]

Work at the Flattops had focused on the earliest period of human occupation in the Petrified Forest. Wendorf turned next to the Twin Buttes site, which represents the period A.D. 600–800. In contrast to the pithouses perched on the rim of the barren Flattop mesa, the village at Twin Buttes rested in a grassy, broad, nearly flat valley, drained by an ephemeral stream called Dry Creek, which joins the Puerco about ten miles away. Two small bentonite cones are the most conspicuous features on the valley floor, and these "twin buttes" give the site its name.[9]

Excavation there indicated that the site probably had been occupied continuously for more than three hundred years, and almost the entire range of human activity was evident at this complex village site.[10] Both Anasazi and Mogollon influences were evident in the pottery—Mogollon brownwares and Anasazi gray. The former, Wendorf believed, had been traded into Twin Buttes from Mogollon centers to the south. In this instance, the trade in ceramics had been more advanced than was earlier believed. He defined Twin Buttes as a large Anasazi Basketmaker III site, whose inhabitants sustained themselves by agriculture supplemented by hunting.[11]

The work at Twin Buttes in the summers of 1949 and 1950 enabled Wendorf to draw important conclusions about the Anasazi-Mogollon frontier. The two cultures did not blend, and Wendorf assigned the site to the Anasazi. Trade between the groups was active, but each retained its own distinctive features.[12] Wendorf believed that all of the brownware, about 40 percent of the total, had been traded into the site. Further, Anna O. Shepherd, who performed chemical tests on the pottery collected at Twin Buttes, confirmed that the brownware and grayware were not made from the same clay sources. She proposes that when the Anasazi moved into the area, perhaps they did not find the kind of clay they had been accustomed to using. They simply ceased making pottery, Shepherd suggests, and obtained some in trade from their homeland and some from the Mogollon people.[13]

After Wendorf's extensive work at Petrified Forest, ensuing excavation tended to be sporadic and generally focused on developing interpretive exhibits for tourists or investigating sites in advance of highway construction. One of the most easily accessible sites for tourists is Puerco Indian Ruin, and Mission 66 provided funds for Albert Schroeder's excavation of several rooms and a kiva in 1958. Schroeder determined that the extensive pueblo was planned and built at one time. Further, when its inhabitants abandoned it, they did so by choice and were not driven out. A similar excavation at the same ruin, sponsored by the Park Service and the Museum of Northern Arizona, took place in the spring of 1967. Calvin Jennings excavated fifteen rooms and two kivas, generally corroborating Schroeder's earlier conclusions. The pottery he found indicated a good deal of trade with the Hopi mesas and with Zuni.[14] A number of additional excavations and surveys have been undertaken over the last two decades. Among the most significant was Nancy Hammack's discovery of three aceramic sites that she described as Archaic (6000 B.C. to A.D. 300). The sites, all on a sand dune ridge that extends south of the Flattops, consisted of sandstone slab concentrations, hearths, small secondary flakes, and occasional sharp-angle thumbnail scrapers. A chert projectile point also was found on the ridge and may be related to the Archaic sites.[15]

By the mid-1980s a fairly coherent framework for the archaeology of Petrified Forest had emerged. More than 330 sites, ranging from Archaic through Pueblo IV, have been recorded within the park's boundaries. A half-dozen have been excavated, and the Flattops, Twin Buttes, Agate House, Puerco Ruin, and two petroglyph districts have been placed on the National Register of Historic Places. Although Petrified Forest sites do not correspond precisely to the Pecos classification periods, a general summary of its inhabitants can be made. Recording of Archaic sites at the park is a recent endeavor that began only in the mid-1970s, and only a few such sites are known. The park has two dozen Basketmaker II locations ranging from single pithouses to villages of twenty-five units; all are located on high bluffs or mesa tops, like the Flattops. The distinctive Adamana brown pottery is found at all known sites. Villages like Twin Buttes exhibit the characteristics of Basketmaker III. At some of these villages, researchers have found remnants of rock and brush agricultural windbreaks, which suggests their inhabitants' means of survival. Their pottery consisted of brownwares, graywares, and black-on-white.[16]

For the pueblo era, the record is not so complete at Petrified Forest. Archaeologists have found no "pure" Pueblo I sites (A.D. 700 or 800 to 950 or 1050), perhaps because of an occupational break or change in settlement pattern in the middle of that time frame. No Pueblo II sites (A.D. 900 or 950 to 1050 or 1100) have been excavated in Petrified Forest, but from settlements elsewhere in the region archaeologists know that this was an era characterized by masonry pithouses and pueblo-like structures. Agate House, rebuilt by Cosgrove in the early 1930s, is characteristic of Pueblo III, and a small Mogollon "campsite" also dates to that time. Both large and small pueblos with kivas or great kivas were evident then; pottery ran the spectrum from graywares and brownwares to black-on-white and polychrome. The region's prehistoric Indian population contracted into a few areas during the latter pueblo centuries, and Petrified Forest was one such location, as evidenced by the occupation of Puerco pueblo. The population then was fully western Pueblo and likely had direct contact with Hopi, Zuni, and Homol'ovi pueblos.[17]

Obviously, archaeological information on Petrified Forest is not complete, but researchers have recorded usable information about site locations, pottery, and architecture. Petrified Forest's prehistoric sites are in good condition. In the past, construction projects disturbed some areas, particularly sites near the new headquarters constructed by Mission 66. Any site near a highway or visitor attraction is subject to some degree of damage, and simple natural erosion also takes its toll on archaeological sites, in the same way that it removes the Chinle Formation to expose the park's fossil trees.

Visitors today are shepherded into a few easily accessible places like the Puerco Indian Ruin and Agate House. The scenery is not so overpowering as it is in Yosemite Valley, Grand Canyon, or Glacier. Even the ruins are not on the scale of those at Chaco Canyon, Canyon de Chelly, or Montezuma Castle. Yet they are representative of the prehistoric cultures of the Colorado Plateau. Interpretive displays tend to be brief and straightforward narratives with comparatively simple illustrations aimed at a broad audience of tourists, few of whom are likely to know much about the region's ancient inhabitants. Still, these ruins easily engage the imagination of any thoughtful visitor, stimulating "the fifth sense of wonder" that archaeologist Walter Hough experienced early in the century.

In the same way that archaeology benefited from federal programs in the 1930s, geology also gained impetus. At Petrified Forest, it was paleontologist Myrl Walker, the reserve's first Park Service naturalist, who shaped research in that field. For Walker, like naturalist John Muir thirty years earlier, Petrified Forest proved to be a place of refuge—in this case a retreat from the tragedies of the Kansas dust bowl. Christmas 1932 had been "a little below average," Walker wrote to his friend Charles W. Gilmore at the Smithsonian Institution. His baby daughter had died only days before the holiday, and the local bank had closed its doors a week later, adding economic woes to the family's sorrow. When the position at Petrified Forest was offered in 1933, he was glad to accept it.[18]

New Deal appropriations had financed the recent construction of a road to Blue Mesa, and the freshly exposed cuts yielded abundant leaves from the late Triassic. The new fossils were all well preserved and represented an important find, given the paucity of such leaves in the Chinle Formation. Between 1934 and 1936 Walker and his CCC assistants gathered there "the finest leaf impressions ever collected from the Triassic of North America," as Walker described their endeavor.[19]

Walker is known for his 1936 excavation of "Walker's Stump" in Blue Forest. With the help of CCC workers, he successfully traced the roots of a large, partially exposed stump to demonstrate that the original tree had grown and been buried at that site.[20] In the course of his observations, Walker also had noticed that numerous *Araucarioxylon arizonicum* specimens exhibited ridges and tunnel-like structures, and he concluded that late Triassic insect larvae were responsible—apparently girding some of the trees while they still lived. At one location in Petrified Forest, a paleobotanist has recently pointed out, at least half of the ancient logs contain such marking.[21]

Scientists had long wondered about Baldwin Möllhausen's observation in 1853 that he had seen petrified stumps still rooted where those ancestral trees originally had grown. Even the more astute observer Lester Frank Ward had been unable to locate such specimens in his 1899 visit to Chalcedony Park, although he later found some near Tanner's Crossing on the Little Colorado. Walker's excavation finally confirmed that some ancient conifers in fact had been growing in Petrified Forest when the Chinle Formation was deposited. Further, some of those trees apparently had died— as do their modern descendants—as the result of insect infestation.

Lyman Daugherty of then San Jose State College also had been drawn to Petrified Forest in the early 1930s, his curiosity piqued by an unusual wood fossil that he had been given. This specimen proved to be a new genus and species, which Daugherty described as *Schilderia adamanica*. Smaller than *Araucarioxylon arizonicum*, the tree rested on a swollen, fluted base.[22] Its discovery, along with Walker's work, added incrementally to the growing body of knowledge about this ancient environment.

Walker was equally interested in animal fossils, and he often used his spare time at the monument to scout the area. Initial excursions turned up only a few teeth, vertebrae, and the like. But in early June 1934, he wrote to Gilmore at the Smithsonian to announce that he had collected a large phytosaur skull and its lower jaws. A smaller skull, that of an adult female that Walker collected west of Jasper Forest, is displayed now at the Rainbow Forest Museum, as are the skull and jaws of the amphibian *Metoposaurus fraasi*, excavated at Devil's Playground. Walker found remains of a third phytosaur south of the Flattops, but he excavated only the lower jaws.[23]

Walker's phytosaurs impressed Gilmore, and the venerable paleontologist journeyed to Petrified Forest in 1937, hoping to find specimens comparable to the one from Devil's Playground. Gilmore's party enjoyed a successful season, finding excellent specimens both near Camp's old site at Billings Gap and near Twin Buttes. The last discovery of the 1940s came at the hands of a local collector, who found a large phytosaur skull and lower jaws just outside the monument near Devil's Playground. After University of California scientists studied and cleaned the specimen, the discoverer donated it to the Mesa Southwest Museum in Arizona.[24]

Although a few remarkable specimens had been found in the 1930s, the search for vertebrate fossils had gradually abated. The 1920s and 1930s had been successful years for Barnum Brown, Charles Mehl, Samuel Welles, Charles Camp, and others. Camp's work in the Chinle Formation came to an end in 1934, and only isolated discoveries followed. When a Navajo resident of the Little Colorado Valley found a large skull in Frank Ward's old "bone bed" near Cameron, the news was important enough to send Barnum Brown and his associate R. T. Bond of the American Museum of Natural History on another expedition to the site. They were well rewarded, for they recovered the largest known phytosaur skull—a specimen that measured four feet, eight inches in length. Edwin Colbert described it in 1947 under the name *Machaeroprosopus gregorii*.[25] In general, though, the following decades were devoted not to more expeditions but rather to the study and identification of existing fossils.

At Petrified Forest, Myrl Walker was entrusted with responsibility for developing interpretive displays featuring the recently unearthed fossils as well as items found at archaeological sites. Walker proposed separate museums devoted to paleontology, ethnology, and contemporary Native American arts and crafts, but his plan received little support from the Park Service. Erik Reed, the agency's regional archaeologist, dismissed the need for any exhibits featuring anthropology and maintained that visitors would be content with scenery and geological sites. "When people visit a park, they want to see a park," he wrote in a special report on Petrified Forest.

"If they wanted to see a museum, they'd go to, or stay in, the cities."
Beyond protecting petroglyphs and perhaps expanding the Puerco Indian
Ruin, Reed opposed any additional educational endeavors in archaeology.[26]

Reed's comment about museums at national parks and monuments
raised an important issue: how best to enhance visitors' understanding and
appreciation of scientific reserves like Petrified Forest, particularly when
they lacked the amenities that many vacationers anticipated. Scenery,
camping, and recreation obviously figured in tourists' plans; museums and
interpretive displays probably did not, as Reed argued. Still, visitors to Petrified Forest needed some kind of educational and interpretive programs
to capture their imagination and stimulate their sense of wonder and curiosity. Otherwise, the fossil logs and occasional phytosaur displays would
represent nothing more than interesting roadside attractions. By the
1930s, scientists already had shown that Petrified Forest represented more
than colorful stone trees. The place was rich in fossils that defined a unique
ancient environment, and these held the keys to a novel national park
experience.

Research at Petrified Forest ceased during World War II, as did most
operations, and work in geology was not fully reestablished until the
1960s. A few noteworthy discoveries occurred in the interim. In 1958,
park naturalist Philip F. Van Cleve came across a well-preserved footprint
of a three-toed dinosaur at Blue Mesa—a particularly important find, since
it established for the first time that dinosaurs had inhabited the present
park. The specimen, unfortunately, was destroyed in transit to Berkeley.
Several years later a geologist discovered a large dinosaur footprint in the
Newspaper Rock Sandstone west of the Teepees. But he did not collect the
specimen, and his subsequent efforts to relocate it were all in vain.[27]

Various small specimens, such as teeth and scales, were found during
the 1960s. In one instance, examination of the stony matrix encasing phytosaur teeth yielded the scales of bony fish, teeth from ancient sharks, and
also the teeth of small reptiles. Enough paleontological work had occurred
at Petrified Forest by the 1970s to warrant a complete survey of the park.
In 1978 and 1979, personnel from the Museum of Northern Arizona
mapped old vertebrate fossil locations and also discovered a number of
new sites. The collections contained mostly phytosaur and metoposaur
bones, which now are housed at the Museum of Northern Arizona.

When new research expanded at Petrified Forest in the 1980s, it actually grew out of the early work of Charles Camp in the 1920s and 1930s. Camp and his students had published their findings in various professional papers, but much of Camp's material from the Chinle in Arizona and New Mexico had never been studied. In the late 1970s, Robert Long of the Museum of Paleontology at the University of California began reorganizing and studying the Chinle collections that Camp had deposited at Berkeley a half-century earlier. Camp's field notes were extensive and meticulous, with literally hundreds of pages devoted to his work in Petrified Forest. The renowned scientist also had photographed various locations, and in August and September of 1981 researchers from the Museum of Paleontology used the old photos to find some of Camp's original sites.[28]

The abbreviated 1981 season at Petrified Forest produced a number of important discoveries. Just south of Jasper Forest, researchers found the first undoubted dinosaur bones in Petrified Forest, and they collected remains of both plant-eating prosauropods and meat-eating theropod dinosaurs. These are among the earliest dinosaurs that have been found anywhere. The same site included a large concentration of armor, representing the aetosaur *Calyptosuchus wellesi*. In addition, the first Petrified Forest records of a spiked aetosaur were unearthed at Jasper Forest and at Crystal Forest. Aetosaurs were unusual reptiles, bearing heavy armor and resembling the modern armadillo. They had been considered rare within the boundaries of the present park, but the 1981 party found remains at a large number of sites.[29]

Long and some members of the initial party returned the next summer and discovered the productive Dinosaur Hill Quarry southeast of Lacey Point. Here they found a partial skeleton of the carnivore *Coelophysis*, along with bones of prosauropod dinosaurs. Additional remains of dinosaurs and other ancient animals were discovered west of Crystal Forest, along with remains of other ancient animals. In two locations—the Flattops and Black Forest—researchers found the bones of the first coelacanth fishes in Petrified Forest.[30]

The 1983 field season was another successful venture, and a year later Long guided another group to Dinosaur Hill. Graduate student Bryan Small of Texas Tech joined the party, and in the course of the explorations he came across the remains of "Gerti"—the small, long-legged, carnivorous dinosaur belonging to the staurikosaur family (see chapter 1). Additional discoveries—phytosaurs, *Placerias*, and *Metoposaurus*—followed. Petrified Forest Superintendent Edward Gastellum discovered in Blue Forest the first microvertebrate site in the park. A wealth of these tiny vertebrates had been discovered earlier at Camp's *Placerias* Quarry near St. Johns, and it seemed logical that such organisms should also occur forty miles to the north in Petrified Forest. Scientists had searched the park for years with no success—until Superintendent Gastellum inadvertently happened upon the site.

Gastellum actively encouraged research at Petrified Forest, continuing a commitment that his immediate predecessor, Roger Rector, had initiated. The accomplishments of archaeologists, paleontologists, paleobotanists, and others in the 1980s effectively established scientific inquiry as a continuing process at the park. The importance of research was verified in 1986, when a scientific advisory committee convened to discuss research at Petrified Forest, and members produced a list of topics in cultural and natural history that merited attention. More important, they identified as their goal the presentation of "a more complete picture of the paleo-environment and history of man in Petrified Forest."[31]

The statement recognized that a major transformation had taken place at Petrified Forest. Once an incidental endeavor, science was now virtually reshaping the identity of the park. The single-minded protection of fossil trees had given way to a dynamic investigation of the Chinle Formation, and the findings of archaeologists and paleontologists today offer visitors a much more sophisticated perspective on this ancient landscape. In a subtle way, scientists and Park Service personnel have identified and developed a unique environmental resource. For Americans who have become increasingly conscious of environmental issues and more cognizant of the complexity of ecological relationships, this new commitment offers a chance to expand their understanding of the earth and its evolving environment. The park not only exhibits the colorful trunks of fossil trees but incorporates a view of a complete ancient ecosystem consisting of plants and animals that can now be recognized in the Chinle Formation as it is exposed in the park. As one prominent researcher points out, "a clear understanding of the ecological setting is being pieced together, the first time such an achievement has materialized for Triassic faunas anywhere in the world." [32]

After a hesitant start and intermittent progress earlier in the century, science is today an integral feature of Petrified Forest and contributes to defining a particular national park experience at the reserve. Visitors always will want to wander along the paths that wind among the petrified logs and prehistoric ruins. And no doubt they still will carry off a certain amount of souvenir petrified wood. But as scientists and interpretive specialists introduce casual visitors to the continuing accomplishments of scientific discovery, Petrified Forest can finally provide visitors with a unique experience. The park does not have the monumental scenery of Yosemite or Glacier, nor can it offer extensive recreational opportunities like those available in the old "crown jewel" national parks. Petrified Forest is a place to encounter a Triassic environment that overwhelms the visitor. It offers more than an opportunity to view landscape as it existed before Americans traveled and settled in the Southwest. Petrified Forest's environment offers a perspective on the earth before humans appeared at all.

EPILOGUE:
THE FUTURE OF THE PAST

Park Service officials and their insistent critics have differed over the kind of experience visitors should have in America's national parks. Devereux Butcher, F. Fraser Darling, Noel D. Eichhorn, and others in the 1960s complained of the agency's tendency to bend to the wishes of tourists and concessionaires, often at the expense of the environment. Edward Abbey shared that perspective and in *Desert Solitaire* delivered a sharp critique of "industrial tourism." Insulated in their automobiles and recreational vehicles, modern tourists swarm into the national parks during the summer months, he wrote, but these vacationlands offer not solitude or relaxation but rather traffic congestion and crowded campgrounds. The parks are hard-pressed to accommodate these people, and tourists burden both the facilities and the personnel, not to mention the threat their numbers present to the essential integrity of many parks. The real victims are the tourists themselves, Abbey pointed out. "They are being robbed and are robbing themselves." So long as visitors refuse to venture outside their vehicles, they can never discover the treasures of national parks. Nor will they ever escape the stress and frustration of modern urban living, which presumably induced them to undertake their motorized pilgrimages. Abbey's solution was simple enough: "No more cars in the parks. Let the people walk." [1]

Additional recommendations came in the following years, the most thoughtful in Joseph Sax's *Mountains without Handrails: Reflections on the National Parks*, published in 1980. Like Abbey, Sax questions the use of vehicles in the parks. The issue is not transportation but rather the pace of the trip through any reserve. Even at a leisurely speed of forty miles per hour, the visitor's ability to concentrate on natural scenes and to perceive details is reduced severely. Therefore, he too advocates discouraging motorized travel. National parks are preserved "not to keep people in their cars," he writes, "but to lure them out; to encourage a close look at the infinite detail and variety that the natural scene provides." [2] How else will visitors experience the character of a dense forest or an alpine lake—or, in the case of Petrified Forest, an ancient landscape?

Such critiques are valid. Even extensive reserves like Yellowstone, Glacier, Yosemite, and Grand Canyon cannot provide travelers with more than a glimpse of the park's terrain or inspire much appreciation for its unique characteristics as long as people remain insulated in their vehicles. These recommendations are even more important for natural and scientific parks like Petrified Forest, where the focus on detail is critical and nearly impossible to achieve through the windshield of an automobile. Only two hours and twenty minutes are required to make the complete trip from north to south across Petrified Forest, a distance of twenty-eight miles along a modern highway with numerous turnouts and spur roads that connect with such sites as Jasper Forest, Blue Mesa, and the Long Logs. Visitors are restricted to park trails, which provide easy access to archaeological and natural points of interest, but first they have to be enticed out of their vehicles.

A park that is not characterized by monumental scenery faces certain difficulties in capturing the attention of visitors. In the case of Petrified Forest, scientific discoveries—regardless of their intrinsic interest and global significance—may well elude the average tourist. Not many people, after all, have any context for understanding the natural phenomena evident there. The aesthetic aspects of the park are impressive, and anyone who walks even a short distance from the main road can wander among immense prostrate petrified logs and perhaps find a fossil bone or admire a petroglyph etched on a rock. But without some broader interpretive framework to focus their attention, people often experience Petrified Forest as an immense collection of natural and cultural oddities—"freaks of nature," as nineteenth-century magazines described them. The essential task of the Park Service is to enhance the visitor's experience by providing a broader understanding of the Triassic period of the earth's history and its importance today.

Visitors to northern Arizona are treated to views of the Painted Desert from a number of places along Interstate Highway 40, which virtually bisects Petrified Forest National Park. The expansive vistas from within the park make this undeveloped, colorful landscape an ideal setting in which to present a broad overview to visitors. About 65 percent of them enter Petrified Forest via Interstate 40 at the north end of the park; of this group, perhaps as many as one-third never venture beyond the Painted Desert Visitor Center and the Fred Harvey operation, the Painted Desert Oasis. The current visitor center functions only as a regional information center and offers tourists little explanation and limited interpretation about the Triassic environment.

The Park Service hopes to lure these travelers about a mile farther into the park, to a new visitor center on the rim of the Painted Desert at Tiponi Point. Removed from the distractions of Interstate 40, people would not only be treated to a remarkable panorama of the Painted Desert but would also be given immediate access to scenic walks along the desert rim or even down to the desert floor. Within fifteen minutes, visitors could follow a trail into another world free of the sights and sounds of modern America. The Painted Desert, in short, is an easily accessible wilderness, offering both novices and expert hikers the opportunity to undertake a primitive encounter in its extensive badlands. The desert landscape itself focuses attention on geology, for it exhibits developments that occurred 215 to 230 million years ago. At the new visitor center, interpretation would be expansive, focusing on the earth processes and phenomena, such as continental drift, evolution, fossilization, and uplift and erosion, that shaped the paleoecology. As with any ecological unit, it is not the individual features that are important—and at Petrified Forest the objectives are to enhance understanding and appreciation of the park's environment. The Triassic period, tourists would learn, was a time of critical transition, and the alien plants and animals of that era carried the seeds of life today.[3]

Beyond such interpretive displays (which travelers typically encounter in parks and monuments across the country), Petrified Forest would include an additional dimension to introduce visitors to the scientific processes themselves, as reflected in the research that continues in the park. "It would be a disservice to visitors to present a comprehensive picture of the Triassic period as if scientists knew everything about it," a recent Park Service publication states, "when, in fact, new discoveries are being made every year."[4] A proposed research center adjacent to the visitor center would be open to the public, and naturalists or rangers would guide visitors to excavation sites as fieldwork was under way, encouraging people to experience some of the excitement associated with scientific research in this ancient environment. In the end, the proposed Tiponi Point visitor and research center has the potential to offer a special park experience—one based on an actual encounter, however brief, with the environment of the Triassic. Visitors, then, ought to depart the park with a heightened appreciation for scientific discovery, and perhaps a bit humbled, too, by the understanding of their relatively small place in the earth's history, which is visible here back some 200 million years.

The development at Painted Desert is the most dramatic aspect of the recently proposed changes at Petrified Forest. A similar interpretive emphasis would focus on archaeological resources, and the Park Service's Western Archeological and Conservation Center in Tucson would oversee all such research. The historic Painted Desert Inn is scheduled for rehabilitation, and administrative and maintenance facilities need to be expanded and in some cases to be replaced.

The success of research in the park was one of several factors that prompted officials to reevaluate its current boundaries. The portion of the Triassic Chinle Formation encompassed within the park is only a small segment of an extensive geological strata in the Southwest. Like most park boundaries across the country, those at Petrified Forest were drawn as straight lines that followed traditional survey points and ignored environmental considerations. Although the lines embraced undeniably valuable collections of fossil trees, the boundaries no longer encompass all of the valuable cultural resources that emerged as a result of the 1980s research. Important paleontological, paleobotanical, and archaeological sites rest outside the park's boundaries.

The most important aspect of the ancient environment in Petrified Forest is the Chinle escarpment, which runs in an east-west direction and crosses the park around Blue Mesa and Jasper Forest. This outcrop of the Chinle Formation contains not only petrified wood but also leaf imprints, pollens, the earliest sample of amber, and even nonmineralized tissues of more than 140 plants, most of which were herbaceous rather than woody. Scientists also have found embedded in the escarpment the fossil remains of more than fifty animals, both vertebrates and invertebrates. Taken together, these remains constitute "the best record of the Triassic period ecosystem found anywhere in the world."[5] Only six miles of the twenty-two-mile-long escarpment are now within the park's boundaries, and the ephemeral stream Dry Creek has eroded through the formation to isolate east Jasper and Blue Mesas as remnants of the continuous escarpment. The Chinle outcrops in the park have been accessible for research and serve as the standard reference for evaluating all Triassic sites throughout the world. But to the east and west of the park are continuous parts of the Chinle escarpment that scientists believe are even more valuable than the remnant protected by the park's boundaries.

Triassic fossils are nonrenewable resources. Once the remainder of the Chinle Formation erodes away, the source of such fossils will be gone. Vertebrate fossils pose a special problem, for unlike other nonrenewable cultural resources they cannot be preserved by leaving them alone. Preserving these bones requires excavation, preparation, and careful storage. Otherwise, as fossils erode out of the ground, exposure to the elements causes them to oxidize and disintegrate. Skeletal remains, paleontologists point out, begin to break up even before their exposure on the surface, so preservation depends on early detection and subsurface excavation.[6]

Also beyond the boundaries are hundreds of archaeological sites relating to several prehistoric cultures. Puerco Ridge and the drainages of Dead Wash and the Puerco River have yielded isolated artifacts perhaps ten thousand years old. Mammoth bone, too, has been discovered. Rare Paleo-Indian sites are intermixed with Basketmaker villages, and the area also embraces Pueblo religious and community centers that contain great kivas and other monumental architecture. Rock art panels are also present, along with petrified wood quarries and Navajo sites. These archaeological finds are as important as those within the park, and possibly more so. Further research will elaborate trade networks and perhaps fill in the missing elements in the chronology between prehistoric and historic peoples.

The same terrain that is so rich in paleontological and archaeological sites also represents an important visual resource at Petrified Forest. Landscape pays no attention to the boundaries that typically follow section lines, and visitors easily get the impression that the park is much larger than it really is. The views from the rim of the Painted Desert, Blue Mesa, and Jasper Forest embrace terrain that extends well beyond the park. In some instances, where the natural surface has remained undisturbed, visitors perceive the park as extending virtually to the horizon. People may well enjoy the illusion and depart believing that the panorama is actually secure within park boundaries. But in fact, the opposite is true, and such natural vistas exist not because of careful management but simply by chance: neighboring landowners, for whatever reasons, have not developed their property.

For more than a century, most of the adjacent land has been reserved for grazing—a compatible use that has not threatened scientific resources. Forage around Chinle outcrops is poor, and cattle normally avoid those areas. But, as land use patterns have changed over the last few decades, adjacent scenic vistas are indeed threatened by mineral exploration and by mines for which there are no reclamation plans. In other instances, some landowners have divided their range into smaller ranchettes to appeal to a broader range of buyers. None of these uses are compatible with long-term preservation of paleontological and archaeological resources, and all represent some degree of threat to the environment in the vicinity of the park.

Most threatening is the proposal to construct a large landfill to dispose of solid wastes from the East Coast. To be located about eight miles east of Blue Mesa at the headwaters of Ninemile Wash, the landfill initially would cover one square mile. But it could be expanded to fifty-three square miles to become the world's largest landfill. As such, it would threaten paleontological and archaeological resources and also raise questions about maintaining the quality of air and water at Petrified Forest National Park. The landfill would generate considerable dust, which would obscure the scenic vistas visible from Blue Mesa and also drift into the park itself. If wastes are incinerated at the site, even more pollutants would enter the air around the park and likely contaminate surface and groundwater. In addition, such a landfill would introduce alien species of plants and animals into the region's short-grass prairie ecosystem.[7]

Including adjacent areas in the present national park is the only way to protect important scientific resources while also preserving scenic vistas, air quality, wilderness areas, and part of the short-grass prairie ecosystem in the vicinity. The Park Service has proposed a boundary expansion to embrace critical resources. The land in question belongs to the Bureau of Land Management, the state of Arizona, and a number of private parties; in all the total comprises 97,800 acres.[8] Expansion would guarantee the long-term integrity of the park and also enhance visitors' overall experience.

Years ago, the phrases "petrified forest" and "chalcedony park" conjured up images of immense stone trees, and more imaginative people fully expected to encounter standing groves of petrified trees—perhaps not an unwarranted expectation in an area drained by Lithodendron Wash. The idea of a petrified forest still intrigues people, of course, and hundreds of thousands of visitors drive through the park every year. But, instead of preserving these fossil trees as remarkable icons of the past, to be admired solely because of their age, we now see them and other fossils as crucial means to more fully understand the past and the place of humans in our environment. Rather than existing merely as a monument to an ancient environment, Petrified Forest National Park today functions as a laboratory for better understanding the Triassic period of the earth's history. The past at this reserve is an ever-expanding phenomenon—one that continually adds to our knowledge about the present.

NOTES

Introduction

1. Alfred Runte, *National Parks: The American Experience*, 5th ed. (Lincoln: University of Nebraska Press, 1987), 3. Runte's work has influenced much of the recent writing on national parks. The book provides an important cultural context for understanding the origins and development of national parks in this country; see his prologue and chapter 1, pp. 1–32, in particular, for an analysis of cultural nationalism and national parks. John Ise's earlier study, *Our National Park Policy: A Critical History* (Baltimore: Johns Hopkins University Press, 1961), is comprehensive but now dated. Much of the volume tends toward administrative and legislative history and offers little interpretive context. Freeman Tilden's *The National Parks* (New York: Knopf, 1983) offers short essays on individual parks, monuments, historic sites, seashores, military parks, battlefields, and other sites—nearly two hundred in all. It will appeal to general readers and tourists. Anne Hyde's recent book, *An American Vision: Far Western Landscape and National Culture, 1820–1920* (New York: New York University Press, 1990), provides an important perspective on the connection between culture and the terrain of the West. Two older studies that help establish a cultural context for parks are Hans Huth, *Nature and the American: Three Centuries of Changing Atti-*

tudes (Lincoln: University of Nebraska Press, 1990), and Roderick Nash, *Wilderness and the American Mind* (New Haven: Yale University Press, 1982). Readers also will want to consult Nash's "The American Invention of National Parks," *American Quarterly* 22 (Fall 1970): 726–35, and Richard W. Sellers, Alfred Runte, and others, "The National Parks: A Forum on the 'Worthless Lands' Thesis," *Journal of Forest History* 27 (July 1983): 130–45.

Works on national monuments are not so numerous, although Hal Rothman, in *Preserving Different Pasts: The American National Monuments* (Urbana: University of Illinois Press, 1989), has produced a solid analysis of those reserves. He also is the author of two important articles—"Second-Class Sites: The National Monuments and the Growth of the Park System," *Environmental Review* 10 (Spring 1986): 45–56, and "Forged by One Man's Will: Frank Pinkley and the Administration of the Southwestern National Monuments, 1923–1932," *Public Historian* 8 (Spring 1986): 83–100. In *The Antiquities Act of 1906* (Washington, D.C.: National Park Service, 1971), Ronald F. Lee discusses the legislation that established the national monuments. Rothman devotes a full chapter to the Antiquities Act in *Preserving Different Pasts*, providing an analysis based on current research.

A number of writers have focused on science and the national parks. For research at prehistoric sites, readers should consult Robert H. and Florence C. Lister, *Those Who Came Before: Southwestern Archaeology in the National Park System* (Tucson: University of Arizona Press, 1983). This richly illustrated volume contains a short discussion of archaeology at Petrified Forest. Geology is covered in William H. Matthews III, *A Guide to the National Parks: Their Landscape and Geology*, vol. 1, *The Western Parks* (Garden City, N.Y.: Natural History Press, 1968), and Ann G. Harris, *Geology of National Parks* (Dubuque, Iowa: Kendall/Hunt, 1977). Another good introduction to the subject is Halka Chronic, *Pages of Stone: Geology of Western National Parks and Monuments*, vol. 3, *The Desert Southwest* (Seattle: Mountaineers, 1986). The most recent such study is *Science and the National Parks* (Washington, D.C.: National Academy Press, 1992), which examines the importance of science to the parks.

2. Matthews, *Guide to the National Parks*, vol. 1, xiii, ix.

3. John McPhee, *Basin and Range* (New York: Farrar, Straus, Giroux, 1981), 127–29. McPhee uses this example to illustrate geologic time: "With your arms spread wide to represent all time on earth, look at one hand with its line of life. The Cambrian begins in the wrist, and the Permian Extinction is at the outer end of the palm. All of the Cenozoic is in a fingerprint, and in a single stroke with a medium-grained nail file you could eradicate human history" (126). See also Stephen Jay Gould, *Time's Arrow, Time's Cycle: Myth and Metaphor in the Discovery of Geological Time* (Cambridge, Mass.: Harvard University Press, 1987), for additional discussion of deep time.

Chapter 1

1. The new fossil belongs to a family of comparatively small, carnivorous dinosaurs called staurikosaurs; the genus has not yet been described. See Robert A. Long and Rose Houk, *Dawn of the Dinosaurs: The Triassic in Petrified Forest* (Petrified Forest, Ariz., Petrified Forest Museum Association, 1988), 89; and Susan Colclazer, "Dawn of the Dinosaur," *Courier* 30 (August 1985): 1–3.

2. *Phoenix Arizona Republic,* 7 June 1985; *New York Times,* 16 May 1985. See also Larry L. Meyer, "D-Day on the Painted Desert," *Arizona Highways,* July 1986, 5.

3. Matt Walton, "Geology of the Painted Desert and Petrified Forest," *Arizona Highways,* July 1958, 7; Sidney Ash, *Petrified Forest: The Story behind the Scenery* (Petrified Forest, Ariz., Petrified Forest Museum Association, 1986), 6–7.

4. Ash, *Petrified Forest,* 6–8; William J. Breed and George H. Billingsley, "Petrified Forest: The Origins of the Landscape," *Plateau* 51 (1979): 12.

5. Walton, "Geology," 7; Matthews, *Guide to the National Parks,* vol. 1, 295–96.

6. Ash, *Petrified Forest,* 10–11.

7. Edwin H. Colbert, "Ancient Animals of the Petrified Forest," *Plateau* 51 (1979): 24–25.

8. Ash, *Petrified Forest,* 11–12. On the Triassic climate see Allen F. Gottesfeld, "Paleoecology of the Lower Part of the Chinle Formation in the Petrified Forest," in Carol S. Breed and William J. Breed, eds., *Investigations in the Triassic Chinle Formation,* MNA Bulletin No. 47 (Flagstaff, Ariz.: Museum of Northern Arizona, 1972), 71.

9. Ash, *Petrified Forest,* 8–11; see also Breed and Billingsley, "Petrified Forest: Origins," 15–16.

10. Descriptions of petrifications occur in most of the sources on Petrified Forest. Sidney Ash covers the process clearly in *Petrified Forest,* 12.

11. Charles W. Barnes, "A Forest of 180 Million Year Old Trees," *Arizona Highways,* June 1975, 16.

12. Ash, *Petrified Forest,* 12.

13. Gottesfeld, "Paleoecology," 66–67.

14. Ash, *Petrified Forest,* 18.

15. Ibid., 22–23; also see Ash, "The Search for Plant Fossils in the Chinle Formation," in *Investigations in the Triassic Chinle Formation,* 45–58.

16. Long and Houk, *Dawn of the Dinosaurs,* includes unique illustrations of Triassic plants and animals by Doug Henderson and should be consulted; see also Ash, *Petrified Forest,* 26–27.

17. Colbert, "Ancient Animals," 25.

18. Ibid., 26–27.

19. Ash, *Petrified Forest*, 26–27; Colbert, "Ancient Animals," 25. *Chinlea* was a small coelacanth, a species that was thought to have become extinct about 60 million years ago. In 1938, though, a now famous living coelacanth, *Latimeria*, was found off the east coast of Africa.

20. The following material on Triassic animals comes from Colbert, "Ancient Animals," 25–29, and Ash, *Petrified Forest*, 26–29, unless otherwise noted.

21. Colbert, "Ancient Animals," 27. The classic study of phytosaurs is Charles Lewis Camp, *A Study of the Phytosaurs*, Memoirs of the University of California, vol. 10 (Berkeley: University of California Press, 1930).

22. Timothy Rowe, "*Placerias*: An Unusual Reptile from the Chinle Formation," *Plateau* 51 (1979): 30–32.

23. William J. Breed, *The Age of Dinosaurs in Northern Arizona* (Flagstaff: Museum of Northern Arizona, 1968), 10–11. The most recent study is Edwin H. Colbert, *The Triassic Dinosaur Coelophysis*, Bulletin Series No. 57 (Flagstaff: Museum of Northern Arizona Press, 1989).

24. Colbert, "Ancient Animals," 29.

25. For a recent, brief survey of the Anasazi see J. Richard Ambler, *The Anasazi: Prehistoric People of the Four Corners Region* (Flagstaff: Museum of Northern Arizona, 1989); also see Robert H. Lister and Florence C. Lister, *Those Who Came Before: Southwestern Archeology in the National Park System* (Tucson: University of Arizona Press, 1983). A regional perspective is provided in John C. McGregor, *Southwestern Archaeology* (Urbana: University of Illinois Press, 1965). Although the Pecos Classification suffers from a number of flaws, it still is widely used as a quick reference to the level of Anasazi development. It breaks down Anasazi prehistory into the following classifications: Basketmaker II, 100 B.C. to A.D. 500 to 700 (at the 1927 Pecos Conference, archaeologists postulated a Basketmaker I stage as an antecedent to following periods, although they had little specific information); Basketmaker III, 500 to 700 or later; Pueblo I, 700 to 900; Pueblo II, 900 to 1100 or 1170; Pueblo III, 1000 or 1120 to 1200 or 1300; Pueblo IV, 1300 to 1598; and Pueblo V, the historic period following the arrival of the Spanish. For descriptions see, Ambler, pp. 2–4; other scholars provide somewhat different dates for the Pecos periods.

26. Yvonne G. Stewart, *An Archeological Overview of Petrified Forest National Park* (Tucson: Western Archeological and Conservation Center, 1980), 79–80.

27. A recent survey of the Sinagua is Christian E. Downum, "The Sinagua," *Plateau* 63 (1992): 2–31; also see Downum's "One Grand History: A Critical Review of Flagstaff Archaeology, 1851–1988" (Ph.D. diss., University of Arizona, 1988).

28. Yvonne Stewart, *Archeological Overview*, 54.

29. A number of sources discuss archaeology in Petrified Forest National Park. Lister and Lister discuss the significance of archaeology in the southwestern parks in

Those Who Came Before, 159; a recent and comprehensive study is Yvonne Stewart, *Archeological Overview*; Ash provides a brief survey of the area's ancient inhabitants in *Petrified Forest*, 31–39. For developments over the last few years, see Jeffrey F. Burton, *Days in the Painted Desert and the Petrified Forests of Northern Arizona: Contributions to the Archeology of Petrified Forest National Park*, 1988–1992 (Tucson: Western Archeological and Conservation Center, 1993).

Chapter 2

1. Senate, *Journal of a Military Reconnaissance from Santa Fe, New Mexico, to the Navajo Country, Made in 1849 by James H. Simpson*. 31st Cong., 1st sess., 1850, Exec. Doc. 64: 98, 147. Earlier in that same expedition, Simpson had a chance to explore Chaco Canyon, where he documented seven of the canyon's major ruins as well as several smaller ones. On his fossil discovery at Canyon de Chelly, see also Ash, "Search for Plant Fossils," 46.

2. Senate, *Report of an Expedition down the Zuni and Colorado Rivers, by Captain L. Sitgreaves*, 32nd Cong., 2nd sess., 1853, Exec. Doc. 59, 7; Andrew Wallace, "Across Arizona to the Big Colorado: The Sitgreaves Expedition of 1851," *Arizona and the West* 26 (Winter 1984): 332–33, see map opposite p. 336; see also Ash, "Search for Plant Fossils," 47.

3. Senate, *Report of an Expedition down the Zuni and Colorado Rivers, by Captain L. Sitgreaves*, 36; Richard H. Kern Diary of the Sitgreaves Expedition, September 29, 1851, copy in files of Andrew Wallace, Northern Arizona University.

4. In 1987 a researcher inadvertently came across the specimen in the Academy's paleobotany collection. A small label identified the donor as Woodhouse and its source as the Little Colorado River in New Mexico Territory. This unimposing specimen represents "perhaps the oldest surviving collected piece of wood from the Triassic of Arizona." See Earle E. Spamer, "A Historic Piece of Petrified Wood from the Triassic of Arizona," *Mosasaur* 4 (December 1988): 1–2.

5. William H. Goetzmann, *Army Exploration in the American West, 1803–1863* (Lincoln: University of Nebraska Press, 1979), 307–8.

6. Senate, *Reports of Explorations and Surveys, to Ascertain the Most Practicable and Economical Route for a Railroad from the Mississippi River to the Pacific Ocean*, vol. 3, *Route Near the Thirty-fifth Parallel, under the Command of Lieut. A. W. Whipple, Topographical Engineers, in 1853 and 1854*, 33rd Cong., 2nd sess., 1856, Exec. Doc. 78, 73–74. Hereafter cited as *Whipple Report*. Also, Amiel Weeks Whipple Journal, December 2, 1853 (Oklahoma Historical Society, Oklahoma City). Whipple's career is covered in Grant Foreman, ed., *A Pathfinder in the Southwest* (Norman: University of Oklahoma Press, 1941).

7. Whipple Journal, December 3, 1853. Whipple's description of the wood at

the Black Forest as "rich and bright" is puzzling. Dr. Sidney Ash of Weber State University has studied the geology of Petrified Forest for years and in the process has developed a detailed knowledge of the terrain. His examination of Whipple's map and journals has led him to question whether the wood that Whipple described actually was in the Black Forest. Ash notes that the expedition's camp 77 was situated in the Puerco River Valley several miles from Lithodendron Wash; therefore the wood described by Whipple could have come from the lower part of the Chinle Formation, which is roughly equivalent to the beds that contain the brilliantly colored logs of Rainbow Forest. According to Ash's analysis, Whipple descended into Lithodendron Creek (now Lithodendron Wash) some distance to the southwest, roughly where Interstate 40 now crosses the wash. As the men followed the wash to the Puerco River, according to Ash, they moved lower and lower into the Chinle formation and could have found a large amount of colorful wood in place. Another possibility is that the wood was simply "float" that had washed down the Puerco from Jasper Forest or some other locality to the east. Sidney R. Ash, letter to author, November 13, 1989.

8. [Heinrich] Baldwin Möllhausen, *Diary of a Journey from the Mississippi to the Coasts of the Pacific*, vol. 2 (1858; reprint, New York: Johnson Reprint Corp., 1969), 119.

9. Ibid., 120.

10. Ibid., 120–21.

11. George P. Merrill, *The First One Hundred Years of American Geology* (1924; reprint, New York: Hafner Publishing Co., 1964), 315–16. W. P. Blake was a professor of geology at the University of California and later served as director of the Arizona School of Mines at Tucson. For additional information on Jules Marcou, see Merrill, 108–10.

12. Jules Marcou, "Resume and Field Notes," in *Whipple Report*, 151. See also Ash, "Search for Plant Fossils," 47–48; J. H. Stewart, F. G. Poole, and R. F. Wilson, *Stratigraphy and the Origin of the Chinle Formation and Related Upper Triassic Strata in the Colorado Plateau Region* (Washington, D.C.: Government Printing Office, 1972), 172; Lyman H. Daugherty, *The Upper Triassic Flora of Arizona* (Washington, D.C.: Carnegie Institution, 1941), 38.

13. Ash summarizes briefly the disagreement between Marcou and Blake in "Search for Plant Fossils," 47–48. Blake's own lengthy account, "Report on the Geology of the Route," is in the *Whipple Report*, part 4. The Triassic as an interpretive division in the prehistoric time scale had been established only in 1834, the work of Friedrich August von Alberti in western Germany. See William B. N. Berry, *Growth of a Prehistoric Time Scale, Based on Organic Evolution* (Palo Alto, Calif.: Blackwell Scientific Publications, 1987), 78–79.

14. See T. G. Manning, *Government in Science: The U.S. Geological Survey, 1867–1894* (Lexington: University of Kentucky Press, 1967), 22.

15. Hyde, *An American Vision* 55–56.

16. Ash, "Search for Plant Fossils," 49–50.

17. Senate, *Report upon the Colorado River of the West, Explored in 1857 and 1858 by Lieutenant Joseph C. Ives*, 36th Cong., 1st sess., 1861, Exec. Doc. 90, 75, 79–80; also Ash, "Search for Plant Fossils," 50–51. Möllhausen's account is in *Reisen in die Felsengebirge Nord-Amerikas bis zum Hochplateau von Neu-Mexico*, vol. 2 (Leipzig: Otto Purfuerst, 1860), 182; for additional information on Möllhausen see David H. Miller, "Baldwin Möllhausen: A Prussian's Image of the American West" (Ph.D. diss., University of New Mexico, 1970), and Preston Albert Barbara, *Baldwin Möllhausen, The German Cooper* (Philadelphia, 1914).

18. Wyman D. Walker, "F. X. Aubrey: Santa Fe Freighter, Pathfinder, and Explorer," *New Mexico Historical Review* 7 (January 1932): 31; House, *Wagon Road from Fort Defiance to the Colorado River*, 35th Cong., 1st sess., 1858, Exec. Doc. 124, 40; Emmanuel Henry Dieubonné Domenach, *Seven Years' Residence in the Great Deserts of North America*, vol. 1 (1860; reprint, New Haven: Research Publications, 1975), 215.

19. National Museum, "Information Concerning Some Fossil Trees in the United States Museum," *Proceedings of the United States National Museum* (Washington, D.C.: Government Printing Office, 1882), 1–3.

20. National Museum, "New Species of Fossil Wood (*Araucarioxylon arizonicum*) from Arizona and New Mexico," *Proceedings of the United States National Museum* (Washington, D.C.: Government Printing Office, 1888), 1–2.

21. Edwin H. Colbert, *Wandering Lands and Animals: The Story of Continental Drift and Animal Populations* (New York: Dover Publications, 1973), 21–22, 112–13; also see Colbert's *Dinosaurs: Their Discovery and Their World* (New York: E. P. Dutton, 1961).

22. H. C. Hovey, "A Visit to Chalcedony Park, Arizona," *Scientific American*, 23 July 1892, 55.

23. Ibid.

24. Ibid.

25. S. A. Miller, "The Petrified Forest of Arizona," *Cincinnati Society of Natural History* 17 (April 1894), 56-58.

26. George F. Kunz, *Gems and Precious Stones of North America* (1892; reprint, New York: Dover Publications, 1968), 141–42; also see his "Agatized and Jasperized Wood of Arizona," *Popular Science Monthly*, January 1886, 367.

27. "A Petrified Forest in Arizona," *Scientific American Supplement* no. 714, 7 September 1889, 11412.

28. "A Petrified Forest," *Cambrian* 15 (November 1895): 342.

29. C. F. Holder, "Stone Forests," *Frank Leslie's Popular Monthly*, March 1887, 378.

30. Charles F. Lummis, "Stone Trees: A Forest Gone to Bed," *Santa Fe Magazine*, June 1912, 35.

31. Charles F. Lummis, *Some Strange Corners of Our Country: The Wonderland of the Southwest* (New York: Century Co., 1901), 20–25.

32. Adam Clark Vroman, notes on backs of photographs no. 16, General View Petrified Forest (Arizona), and no. 17, in Petrified Forest (Arizona), 1895; Album 86 (Huntington Library, San Marino, California).

33. Ibid., photo no. 18, The Bridge, Petrified Forest (Arizona).

34. For discussions of economic development and the threats to national parks, see Richard A. Bartlett, *Yellowstone: A Wilderness Besieged* (Tucson: University of Arizona Press, 1985), 86; H. Duane Hampton, *How the U.S. Cavalry Save Our National Parks* (Bloomington: Indiana University Press, 1971), 39–41; Alfred Runte, *Yosemite: The Embattled Wilderness* (Lincoln: University of Nebraska Press, 1990), 49, 52; and Susan R. Schrepfer, *The Fight to Save the Redwoods: A History of Environmental Reform, 1917–1978* (Madison: University of Wisconsin Press, 1983), 7.

35. William Adams to William A. J. Sparks, 10 August 1886, National Archives, Record Group 79 (hereafter cited as NA, RG 79), National Monuments, Petrified Forest, file 12.

36. Ibid. In all, Adams filed 119 claims, following precisely the 1872 Mining Law by giving each claim a separate name and marking it with stakes.

37. Tom M. Bowers to Commissioner, General Land Office, 25 August 1886; John Mason to Commissioner, General Land Office (hereafter, GLO), 25 April 1988, NA, RG 79, National Monuments, Petrified Forest, file 12. Also see *Holbrook Tribune-News*, 7 December 1956. The issue of valuable minerals is discussed in John D. Leshy, *The Mining Law: A Study in Perpetual Motion* (Washington, D.C.: Resources for the Future, 1987), 90. See also Rocky Mountain Mineral Law Foundation, *The American Law of Mining*, vol. 1, Titles I–V (Albany, N.Y.: Matthew Bender and Co., 1960), 166–68, for the current determination of substances that would qualify as mineral deposits. The list begins with alum and ends with uranium; petrified wood is not included.

38. *A Historical and Biographical Record of the Territory of Arizona* (Chicago: McFarland and Poole, 1896), 529–30; J. H. Drake to John Muir, 4 December 1906, John Muir Papers, 1858–1957 (microform, University of the Pacific), roll 16.

39. "The Petrified Forest of Arizona," *Natural Science News*, 7 December 1895, 178.

40. Kunz, *Gems and Precious Stones of North America*, 320–21.

41. Arizona (Territory), *Acts, Resolutions, and Memorials of the Eighteenth Legislative Assembly*, House Memorial No. 4, 11 February 1895.

42. D. R. Francis to Commissioner, GLO, 8 December, 11 December, and 15 December 1896; NA, RG 79, National Monuments, Petrified Forest, file 12.

Chapter 3

1. The vandalism and theft at prehistoric ruins and the Antiquities Act are covered in Ise, *Our National Park Policy*, 143–62, and Rothman, *Preserving Different Pasts*, 6–51.

2. Will Barnes to John D. Benedict, 10 October 1898, NA, RG 79, National Monuments, Petrified Forest, file 12 1 5.

3. John D. Benedict to Commissioner, GLO, 2 December 1898, NA, RG 79, National Monuments, Petrified Forest, file 12 1 5; *Congressional Record*, 56th Cong., 1st sess., 1900, 33, pt. 5 : 3892.

4. S. J. Holsinger to Commissioner, GLO, 18 November 1899, NA, RG 79, National Monuments, Petrified Forest, file 12 1 5.

5. Charles F. Lummis, "In the Lion's Den," *Land of Sunshine*, October 1899, 291–92; "Agate Bridge," *Arizona Graphic*, 4 November 1899, 2.

6. Smithsonian Institution, "The Petrified Forests of Arizona," by Lester F. Ward, *Annual Report*, 1899 (Washington, D.C.: Government Printing Office, 1901), 293. Ward is perhaps better known as the author of *Dynamic Sociology* (1883) and as a sociologist at Brown University.

7. Ibid., 293–94.

8. *Congressional Record*, 56th Cong., 1st sess., 1900, 33, pt. 5 : 3892. The initiative for this measure came from the Interior Department, and Commissioner Binger Hermann actually drew up the original draft to set aside forty thousand acres.

9. *Congressional Record*, 57th Cong., 1st sess., 1902, 35, pt. 4 : 4049; Runte, *National Parks*, 49, 65; also see Sellers, Runte, and others, "The National Parks: A Forum," 130–45.

10. *Congressional Record*, 59th Cong., 1st sess., 1906, 40, pt. 10 : 9558. See also John F. Lacey, "The Petrified Forest National Park In Arizona," in L. H. Pammel, ed., *Major John F. Lacey: Memorial Volume*, (Des Moines: Iowa Park and Forestry Association, 1915; reprint, Cedar Rapids: Torch Press, n.d.), 203, 205–6. A recent survey of Lacey's contributions as a conservationist is Annette Gallagher, "Citizen of the Nation: John Fletcher Lacey, Conservationist," *Annals of Iowa* 46 (1981): 9–24.

11. Rothman, *Preserving Different Pasts*, 59. Although Petrified Forest and other natural sites, such as Devil's Tower, evoke some degree of cultural nationalism, they clearly never were large or as spectacular as the national parks. As Rothman notes on page 91, they reflected little of the grandeur of the American West. See also Ise, *Our National Park Policy*, 136–42; Runte, *National Parks*, 213–18; and Joseph L. Sax, *Mountains without Handrails: Reflections on the National Parks* (Ann Arbor: University of Michigan Press, 1980), 6–7.

12. William C. Everhart, *The National Park Service* (Boulder, Colo: Westview Press,

1983), 128–29; H. Duane Hampton, "Opposition to National Parks," *Journal of Forest History* 25 (January 1981): 41; Robert W. Righter, "National Monuments to National Parks," *Western Historical Quarterly* 20 (August 1989): 299–300.

13. Ise, *Our National Park Policy*, 147–53. Although a bit dated, the source is still valuable. More recent and comprehensive is Rothman's *Preserving Different Pasts*; see his third chapter for a summary of the background to passage of the Antiquities Act. See also Lee, *The Antiquities Act of 1906*.

14. Ise, *Our National Park Policy*, 151.

15. Department of the Interior, General Land Office, *Circular Relating to Historic and Prehistoric Ruins of the Southwest and Their Preservation*, by Edgar L. Hewett (Washington, D.C.: Government Printing Office, 1904), 9.

16. General Land Office, *Circular*, 11–12. Casa Grande ruins in southern Arizona received congressional appropriations to repair the structure and maintain it in 1889, and President Benjamin Harrison in 1892 established Casa Grande Ruins Reservation. The designation was not a precedent for the national monuments, however, since it was clearly a single act restricted to 160 acres that included the ruins.

17. Runte, *National Parks*, 73.

18. Rothman, *Preserving Different Pasts*, 46.

19. *U.S. Statutes at Large* 34 (1906), Stat. 225.

20. *U.S. Statutes at Large* 34 (1906), Stat. 3266.

21. See Righter's "National Monuments to National Parks," 282.

22. S. J. Holsinger to Commissioner, GLO, 15 October 1900, NA, RG 79, National Monuments, Petrified Forest, file 12 1 5; Holsinger to Commissioner, GLO, 17 March 1903, NA, RG 79, box 746, file 12 1 5; Holsinger to Commissioner, GLO, 12 May 1903, NA, RG 79, file 12 1 5.

23. Holsinger to Commissioner, GLO, 17 March 1903; also W. A. Richards to Secretary of the Interior, November 1905, NA, RG 79, box 746, file 12 2 5; Holsinger to Commissioner, GLO, 13 May 1905, NA, RG 79, National Monuments, Petrified Forest, file 12 1 5.

24. Richards to Secretary of the Interior, November 1905, NA, RG 79, file; 12 1 5, pt. 3.

25. Charles D. Walcott to Secretary of the Interior, 26 October 1907, NA, RG 79, box 746, file 12 2 5.

26. Report on Petrified Forest National Monument by C. W. Hayes, 10 February 1908, NA, RG 79, box 746, file 12 1 5.

27. Ibid.

28. Petrified Forest National Monument, Custodian's Monthly Report, February 1909, NA, RG 79, National Monuments, Petrified Forest, file 12 1 5, pts. 1–5; Karl

R. A. Stevenson to Secretary of the Interior, 10 January 1910, National Monuments; Petrified Forest, file 1215, pts. 1–5.

29. George P. Merrill, Report and Recommendations Relative to the Fossil Forests of Arizona, May–June 1911, RG 79, box 746, file 1215, pt. 4.

30. Ibid.

31. *U.S. Statutes at Large* 37 (1911), Stat. 1716.

32. S. L. Gillan to Commissioner, GLO, 9 February 1912, NA, RG 79, National Monuments, Petrified Forest, pts 1–5, file 1215; *Petrified Forest Arizona* (pamphlet; Chicago: Atchison, Topeka, and Santa Fe Railway Co., 1912).

33. Alfred Runte, *Trains of Discovery: Western Railroads and the National Parks* (Flagstaff, Ariz.: Northland Press, 1984), 7, 12–14.

34. Runte, *Trains of Discovery*, 17; Earl Pomeroy, *In Search of the Golden West: The Tourist in Western America* (New York: Knopf, 1957), 112.

35. Charles F. Lummis, "Stone Trees: A Forest Gone to Bed," *Santa Fe Magazine*, June 1912, 41.

36. *Petrified Forest Arizona.*

37. C. W. Bruce to Secretary of the Interior, 25 November 1913, NA, RG 79, box 746, file 1215.

38. Roy G. Mead to Commissioner, GLO, 29 May 1914, NA, RG 79, box 746.

39. Chester B. Campbell to Horace M. Albright, 1 June 1915, NA, RG 79, box 756, file 1215.

40. Bo Sweeney to Chester B. Campbell, 30 August 1915, and Chester B. Campbell to Secretary of the Interior, 13 June 1916, NA, RG 79, box 746, file 1215; Horace Albright to Edward Chambers, 2 May 1917, and Chester B.Campbell to National Park Service, 26 September 1917, NA, RG 79, National Monuments, Petrified Forest, file 1215, pts. 6–9.

41. Everhart, *The National Park Service*, 18.

Chapter 4

1. For a brief discussion of the investigations of fossil plants see Ash, "Search for Plant Fossils," 45–68; on vertebrates see Samuel P. Welles, "Collecting Triassic Vertebrates in the Plateau Province," *Journal of the West* 8 (April 1969): 231–46. In the Breed and Breed anthology, also see Welles, "Fossil Hunting for Tetrapods in the Chinle Formation: A Brief Pictorial History," pp. 13–18.

2. Smithsonian Institution, "Petrified Forests of Arizona," 295–96. Some of the petrified logs at Chalcedony Park undoubtedly eroded out of the plateau that Ward described. The source of the petrified logs, though, is considered to be the

ancient mountains that surrounded the park in the Triassic Period when the Chinle Formation was deposited.

3. Ibid., 299–300.

4. Ibid., 300–301.

5. Welles, "Fossil-Hunting for Tetrapods in the Chinle Formation," in Breed and Breed, 13. For a more detailed account see Welles, "Collecting Triassic Vertebrates," 237.

6. U.S. Geological Survey (USGS), Monographs, "Status of the Mesozoic Floras of the United States," second paper by Lester F. Ward (Washington, D.C.: Government Printing Office, 1905), 34; also Ash, "Search for Plant Fossils," 54.

7. GS Monographs, "Status of Mesozoic Floras," 34–35; Ash, "Search for Plant Fossils," 55.

8. Walter Hough, "Ancient Peoples of the Petrified Forest of Arizona, Harper's Monthly Magazine 105 (1901): 897; see Yvonne Stewart, Archeological Overview, 58–59.

9. Smithsonian Institution, "Archaeological Fieldwork in Northeastern Arizona: The Museum-Gates Expedition of 1901," by Walter Hough, Annual Report, 1901 (Washington, D.C.: Government Printing Office, 1903), 312–15; and Hough, "Ancient Peoples," 901. In the latter source, written for a popular audience, Hough's language is considerably more descriptive as he refers to the "Cannibal feast" and the "pueblo of the Cannibals." He adds that it represented "the first material proof of cannibalism among our North-American Indians." He avoids such exuberant narrative and conclusions in the more scientific work for the Smithsonian.

10. Smithsonian Institution, "Museum-Gates Expedition," 319–20, 322; Hough, "Ancient Peoples," 897.

11. Yvonne Stewart, Archeological Overview, 58–59.

12. Petrified Forest Arizona; Alice Cotton Fletcher, "Along the Way I Met John Muir," John Muir Papers, 1858–1957 (microform, University of the Pacific), reel 51, Series V, E: 57. Hereafter cited as John Muir Papers.

13. Wanda Muir to John Muir, 13 May 1906 and 23 May 1906, John Muir Papers, reel 16.

14. Fletcher, "Along the Way."

15. Fletcher, "Along the Way." The account is a warm, sympathetic recollection of Alice Cotton Fletcher's short acquaintance with Muir, but it poses certain problems. The typescript is undated, although it clearly is a reminiscence, probably written decades after the event. In fact, it was produced at a New Hampshire nursing home, and the passage of time may have affected the author's accuracy. As for the Cosmopolitan articles, Muir did correspond with F. Bailey Millard, explaining that he intended to write "the little article you want." 25 September 1905, John Muir Papers, reel 15.

16. Louie Muir to Wanda Muir, in Jean H. Clark and Shirley Sargent, eds., *Dear Papa: Letters between John Muir and His Daughter Wanda* (Fresno, Calif.: Panorama West Books, 1985), 86–87. John Muir to J. E. Calkins, 8 April 1906, John Muir Papers, reel 16.

17. Muir to J. E. Calkins, 8 April 1906.

18. John Muir to Robert Underwood Johnson, 21 December 1905, John Muir Papers, reel 15.

19. John Muir to Florence Merriam Bailey, 15 February 1906; John Muir to James Murdock, 19 February 1906; John Muir to J. E. Calkins, 8 April 1906, John Muir Papers, reel 16.

20. Linnie Marsh Wolfe, ed., *John of the Mountains: The Unpublished Journals of John Muir* (Madison: University of Wisconsin Press, 1979), 94–95. John Muir to Helen and Wanda Muir, 3 June 1906 and 4 June 1906, John Muir Papers, reel 16; John Muir to John J. Byrne, 12 September 1906, NA, RG 79, box 746, file 12 1 5.

21. The explanation comes after a brief excursion through Muir's "Sigillaria Grove" in Petrified Forest with Dr. Sidney Ash in June of 1989. The confusion over Muir's *Sigillaria* was eliminated in 1910 when Edward C. Jeffrey of Harvard described a new genus and species of fossil plant. From a specimen of wood collected in the vicinity of Petrified Forest, Jeffrey named *Woodworthia arizonica*. Its surface is marked with small pits, and these may have misled Muir into identifying specimens of that species as *Sigillaria*. For an illustration of *Woodworthia*, see Long and Houk, *Dawn of the Dinosaurs*, 76–77.

22. John Muir to Helen and Wanda Muir, 13 May 1906, John Muir Papers, reel 16.

23. "Among the World's Workers: A Conversation with John Muir," *World's Work*, November 1906, 8250.

24. W. H. Simpson to John Muir, 9 May 1906 and 31 May 1906; Wanda Muir to John Muir, 13 May 1906, John Muir Papers, reel 16.

25. John Muir to Robert Underwood Johnson, 10 June 1906, John Muir Papers, reel 16.

26. No evidence of Muir's role in promoting Petrified Forest National Park surfaces in any of the pertinent collections: the John Muir Papers (microform), the John Muir Collection, 1902–1955, at the Huntington Library; the John Fletcher Lacey Papers at the Iowa State Historical Society, and the Theodore Roosevelt material at the Library of Congress. Nor does Record Group 79 at National Archives indicate any role for Muir. Indeed, the only source to credit Muir with establishing Petrified Forest National Park is Alice Cotton Fletcher's manuscript, "Along the Way I Met John Muir." Fletcher states that when Muir learned of the plans to crush petrified wood into industrial abrasives, he made a special trip to Washington, "where

he worked untiringly until he obtained the necessary papers to show conclusively that the Petrified Forest of Arizona was to be made into a National Park." Nor is there any evidence that Muir used his friendship with Theodore Roosevelt to promote the park cause.

27. John Muir to John J. Byrne, 12 September 1906; Frank Bond to John Muir, 28 December 1906; John Muir Papers, reel 16.

28. John Muir to James Murdock, 12 February 1906; John Muir to Robert Underwood Johnson, 19 October 1906, John Muir Papers, reel 16.

29. Robert Underwood Johnson to John Muir, 3 June 1906, John Muir Papers, reel 16.

30. Robert Underwood Johnson to John Muir, 3 June 1906; John Muir to C. Hart Merriam, 15 December 1906; John Muir to John C. Merriam, 26 January 1907; John C. Merriam to John Muir, 17 May 1907, John Muir Papers, reel 16.

31. See Peter Wild, "Months of Sorrow and Renewal: John Muir in Arizona, 1905–1906," *Journal of the Southwest* 29 (Spring 1987): 20–40.

32. Modern writers have sought to ascertain Muir's significance in Petrified Forest; see Meyer, "D-Day on the Painted Desert," 8.

33. Welles, "Collecting Triassic Vertebrates," 234.

34. Camp, *Study of Phytosaurs*, 12.

35. Janet Lewis Zullo, "Annie Montague Alexander: Her Work in Paleontology, *Journal of the West* 8 (April 1969): 183–84; See also "Biographical Sketch of Annie M. Alexander," Annie Montague Alexander Collection, Bancroft Library, University of California, Berkeley, California.

36. Welles, "Collecting Triassic Vertebrates," 235–37; also Robert A. Long, notes, p. 14–15 (copy in author's possession).

37. Welles, "Collecting Triassic Vertebrates, 235.

38. Colbert, *Dinosaurs*, 60. Illustrations of phytosaurs appear in Houk and Long, *Dawn of the Dinosaurs*, 28–29, 36–37, 38–39, 56–57, 76–77, and 78–79.

39. Colbert, *Wandering Lands and Animals*, 23–24.

Chapter 5

1. John A. Jakle, *The Tourist: Travel in Twentieth-Century North America* (Lincoln: University of Nebraska Press, 1985), 107; Emily Post, *By Motor to the Golden Gate* (New York: D. Appleton and Co., 1910), 183–84.

2. Jakle, *The Tourist*, 70–71; Peter Schmitt, *Back to Nature: The Arcadian Myth in Urban America* (New York: Oxford University Press, 1969), 161.

3. Quoted in Runte, *National Parks*, 156–57.

4. Schmitt, *Back to Nature*, 159; Jakle, *The Tourist*, 103–4.

5. Warren James Belasco, *Americans on the Road: From Autocamp to Motel*, 1910–1945 (Cambridge, Mass.: MIT Press, 1979), 20, 23.

6. Donald C. Swain, *Wilderness Defender: Horace M. Albright and Conservation* (Chicago: University of Chicago Press, 1970), 134–35.

7. *The Petrified Forest, Adamana, Arizona* (brochure, 1920), NA, RG 79, National Monuments, Petrified Forest, file 12, pt. 7.

8. Belasco, *Americans on the Road*, 137.

9. Arno B. Cammerer to Charles L. Gable, 9 June 1925, NA, RG 79, National Monuments, Petrified Forest, file 204; Frank Pinkley to Stephen Mather, 16 September 1919, NA, RG 79, National Monuments, Petrified Forest, file 12; Arno Cammerer to Charles Gable, 9 June 1925, NA, RG 79, NPS Monuments, Petrified Forest, file 204.

10. Susan C. Kelly, *Route 66: The Highway and Its People* (Norman: University of Oklahoma Press, 1988), 36–37; also see Michael Wallis, *Route 66: The Mother Road* (New York: St. Martin's Press, 1990).

11. William Nelson, Report on the Petrified Forest National Monument, May 1918, NA, RG 79, box 747, file 11.

12. Frank Pinkley to Stephen Mather, 4 March 1919, NA, RG 79, box 747, file 1215.

13. Ibid.

14. A. E. Demary to Stephen Mather, 25 March 1919, NA, RG 79, box 746.

15. Arno Cammerer to Carl Hayden, 1 December 1923, NA, RG 79, box 747, file 12; Rothman, *Preserving Different Pasts*, 127–28.

16. Frank Pinkley to Director, National Park Service (NPS), 1 December 1919, NA, RG 79, box 747, file 1215.

17. Ibid.

18. William Nelson to Director, NPS, 22 July 1920 and 17 October 1920; A. B. Cammerer to Stephen T. Mather, 13 October 1920; NA, RG 79, box 747, file 1215; Petrified Forest National Monument, Annual Report, 1922, NA, RG 79, National Monuments, Petrified Forest, file 12, pts. 6–9.

19. William Nelson to Director NPS, 7 July 1922, NA, RG 79, NPS Monuments, Petrified Forest, box 597, file 201-06.

20. Rothman, *Preserving Different Pasts*, 101–2.

21. Ibid., 75.

22. Dean MacCannell, *The Tourist: A New Theory of the Leisure Class* (New York: Schocken Books, 1976), 136; also Jakle, *The Tourist*, 23–26.

23. Irvin S. Cobb, *Roughing It De Luxe* (New York: George H. Doran Co., 1913), 45.

24. William Nelson to Director, NPS, 7 July 1922, NA, RG 79, NPS Monuments, PEFO, box 597, file 201-06, pt. 1.

25. Arno Cammerer to William Nelson, 13 July 1922 and 25 July 1922, NA, RG 79, NPS Monuments, Petrified Forest, box 597, file 201-06.

26. William Nelson to Director NPS, 17 July 1922, NA, RG 79, NPS Monuments, box 597, PEFO, 1921–1932, file 201-06, pt. 1.

27. William Nelson to Director NPS, 29 July 1922, NA, RG 79, box 747, file 12 1 5.

28. Arno Cammerer to Charles Gable, 9 June 1925, NA, RG 79, box 597, NPS Monuments, Petrified Forest, file 204.

29. Frank Pinkley to Stephen Mather, 16 September 1922, NPS Monuments, Petrified Forest, file 204.

30. See Hal Rothman, "Second-Class Sites," 45–56.

31. Arno Cammerer to Carl Hayden, 1 December 1923, NA, RG 79, box 747, file 12.

32. Southwestern National Monuments, Monthly Report, October 1923, Western Archeology and Conservation Center (WACC), Tucson, Ariz.

33. Southwestern National Monuments, Monthly Report, December 1923, WACC; William Nelson to Director, NPS, [?] 1923, NA, RG 79, box 747, file 12.

34. L. Caldwell to Carl Hayden, 23 November 1923, NA, RG 79, box 747, file 12 1 5.

35. William Nelson to Director, NPS, n.d. 1923; Frank Pinkley to William Nelson, 3 January 1924, NA, RG 79, box 747, file 12 1 5.

36. Southwestern National Monuments, Monthly Reports, March, May, and June 1924, WACC; see also Rothman, *Preserving Different Pasts*, 120–24.

37. William Nelson to Director NPS, 15 March 1922, NA, RG 79, NPS Monuments Petrified Forest, file 201; Anna M. Marleau to Stephen T. Mather, 25 November 1924, NA, RG 79, box 747, file 204; Arno Cammerer to Frank Pinkley, 7 January 1925, NA, RG 79, NPS Monuments, box 597, file 204.

38. Arno Cammerer to Frank Pinkley, 7 January 1925, NA, RG 79, NPS Monuments, box 597, file 204.

39. Mrs. Henry Henderson to Frank Pinkley, 1 June 1925; Clark M. Terry to Frank Pinkley, 1 June 1925; Arno Cammerer to William Nelson, 25 August 1925 and 2 November 1925; Frank Pinkley to Stephen Mather, 27 August 1925 and 15 September 1924; NA, RG 79, box 597, file 204.

40. Frank Pinkley to Stephen Mather, 12 April 1926, NA, RG 79, NPS Monuments, Petrified Forest, file 201.

41. Arno Cammerer to L. W. Douglas, 28 April 1929, NA, RG 79, box 747.

42. Arno Cammerer letter, 4 June 1929, NA, RG 79, NPS Monuments, Petrified Forest, box 597, file 204-010.

43. Arno Cammerer to F. A. Kittredge, 13 May 1929, NA, RG 79, NPS Monuments, file 207.

44. Arthur Demaray to George D. Pratt, 15 June 1929, NA, RG 79, NPS Monuments, box 597, file 204.

45. See Horace M. Albright's reminiscences, *The Birth of the National Park Service: The Founding Years, 1913–1933*, as told to Robert Cahn (Salt Lake City: Howe Brothers, 1985).

46. M. R. Tillotson to Horace M. Albright, 27 May 1929, NA, RG 79, NPS Monuments, Petrified Forest, box 597, file 204-010.

47. T. S. Palmer to Horace M. Albright, 2 August 1929, NA, RG 79, NPS Monuments, Petrified Forest, box 599, file 857.

48. Ibid.

49. M. R. Tillotson, Report on Petrified Forest National Monument, 9 September 1929, NPS Monuments, Petrified Forest, box 597, file 204-010.

50. Ibid.

51. Ibid.

52. Ibid.

53. Ibid.

54. Schmitt, *Back to Nature*, 162.

Chapter 6

1. Charles J. Smith, Petrified Forest National Monument, 22 March 1932, NA, RG 79, box 2331, file 207. Also see "Address, by Charles F. Smith," Fiftieth Anniversary of Petrified Forest National Monument, 8 December 1956; copy in Petrified Park National Park Library (PFNPL). Also see the account by Smith's wife, Dama Margaret Smith, *I Married a Ranger* (Stanford: Stanford University Press, 1931), 2–3, 6.

2. Horace M. Albright to Secretary of the Interior, 18 December 1929, NA, RG 79, NPS Monuments, Petrified Forest, box 597.

3. Smith, Petrified Forest National Monument, 22 March 1932, NA, RG 79, box 2331, file 207; Smith, "Address." In all, the land company held 12,792 acres within the monument, which was exchanged for land valued at $88,000, according to Smith. The land was deeded to the federal government in June 1933.

4. Smith, Petrified Forest National Monument, 22 March 1932, NA, RG 79, box 2331, file 207; *U.S. Statutes at Large* 16 (1930), Stat. 3040.

5. Charles E. Peterson, Report on Petrified Forest National Monument, January 1930, NA, RG 79, NPS Monuments, Petrified Forest, box 597.

6. D. H. Thomas, *The Southwestern Indian Detours: The Story of the Fred Harvey / Santa Fe*

Railway Experiment in "Detourism" (Phoenix, Ariz.: Hunter Publishing Co., 1978), 44, 90; Petrified Forest National Monument (PFNM), Superintendents Monthly Report, June 1930. Since accommodating these detours required delaying regular trains, some travelers were understandably irate at the delay, Thomas points out in *Southwestern Indian Detours*, 90.

7. Thomas, *Southwestern Indian Detours*, 59–63, 224, 261–63.

8. PFNM, Superintendents Monthly Report, September 1930. Statistics relating to the number of visitors at Petrified Forest are taken from Superintendents Annual Reports, which reflect numbers for fiscal years. These can differ from the annual totals compiled by the Park Service.

9. Rose Houk, *The Painted Desert: Land of Light and Shadow* (Petrified Forest National Park, Ariz.: Petrified Forest Museum Association, 1990), 22–23; National Park Service, The Painted Desert Inn: Evaluation of Structures and Cultural Resources (San Francisco: NPS Western Regional Office, 1974), 13. Lore estimated that some 70,000 people had visited the Painted Desert in 1930.

10. Charles J. Smith to Conrad L. Wirth, 18 May 1931, copy in Painted Desert Inn History File, PFNPL; Smith to Wirth, 8 June 1931, NA, RG 79, NPS Monuments, Petrified Forest, box 598, file 601-1.

11. Conrad Wirth Memo, 3 June 1931, NA, RG 79, NPS Monuments, Petrified Forest, box 598, file 602-1.

12. Charles J. Smith to Director NPS, 8 June 1931, NA, RG 79, NPS Monuments, Petrified Forest, box 598, file 602-1.

13. Roger W. Toll to Director NPS, 21 March 1932, NA, RG 79, NPS monuments, Petrified Forest, box 598, file 602-1.

14. Roger W. Toll to Horace Albright, 14 March 1932, NA, RG 79, NPS Monuments, Petrified Forest, box 598, file 602-1. The Painted Desert Inn was comparable to El Tovar only as a symbol. The Grand Canyon's elegant hotel initially had more than a hundred rooms and could accommodate 250 guests. Painted Desert Inn was modest in comparison; even after its remodeling in the 1930s, it had only six guest rooms.

15. U.S. *Statutes at Large* 47 (1932), Stat. 2532; Superintendents Monthly Report, October 1932, PFNPL.

16. Southwestern National Monuments, Monthly Reports, March 1932, May 1932, WACC.

17. Southwestern National Monuments, Monthly Report, September 1932, WACC; Thomas, *Southwestern Indian Detours*, 273–74, 305–7.

18. Kelly, *Route 66*, 37, 71–72; also Wallis, *Route 66*, 179–82.

19. Southwestern National Monuments, Monthly Report, February 1933, WACC.

20. Harold L. Ickes to Julia B. Miller, 24 July 1933, NA, RG 79, box 2330, file 204.

21. Harold L. Ickes to Julia Miller, 24 July 1933; Julia Miller to Harold L. Ickes, 15 August 1933; Julia Miller to Arno B. Cammerer, 15 August 1933; NA, RG 79, box 2330, file 204.

22. Charles J. Smith to Director NPS, 5 August 1933; Secretary Ickes to A. B. Cammerer, 26 August 1933; NA, RG 79, box 2330, file 204.

23. Paul F. Cutter to Director, NPS, 10 August 1934, NA, RG 79, box 2332, file 204.

24. Harold Sellers Colton, "Racking My Brain: An Autobiography," pt. 4, manuscript at the Library of the Museum of Northern Arizona, Flagstaff, Ariz.; also see Rothman, *Preserving Different Pasts*, 130.

25. Louis R. Gladdis to Secretary of the Interior, 11 October 1934, NA, RG 79, box 2330, file 204.

26. Kelly, *Route 66*, 111, 168; Jakle, *The Tourist*, 146.

27. Richard Lowitt, *The New Deal and the West* (Bloomington: Indiana University Press, 1984), 219.

28. Donald C. Swain, "The National Park Service and the New Deal, 1933–1940," *Pacific Historical Review* 41 (August 1972): 323–27.

29. Rothman, *Preserving Different Pasts*, 165–66.

30. PFNM, Superintendents Monthly Report, December 1933, PFNPL.

31. Yvonne Stewart, *Archeological Overview*, 82–83, 106–7, 114, 139–48.

32. Southwestern National Monuments, Monthly Reports, April 1934, WACC.

33. A brief survey of the topic is National Park Service, *The Civilian Conservation Corps and the National Park Service, 1933–942: An Administrative History*, by John C. Paige (Washington, D.C.: Government Printing Office, 1985).

34. PFNM Annual Report, 1935, PFNPL.

35. Lorimer H. Skidmore, "Report to the Chief of Planning on the Construction of the Painted Desert Inn at Petrified Forest National Monument," 2, in Painted Desert Inn History File, PFNPL.

36. Ibid., 5; also Harold W. Cole, "Construction History, Painted Desert Inn, Petrified Forest National Monument," 4–5, typescript (5 June 1976) in Painted Desert Inn History File, PFNPL.

37. PFNM, Superintendents Monthly Report, September 1937, PFNPL.

38. Skidmore, "Report to the Chief of Planning," 4.

39. National Park Service, *Painted Desert Inn*, 21.

40. Charles J. Smith to Director NPS, 8 March 1938, NA, RG 79, box 2337, file 601.

41. Newspaper clipping, NA, RG 79, box 2329, file 201.

42. Ibid.

43. Harry G. Slattery to Alva B. Adams, 25 March 1939; Harold Ickes quoted in clipping, RG 79, NA, RG 79, box 2329, file S892.

44. Roger Toll, quoted in Rothman, *Preserving Different Pasts*, 156.

45. Ibid.

46. *St. Johns Observer*, 15 April 1939.

47. PFNM, Annual Reports, 1938 and 1940, PFNPL.

Chapter 7

1. PFNM, Annual Report, 1940; Superintendents Monthly Reports, July 1940 and September 1940. Superintendents Monthly Reports and Annual Reports cited hereafter are located at the Petrified Forest National Park Library (PFNPL), unless otherwise designated.

In addition to the concessionaires at Painted Desert Inn and Rainbow Forest, the Park Service had granted a single grazing permit on 6,880 acres and a special use permit on a single acre. Hunter Clarkson also retained his permit to transport tourists through the monument, but his operation was not actively involved.

2. PFNM, Annual Report, 1943.

3. Kelly, *Route 66*, 148–49. Cynthia Troup's husband, Bobby, composed the lyrics to "Get Your Kicks on Route 66" during the course of their 1946 journey to Los Angeles.

4. PFNM, Annual Report, 1945; Annual Report, FY 1947.

5. PFNM, Annual Report, 1947; Virginia L. Grattan, *Mary Colter: Builder upon the Red Earth* (Flagstaff, Ariz.: Northland Press, 1980), 102–3.

6. Grattan, *Mary Colter*, 102–3; Fred Kabotie, "The Zuni Salt Lake Trip Mural," typescript in Painted Desert Inn History File. PFNPL.

7. PFNM, Annual Report, FY 1947.

8. Ibid., Annual Report, FY 1947, and Annual Report, FY 1949.

9. PFNM, Annual Report, FY 1948.

10. PFNM, Annual Report, 1950–51; Superintendents Monthly Reports, November 1950, December 1950, May 1951.

11. Kelly, *Route 66*, 158.

12. Ibid.

13. PFNM, Annual Report, FY 1943; Superintendents Monthly Reports, June 1951, July 1951, August 1951.

14. PFNM, Annual Report, FY 1943; PFNM, Superintendents Monthly Reports, September 1950, January 1953, March, 1953, August 1953.

15. PFNM, Annual Report, FY 1952–53; Monthly Report, April 1953.

16. PFNM, Superintendents Monthly Report, November 1955 and June 1956.

17. Conrad L. Wirth, Parks, Politics, and the People (Norman: University of Oklahoma Press, 1980), 226–27, 234.

18. Ibid., 234. Charles Stevenson, "The Shocking Truth about Our National Parks," Reader's Digest, January 1955, 45; Bernard De Voto, "The Easy Chair," Harper's Monthly, October 1953, 50–52. See also De Voto's "Easy Chair" column, February 1954, 12–17.

19. Wirth, Parks, Politics, and the People, 239–43, 256.

20. F. Fraser Darling and Noel D. Eichhorn, "Man and Nature in the National Parks," National Park Magazine 43 (April 1969): 17; Devereux Butcher, "Resorts or Wilderness?" Atlantic, February 1961, 45–51.

21. Runte, National Parks, 212–13.

22. PFNM, Annual Report, FY 1956.

23. Robert E. Merriam to James E. Murray, 13 January 1958, Carl V. Hayden Collection, Hayden Library, Arizona State University; U.S. Statutes at Large 72 (1958), Stat. 69.

24. National Parks and Conservation Magazine, July–September 1957, 127; Devereux Butcher to Conrad Wirth, 12 April 1958, Hayden Collection, Arizona State University.

25. Butcher, "Resorts or Wilderness?" 46, 51.

26. Petrified Forest was a case in point. Rangers there presented interpretive lectures in a twenty-by-thirty-foot room crowded with visitors. People regularly fainted because of the closeness; in 1956, Superintendent Fagergren simply canceled the lectures.

27. PFNM, Superintendents Monthly Report, August 1962.

28. PFNM, Annual Report FY 1963.

29. Department of the Interior, National Park Service, Wilderness Recommendation for Petrified Forest National Park, Arizona (November 1967), 20–22, 31–32, PFNPL.

30. Department of the Interior, National Park Service, Statement for Management, Petrified Forest National Park, May 1988, 12.

31. Department of the Interior, National Park Service, Petrified Forest National Park Natural Resources Management Plan (February 1981 revision), 13.

32. Natural Resources Management Plan, (February 1981 revision), 5, 13; see also John C. Freemuth, Islands under Siege: National Parks and the Politics of External Threats (Lawrence: University Press of Kansas, 1991), 109, which notes a "yellowish-brown layered haze" visible at the park in a 1988 EPA report. In a Class I area, particulate matter may not exceed 0.10 micrograms per cubic meter in a twenty-

four-hour period; sulphur dioxide may not increase beyond 0.5 micrograms in a twenty-four-hour period.

33. Department of the Interior, Statement for Management, Petrified Forest National Park (May 1988), 13.

Chapter 8

1. Albright, Birth of the National Park Service, 270–71; Rothman, Preserving Different Pasts, 174.

2. Matthews, Guide to the National Parks, vol. 1, ix.

3. H. P. Mera, "Observations on the Archaeology of the Petrified Forest National Monument," New Mexico Laboratory of Anthropology Bulletin, Technical Series, no. 7 (1934): 2; also Fred Wendorf, "Early Archaeological Sites in the Petrified Forest National Monument," Plateau 21 (1948): 29–32; and Yvonne Stewart, Archeological Overview, 82–83 and 140–41, for a brief summary of Mera.

4. C. B. Cosgrove, "Report on Excavation, Repair, and Renovation of Agate House and Other Sites." CWA Archaeological Program, Winter 1933–34, 1–10; NA, RG 79, box 2339, file 619-1. A convenient summary and evaluation of the CWA projects appears in Stewart, Archeological Overview, 144–48.

5. Stewart, Archeological Overview, 141, 147–48.

6. A convenient summary of Reed's survey, sponsored by the Park Service and Museum of Northern Arizona, is in Stewart, Archeological Overview, 152–58. Reed's "Special Report on Review of Archaeological Survey Potsherd Collections, Petrified Forest National Monument, Arizona" (Santa Fe, N.M., 1947) is reproduced in Stewart's work as appendix 2, 191–221.

7. Wendorf, "Early Archaeological Sites," 30–32, Archaeological Studies in the Petrified Forest National Monument, MNA Bulletin No. 27 (Flagstaff, Ariz.: Museum of Northern Arizona, 1953), 1, and "The Flattop Site in the Petrified Forest National Monument," Plateau 22 (1950): 43.

8. Wendorf, "Flattop Site," 45–47, 50–51. This is a preliminary report on the Flattop excavation; for more detail see Wendorf's Archaeological Studies and Yvonne Stewart, Archeological Overview, 155–63.

9. Wendorf, Archaeological Studies, 78–80; also see Wendorf, "Archaeological Investigations in the Petrified Forest: Twin Buttes Site, a Preliminary Report," Plateau 24 (1951): 77–78.

10. Stewart, Archeological Overview, 164, 166–68, summarizes Wendorf's work at Twin Buttes; see his Archaeological Studies for additional detail.

11. Wendorf, *Archaeological Studies*, 160–61, 175, and "Twin Buttes Site," 81, 83; Stewart, *Archeological Overview*, 92, 168.

12. Wendorf, *Archaeological Studies*, 175; "Twin Buttes Site," 83.

13. Wendorf, *Archaeological Studies*, 175.

14. Ibid., 171–76.

15. Wendorf, "Twin Buttes Site," 78; also, National Park Service, Petrified Forest National Park, Final General Management Plan / Development Concept Plan / Environmental Impact Statement (Denver: NPS Denver Service Center, 1993), 35–36.

16. Yvonne Stewart, *Archeological Overview*, 116–17.

17. Ibid., 117–19.

18. Myrl Walker, quoted in Long, notes, 16–17.

19. Myrl V. Walker to Harold Bryant, 23 February 1933, PFNM, Park Naturalists Monthly Report, PFNPL; Ash, "Search for Plant Fossils," 56.

20. Gottesfeld, "Paleoecology," 61.

21. Ash, "Search for Plant Fossils," 56.

22. Lyman H. Daugherty, "*Schilderia adamanica*: A New Fossil Wood from the Petrified Forest of Arizona," *Botanical Gazette* 96 (December 1934): 363–66; Ash, "Search for Plant Fossils," 56–57. For an artist's illustration of the fossil, see Long and Houk, *Dawn of the Dinosaurs*, 78–79.

23. Long, notes, 17.

24. Ibid., 18.

25. Welles, "Collecting Triassic Vertebrates," 237.

26. Erik K. Reed, Special Report: Petrified Forest National Monument, Arizona, NA, RG 79, NPS Central Classified File, 1939–1949, box 2331, file 207, Part 1.

27. Long, notes, 19.

28. Ibid., 21.

29. Ibid., 21–22; Long and Houk, *Dawn of the Dinosaurs*, 48–51.

30. Long, notes, 22–23.

31. Department of the Interior, Statement for Management, May 1988, D1-D2.

32. David Gillette, quoted in Department of the Interior, Statement for Management, May 1988, 7.

Epilogue

1. Edward Abbey, *Desert Solitaire: A Season in the Wilderness* (New York: Ballantine Books, 1968), 58–60; also see Michael Frome's more recent work, *Regreening the National Parks* (Tucson: University of Arizona Press, 1992).

2. Sax, *Mountains without Handrails*, 79.

3. Petrified Forest National Park, Final General Management Plan, 1993, 20–21.

4. Ibid., 21, 30.

5. Ibid., 50.

6. Ibid., 28.

7. Ibid., 51.

8. Ibid., 51–52.

BIBLIOGRAPHY

Archival Sources

U.S. Department of the Interior. *Broadcast* (Southwestern National Monuments Newsletter), 1936–1937. WACC.

———. Environmental Assessment. Natural Resources Management Plan. Petrified Forest National Park, Arizona, 1974. PFNPL.

———. Historical Reports—PEFO. 1932. Petrified Forest National Park Library (PFNPL).

———. Master Plan for Petrified Forest National Park, 1965. PFNPL.

———. Naturalist Division Monthly Reports, 1938–1940. PFNPL.

———. Park Naturalists Monthly Reports, 1935–1956. PFNPL.

———. Petrified Forest National Monument. Album, 1957. Petrified Forest National Park Library (PFNPL).

———. Petrified Forest National Park. Environmental Improvement Demonstration Project (Rainbow Forest), 1970. PFNPL.

———. Petrified Forest National Park Natural Resources Management Plan, February 1981 Revision. PFNPL.

———. Southwestern National Monuments. Monthly Reports, 1902–1930. Western Archeological and Conservation Center (WACC), Tucson, Arizona.

————. Statement for Management. Petrified Forest National Park, Arizona, 1976.
    PFNPL.
————. Statement for Management. Petrified Forest National Park, Arizona, 1988.
    PFNPL.
————. Superintendents Annual Reports, 1933–1963. PFNPL.
————. Superintendents Monthly Reports, 1929–1940. PFNPL.
————. Wilderness Recommendation for Petrified Forest National Park, Arizona,
    November 1967. PFNPL.
U.S. National Archives, Record Group 79, Records of the National Park Service.

Manuscripts

Annie Montague Alexander Collection. "Biographical Sketch of Annie M. Alexan-
    der." Photocopy. Bancroft Library, University of California. Berkeley,
    California.
Harold Sellers Colton Autobiography. Museum of Northern Arizona. Flagstaff,
    Arizona.
Fred Harvey Collection. Hayden Library, Arizona State University. Tempe, Arizona.
Carl T. Hayden Collection. Arizona Collection. Hayden Library, Arizona State Uni-
    versity. Tempe, Arizona.
Fred Kabotie. "The Zuni Salt Lake Trip Mural." Typescript of recording. Painted
    Desert Inn—History File. PFNPL.
Robert A. Long. Notes of R. A. Long. Copy in author's possession.
John Muir Collection, 1902–1955. Huntington Library. San Marino, California.
John Muir Papers, 1858–1957. Holt-Atherton Center for Western Studies, Univer-
    sity of the Pacific. Stockton, California. Microform.
Horatio Rust Collection. Huntington Library. San Marino, California.
A. C. Vroman Album. Huntington Library. San Marino, California.
A. C. Vroman Albums. Pasadena City Library. Pasadena, California.
Amiel Weeks Whipple. Journals of Amiel Weeks Whipple, Lieutenant, U.S. Army.
    Pacific Railroad Survey, 1853–1854. Oklahoma Historical Society. Okla-
    homa City, Oklahoma. Microfilm courtesy of Andrew Wallace.

Public Documents

Arizona (Territory). Acts, Resolutions, and Memorials of the Eighteenth Legislative Assembly of the
    Territory of Arizona. Phoenix, 1895.

Bond, Frank. "The Administration of National Monuments." *Proceedings of the National Park Conference Held at Yellowstone National Park, September 11 and 12.* Washington, D.C.: Government Printing Office, 1912.

Congressional Record. 56th Cong., 1st sess., 1900. Vol. 33, pt. 5.

———. 57th Cong., 1st sess., 1902. Vol. 35, pt. 4.

———. 58th Cong., 2nd sess., 1904. Vol. 38, pt. 3.

———. 59th Cong., 1st sess., 1906. Vol. 40, pt. 10.

U.S. Congress. House. *Wagon Road from Fort Defiance to the Colorado River.* 35th Cong., 1st sess., 1858. Exec. Doc. 124.

———. Senate. *Journal of a Military Reconnaissance from Santa Fe, New Mexico, to the Navajo Country, Made in 1849 by James H. Simpson.* 31st Cong., 1st sess., 1850. Exec. Doc. 64.

———. Senate. *Report of an Expedition down the Zuni and Colorado Rivers, by Captain L. Sitgreaves.* 32nd Cong., 2nd sess., 1853. Exec. Doc. 59.

———. Senate. *Report upon the Colorado River of the West, Explored in 1857 and 1858 by Lieutenant Joseph C. Ives.* 36th Cong., 1st sess., 1861. Exec. Doc. 90.

———. Senate. *Reports of Explorations and Surveys, to Ascertain the Most Practicable and Economical Route for a Railroad from the Mississippi River to the Pacific Ocean.* Vol. 3, *Route Near the Thirty-Fifth Parallel, under the Command of Lieut. A. W. Whipple, Topographical Engineers, in 1853 and 1854.* 33rd Cong., 2nd sess., 1856. Exec. Doc. 78.

U.S. Department of the Interior. U.S. Geological and Geographical Survey of the Territories. *Report on the Geology of the Eastern Uinta Mountains and a Region Thereto.* Washington, D.C.: Government Printing Office, 1876.

——— General Land Office. *Circular Relating to Historic and Prehistoric Ruins of the Southwest and their Preservation, by Edgar L. Hewett.* Washington, D.C.: Government Printing Office, 1904.

———. Geological Survey. *Twentieth Annual Report, 1998–99. Part 2, General Geology and Paleontology.* Washington, D.C.: Government Printing Office, 1900.

———. *Monographs.* XLVIII, part 1: Text. Washington, D.C.: Government Printing Office, 1905.

———. National Park Service. *The Painted Desert Inn: Evaluation of Structures and Cultural Resources.* San Francisco: NPS Western Regional Office, 1974.

———. National Park Service. *Petrified Forest National Park. Final General Management Plan / Development Concept Plan / Environmental Impact Statement.* Denver: NPS Denver Regional Center, 1993.

———. *Painted Desert Inn History File.* Typescripts. PFNPL.

U.S. National Museum. "Information Concerning Some Fossil Trees in the United States Museum," by Lt. Col. P. T. Swaine and Lt. J. T. C. Hegewald. Pro-

ceedings of the United States Museum. Washington, D.C.: Government Printing Office, 1882.

———. "New Species of Fossil Wood (*Araucarioxylon arizonicum*) from Arizona and New Mexico," by F. H. Knowlton. *Proceedings of the United States National Museum.* Washington, D.C.: Government Printing Office, 1888.

United States Railroad Administration. *Petrified Forest National Monument, Arizona.* Chicago: Western Lines, 1919.

U.S. Smithsonian Institution. "The Petrified Forests of Arizona," by Lester F. Ward. *Annual Report,* 1899. Washington, D.C.: Government Printing Office, 1901.

———. "Archaeological Fieldwork in Northeastern Arizona: The Museum-Gates Expedition of 1901," by Walter Hough. *Annual Report,* 1901. Washington, D.C.: Government Printing Office, 1903.

Newspapers

Arizona Champion (Flagstaff), 1883–1887; 1888–1896.

Arizona Daily Sun (Flagstaff), 1946–1992.

Arizona Republic (Phoenix), 1931–1992.

Arizona Republican (Phoenix), 1915–1930.

Coconino Sun (Flagstaff), 1899–1945.

Holbrook Argus, 1895–1913.

Holbrook News, 1909–1915.

Holbrook Tribune, 1918–1991.

Holbrook Tribune-News, 1966–1991.

St. Johns Observer, 1939.

Secondary Sources

Books, Dissertations, Pamphlets

Abbey, Edward. *Desert Solitaire: A Season in the Wilderness.* New York: Ballantine Books, 1968.

Albright, Horace M., as told to Robert Cahn. *The Birth of the National Park Service: The Founding Years, 1913–1933.* Salt Lake City: Howe Brothers, 1985.

Albright, Horace M., and Frank J. Taylor. *"Oh, Ranger!" A Book About the National Parks.* Stanford: Stanford University Press, 1928.

Ambler, J. Richard. *The Anasazi: Prehistoric People of the Four Corners Region.* Flagstaff: Museum of Northern Arizona, 1989.

Arizona's National Monuments. Santa Fe, N.M.: Southwestern National Parks and Monuments Association, 1945.

Ash, Sidney. *Petrified Forest: The Story behind the Scenery.* Petrified Forest National Park, Ariz.: Petrified Forest Museum Association, 1986.

Baars, Donald L. *The Colorado Plateau: A Geologic History.* Albuquerque: University of New Mexico Press, 1983.

Barbara, Preston Albert. *Baldwin Möllhausen, The German Cooper.* Philadelphia, 1914.

Bartlett, Richard A. *Yellowstone: A Wilderness Besieged.* Tucson: University of Arizona Press, 1985.

Belasco, Warren James. *Americans on the Road: From Autocamp to Motel, 1910–1945.* Cambridge, Mass.: MIT Press, 1979.

Berry, William B. N. *Growth of a Prehistoric Time Scale, Based on Organic Evolution.* Palo Alto, Calif.: Blackwell Scientific Publications, 1987.

Bieber, Ralph B. *Exploring Southwestern Trails, 1846–1854, by Philip St. George Cooke, William Henry Chase Whiting, and François Xavier Aubrey.* 1938. Reprint, Philadelphia: Porcupine Press, 1974.

Breed, Carol S., and William J. Breed, eds. *Investigations in the Triassic Chinle Formation.* MNA Bulletin No. 47. Flagstaff, Ariz.: Museum of Northern Arizona, 1972.

Breed, William J. *The Age of Dinosaurs in Northern Arizona.* Flagstaff, Ariz.: Museum of Northern Arizona, 1968.

Broderick, Harold J. *Agatized Rainbows: A Story of the Petrified Forest.* Holbrook, Ariz.: Petrified Forest Museum Association, 1951.

Bryant, Keith L., Jr. *History of the Atchison, Topeka, and Santa Fe Railway.* New York: Macmillan, 1974.

Burton, Jeffrey F. *Days in the Painted Desert and the Petrified Forests of Northern Arizona: Contributions to the Archaeology of Petrified Forest National Park, 1988–1992.* Publications in Anthropology no. 62. Tucson: Western Archeological and Conservation Center, 1993.

Cameron, Jenks. *The National Park Service: Its History, Activities, and Organization.* New York: D. Appleton and Co., 1922.

Camp, Charles L. *A Study of the Phytosaurs.* Memoirs of the University of California, vol. 10. Berkeley: University of California Press, 1930.

Chaput, Donald. *François X. Aubrey: Trader, Trailmaker, and Voyager in the Southwest, 1846–1854.* Glendale, Calif.: Arthur H. Clark Co., 1975.

Chronic, Halka. *Pages of Stone: Geology of Western National Parks and Monuments.* Vol. 3, The Desert Southwest. Seattle: Mountaineers, 1986.

Clark, Jean H., and Shirley Sargent, eds. *Dear Papa: Letters between John Muir and His Daughter Wanda.* Fresno, Calif.: Panorama West Books, 1985.

Cobb, Irvin S. *Roughing It De Luxe.* New York: George H. Doran Co., 1913.

Cohen, Michael P. *The Pathless Way: John Muir and American Wilderness.* Madison: University of Wisconsin Press, 1984.

Cohen, Stanley. *The Tree Army: A Pictorial History of the Civilian Conservation Corps, 1933–1942.* Missoula, Mont.: Pictorial Histories Publishing Co., 1980.

Colbert, Edwin H. *The Dinosaur Book: The Ruling Reptiles and Their Relatives.* New York: McGraw-Hill, 1951.

————. *Dinosaurs: Their Discovery and Their World.* New York: E. P. Dutton, 1961.

————. *The Triassic Dinosaur Coelophysis.* Bulletin Series No. 57. Flagstaff, Ariz.: Museum of Northern Arizona, 1989.

————. *Wandering Lands and Animals: The Story of Continental Drift and Animal Populations.* New York: Dover Publications, 1973.

Colbert, Edwin H., and R. Roy Johnson, eds. *The Petrified Forest Through the Ages.* Seventy-fifth Anniversary Symposium. Flagstaff, Ariz.: Museum of Northern Arizona, 1985.

Connally, Eugenia Horstman, ed. *National Parks in Crisis.* Washington, D.C.: National Parks and Conservation Association, 1982.

Darling, F. Fraser, and Noel D. Eichhorn. *Man and Nature in the National Parks: Reflections on Policy.* Washington, D.C.: Conservation Foundation, 1969.

Daugherty, Lyman H. *The Upper Triassic Flora of Arizona.* Contributions to Paleontology, Publication 526. Washington, D.C.: Carnegie Institution, 1941.

Domenach, Emmanuel Henri Dieubonné. *Seven Years' Residence in the Great Deserts of North America.* 2 vols. 1860. Reprint, New Haven: Research Publications, 1975.

Downum, Christian E. "One Grand History: A Critical Review of Flagstaff Archaeology, 1851–1988." Ph.D. diss., University of Arizona, 1988.

Eicher, Don L. *Geologic Time.* Englewood Cliffs, N.J.: Prentice-Hall, 1976.

Euler, Robert Clark. "A Half Century of Economic Growth in Northern Arizona, 1863–1912. Master's thesis, Northern Arizona University, 1947.

Everhart, William C. *The National Park Service.* Boulder, Colo.: Westview Press, 1983.

Fenton, Carroll L., and Mildred A. Fenton. *Giants of Geology.* New York: Doubleday, 1952.

Foreman, Grant, ed. *A Pathfinder in the Southwest: The Itinerary of Lieutenant A. W. Whipple during his Exploration for a Railroad Route from Fort Smith to Los Angeles in the Years 1853 and 1854.* Norman: University of Oklahoma Press, 1941.

Fox, Stephen. *John Muir and His Legacy.* Boston: Little, Brown, 1981.

Freemuth, John C. *Islands under Siege: National Parks and the Politics of External Threats.* Lawrence: University Press of Kansas, 1991.

Frome, Michael. *Regreening the National Parks.* Tucson: University of Arizona Press, 1992.

Goetzmann, William H. *Army Exploration in the American West, 1803–1863*. Lincoln: University of Nebraska Press, 1979.

——. *Exploration and Empire: The Explorer and the Scientist in the Winning of the American West*. New York: Knopf, 1971.

Goetzmann, William H., and William N. Goetzmann. *The West of the Imagination*. New York: W. W. Norton, 1986.

Gould, Stephen Jay. *Time's Arrow, Time's Cycle: Myth and Metaphor in the Discovery of Geological Time*. Cambridge, Mass.: Harvard University Press, 1987.

Grattan, Virginia L. *Mary Colter: Builder upon the Red Earth*. Flagstaff, Ariz.: Northland Press, 1980.

Hampton, H. Duane. *How the U.S. Cavalry Saved Our National Parks*. Bloomington: Indiana University Press, 1971.

Harris, Ann G. *Geology of National Parks*. Dubuque, Iowa: Kendall/Hunt, 1977.

Hartzog, George B., Jr., *Battling for the National Parks*. Mt. Kisco, N.Y.: Moyer Bell, 1988.

A Historical and Biographical Record of the Territory of Arizona. Chicago: McFarland and Poole, 1896.

Houk, Rose. *The Painted Desert: Land of Light and Shadow*. Petrified Forest National Park, Ariz.: Petrified Forest Museum Association, 1990.

Huth, Hans. *Nature and the American: Three Centuries of Changing Attitudes*. Lincoln: University of Nebraska Press, 1990.

Hyde, Anne Farrar. *An American Vision: Far Western Landscape and National Culture, 1820–1920*. New York: New York University Press, 1990.

Ise, John. *Our National Park Policy: A Critical History*. Baltimore: Johns Hopkins University Press, 1961.

Jakle, John A. *The Tourist: Travel in Twentieth-Century North America*. Lincoln: University of Nebraska Press, 1985.

James, Harlean. *Romance of the National Parks*. New York: Macmillan, 1939.

Jones, Anne Trinkle. *Patterns of Lithic Use at AZ Q:1:42, Petrified Forest National Park, Arizona*. Publications in Anthropology no. 25. Tucson: Western Archeological and Conservation Center, 1983.

Kabotie, Fred, and Bill Belknap. *Fred Kabotie: Hopi Indian Artist*. Flagstaff, Ariz.: Northland Press, 1977.

Kelly, Susan C. *Route 66: The Highway and Its People*. Norman: University of Oklahoma Press, 1988.

Kunz, George F. *Gems and Precious Stones of North America*. 1892. Reprint, New York: Dover Publications, 1968.

Lee, Ronald F. *The Antiquities Act of 1906*. Washington, D.C.: National Park Service, 1971.

Leshy, John D. *The Mining Law: A Study in Perpetual Motion.* Washington, D.C.: Resources for the Future, 1987.

Lister, Robert H., and Florence C. Lister. *Those Who Came Before: Southwestern Archaeology in the National Park System.* Tucson: University of Arizona Press, 1983.

Long, Robert, and Rose Houk. *Dawn of the Dinosaurs: The Triassic in Petrified Forest.* Petrified Forest National Park, Arizona: Petrified Forest Museum Association, 1988.

Lowitt, Richard. *The New Deal and the West.* Bloomington: Indiana University Press, 1984.

Lummis, Charles F. *An Appreciation of the Petrified Forest of Arizona.* National Park Series. Chicago: United States Railroad Administration, 1919.

———. *Mesa, Canyon, and Pueblo.* New York: Century Co., 1925.

———. *Some Strange Corners of Our Country: The Wonderland of the Southwest.* New York: Century Co., 1901.

MacCannell, Dean. *The Tourist: A New Theory of the Leisure Class.* New York: Schocken Books, 1976.

McGregor, John C. *Southwestern Archaeology.* Urbana: University of Illinois Press, 1965.

McKee, Edwin D. *Ancient Landscapes of the Grand Canyon Region: The Geology of Grand Canyon, Zion, Bryce, Petrified Forest, and Painted Desert.* Atchison, Kans.: Lockwood-Hazel Co., 1938.

McKnitt, Frank, ed. *Navajo Expedition: Journal of a Military Reconnaissance from Santa Fe, New Mexico, to the Navajo Country Made in 1849 by Lieutenant James H. Simpson.* Norman: University of Oklahoma Press, 1964.

McPhee, John. *Basin and Range.* New York: Farrar, Straus, Giroux, 1981.

Manning, T. G. *Government in Science: The U.S. Geological Survey, 1867–1894.* Lexington: University of Kentucky Press, 1967.

Marcou, Jules. *Geology of North America.* Zurich, 1858.

Matthews, William H. III. *A Guide to the National Parks: Their Landscape and Geology.* Vol. 1, *The Western Parks.* Garden City, N.Y.: Natural History Press, 1968.

Merrill, George P. *The First One Hundred Years of American Geology.* 1924. Reprint, New York: Hafner Publishing Co., 1964.

Miller, David H. "Baldwin Möllhausen: A Prussian's Image of the American West." Ph.D. diss., University of New Mexico, 1970.

Miller, Jimmy H. "A Philadelphia Brahmin in Flagstaff: The Life of Harold Sellers Colton." Ph.D. diss., Northern Arizona University, 1985.

Möllhausen, Baldwin. *Diary of a Journey from the Mississippi to the Coasts of the Pacific.* 2 vols. 1858. Reprint, New York: Johnson Reprint Corp., 1969.

———. *Reisen in die Felsengebirge Nord-Amerikas bis zum Hochplateau von Neu-Mexico.* 2 vols. Leipzig: Otto Purfuerst, 1860.

Muir, John. *The Life and Letters of John Muir*. 2 vols. Edited by William Frederic Bade. Boston: Houghton Mifflin, 1924.

Murphey, Thomas D. *Seven Wonderlands of the American West*. Boston: L. C. Pate, 1925.

Nash, Roderick F. *Wilderness and the American Mind*. New Haven: Yale University Press, 1982.

National Park Foundation. *Mirror of America: Literary Encounters with the National Parks*. Boulder, Colo.: Roberts Rinehart, 1989.

National Park Service. *The Civilian Conservation Corps and the National Park Service, 1933–1942: An Administrative History*, by John C. Paige. Washington, D.C.: Government Printing Office, 1985.

———. *The National Parks: Shaping the System*. Washington, D.C.: NPS Division of Publications, 1985.

Nations, Dale, and Edmund Stump. *Geology of Arizona*. Dubuque, Iowa: Kendall/Hunt, 1981.

Noble, David G. *Ancient Ruins of the Southwest*. Flagstaff, Ariz.: Northland Press, 1981.

Pammel, L. H., ed. *Major John F. Lacey: Memorial Volume*. Des Moines: Iowa Park and Forestry Association, 1915.

Peterson, Charles S. *Take Up Your Mission: Mormon Colonizing along the Little Colorado River, 1870–1900*. Tucson: University of Arizona Press, 1973.

Petrified Forest Arizona. Pamphlet. Chicago: Atchison, Topeka, and Santa Fe Railway Co., 1912.

Pomeroy, Earl. *In Search of the Golden West: The Tourist in Western America*. New York: Knopf, 1957.

Post, Emily. *By Motor to the Golden Gate*. New York: D. Appleton and Co., 1910.

Ranson, Jay Ellis. *Petrified Forest Trails: A Guide to the Petrified Forests of America*. Portland, Ore.: Mineralogist Publishing Co., 1955.

Rocky Mountain Mineral Law Foundation. *The American Law of Mining*. Vol. 1, Titles I–V. Albany, N.Y.: Matthew Bender and Co., 1960.

Rothman, Hal. *Preserving Different Pasts: The American National Monuments*. Urbana: University of Illinois Press, 1989.

Runte, Alfred. *National Parks: The American Experience*. Lincoln: University of Nebraska Press, 1987.

———. *Trains of Discovery: Western Railroads and the National Parks*. Flagstaff, Ariz.: Northland Press, 1984.

———. *Yosemite: The Embattled Wilderness*. Lincoln: University of Nebraska Press, 1990.

Salmond, John A. *The Civilian Conservation Corps, 1933–1942: A New Deal Case Study*. Durham, N.C.: Duke University Press, 1967.

Sax, Joseph L. *Mountains without Handrails: Reflections on the National Parks*. Ann Arbor: University of Michigan Press, 1980.

Schmitt, Peter. *Back to Nature: The Arcadian Myth in Urban America.* New York: Oxford University Press, 1969.

Schrepfer, Susan R. *The Fight to Save the Redwoods: A History of Environmental Reform, 1917–1978.* Madison: University of Wisconsin Press, 1983.

Science and the National Parks. Washington, D.C.: National Academy Press, 1992.

Shankland, Robert. *Stephen Mather of the National Parks.* New York: Knopf, 1951.

Smith, Dama Margaret. *I Married a Ranger.* Stanford: Stanford University Press, 1931.

————. *Petrified Forest National Monument, Arizona.* Holbrook, Ariz., 1930.

Sterling, Kier B. *Last of the Naturalists: The Career of C. Hart Merriam.* New York: Arno Press, 1977.

Stewart, J. H., F. G. Poole, and R. F. Wilson. *Stratigraphy and the Origin of the Chinle Formation and Related Upper Triassic Strata in the Colorado Plateau Region.* GS Professional Paper 690. Washington, D.C.: Government Printing Office, 1972.

Stewart, Yvonne G. *An Archeological Overview of Petrified Forest National Park.* Publications in Anthropology no. 10. Tucson: Western Archeological and Conservation Center, 1980.

Swain, Donald C. *Wilderness Defender: Horace M. Albright and Conservation.* Chicago: University of Chicago Press, 1970.

Tanner, George S., and Morris J. Richards. *Colonization on the Little Colorado: The Joseph City Region.* Flagstaff, Ariz.: Northland Press, 1977.

Thayer, William M. *Marvels of the New West.* Norwich, Conn.: Henry Bill Publishing Co., 1892.

Thomas, D. H. *The Southwestern Indian Detours: The Story of the Fred Harvey / Santa Fe Railway Experiment in "Detourism."* Phoenix: Hunter Publishing Co., 1978.

Tilden, Freeman. *The National Parks.* New York: Knopf, 1983.

Tinker, George. *Northern Arizona and Flagstaff in 1887: The People and Resources.* 1887. Reprint, Glendale, Calif.: Arthur Clark Co., 1969.

Turner, Frederick. *Rediscovering America: John Muir in his Time and Ours.* New York: Viking, 1985.

Wallis, Michael. *Route 66: The Mother Road.* New York: St. Martin's Press, 1990.

Weber, David J. *Richard H. Kern: Expeditionary Artist in the Far Southwest, 1848–1853.* Albuquerque: University of New Mexico Press, 1985.

Wendorf, Fred. *Archaeological Studies in the Petrified Forest National Monument.* MNA Bulletin No. 27. Flagstaff, Ariz.: Museum of Northern Arizona, 1953.

Wirth, Conrad L. *Parks, Politics, and the People.* Norman: University of Oklahoma Press, 1980.

Wolfe, Linnie Marsh. *Son of the Wilderness: The Life of John Muir.* 1945. Reprint, Madison: University of Wisconsin Press, 1978.

————, ed. *John of the Mountains: The Unpublished Journals of John Muir*. Madison: University of Wisconsin Press, 1979.

Articles

"Agate Bridge." *Arizona Graphic* 4 November 1899, 1–2.

"An Agate Forest." *Youth's Companion*, 9 February 1882, 62.

"Among the World's Workers: A Conversation with John Muir." *World's Work*, November 1906, 8249–50.

Ash, Sidney. "The Search for Plant Fossils in the Chinle Formation." In *Investigations in the Triassic Chinle Formation*. MNA Bulletin No. 47, edited by Carol S. and William J. Breed. Flagstaff, Ariz.: Museum of Northern Arizona, 1972.

Baéza, Joan. "Prehistoric Man in the Petrified Forest." *Arizona Highways*, July 1986, 20–27.

Barnes, Charles W. "A Forest of 180 Million Year Old Trees." *Arizona Highways*, June 1975, 13–27.

Breed, William J., and George H. Billingsley. "Petrified Forest: The Origins of the Landscape." *Plateau* 51 (1979): 12–23.

Broderick, Harold J. "Rainbows in Agate from an Ancient Forest." *Arizona Highways*, August 1951, 18–25.

Butcher, Devereux. "Resorts or Wilderness?" *Atlantic*, February 1961, 45–51.

Carroll, Mitchell. "The Story of Our National Monuments." *Art and Archaeology*, July/August 1920, 3–5.

"Chalcedony Park, Arizona." *Arizona Graphic*, 4 November 1899, 1.

"Chalcedony Park, Arizona." *The Great Divide*, October 1892, 166.

Colbert, Edwin H. "Ancient Animals of the Petrified Forest." *Plateau* 51 (1979): 24–29.

Colclazer, Susan. "Dawn of the Dinosaur." *Courier* 30 (August 1985): 1–3.

Conrad, David E. "The Whipple Expedition in Arizona, 1853–1854. *Arizona and the West* 11 (Summer 1969): 147–78.

Dannen, Kent, and Donna Dannen. "Visit the Triassic." *Arizona Highways*, July 1986, 34–39, 43.

Darling, F. Fraser, and Noel D. Eichhorn. "Man and Nature in the National Parks." *National Parks Magazine* 43 (April 1969): 13–24.

Daugherty, Lyman H. "*Schilderia Adamanica*: A New Fossil Wood from the Petrified Forest of Arizona." *Botanical Gazette* 96 (December 1934): 363–66.

De Voto, Bernard. "The Easy Chair." *Harper's Monthly*, October 1953, 50–52.

————. "The Easy Chair." *Harper's Monthly*, November 1954, 12–17.

Downum, Christian E. "The Sinagua." *Plateau* 63 (1992): 2–31.

Forrest, James T. "Edgar Lee Hewett." In *Keepers of the Past*, edited by Clifford L. Lord. Chapel Hill: University of North Carolina Press, 1965.

Funsten, Kenneth. "Adam Clark Vroman and the Forest of Stone." *Arizona Highways*, July 1986, 28–33.

Gallagher, Annette. "Citizen of the Nation: John Fletcher Lacey, Conservationist." *Annals of Iowa* 46 (1981): 9–24.

Gallagher, D. W. "The Petrified Forest In Arizona." *Loretto Magazine*, 10 January 1899, 3–4.

Gottesfeld, Allen F. "Paleoecology of the Lower Part of the Chinle Formation in the Petrified Forest." In *Investigations in the Triassic Chinle Formation*. MNA Bulletin No. 47, edited by Carol S. and William J. Breed. Flagstaff, Ariz.: Museum of Northern Arizona, 1972.

Hampton, H. Duane. "Opposition to National Parks." *Journal of Forest History* 25 (January 1981): 37–45.

Holder, C. F. "Stone Forests." *Frank Leslie's Popular Monthly*, March 1887, 376–82.

Hough, Walter. "Ancient Peoples of the Petrified Forest of Arizona." *Harper's Monthly Magazine* 105 (1902): 897–901.

Hovey, H. C. "The Petrified Forest of Arizona." *Scientific American*, 19 November 1892, 328.

———. "A Visit to Chalcedony Park, Arizona." *Scientific American*, 23 July 1892, 53–56.

Jeffers, Jo. "Petrified Forest." *Arizona Highways*, July 1967, 2–10, 30.

Knowlton, F. H. "The Fossil Forests of Arizona." *American Forestry* 19 (April 1913): 1–12.

Kunz, George F. "Agatized and Jasperized Wood of Arizona." *Popular Science Monthly*, January 1886, 367.

———. "Natural Bridge of Agate." *The Great Divide*, September 1890, 7.

Laetz, Catrien Ross. "Roads and Ruins: A Delicate Balance." *Arizona Highways*, July 1986, 14–19.

Lockwood, Frank C. "Arizona Pioneers: 1854–1864, François Xavier Aubrey." *Arizona Historical Review* 5 (January 1933): 327–32.

Lummis, Charles F. "In the Lion's Den." *Land of Sunshine*, October 1899, 291–92.

———. "Stone Trees: A Forest Gone to Bed." *Santa Fe Magazine*, June 1912, 29–41.

Mackintosh, Barry. "Harold Ickes and the National Park Service." *Journal of Forest History* 29 (April 1985): 78–84.

Mera, H. P. "Observations on the Archaeology of the Petrified Forest National Monument." *New Mexico Laboratory of Anthropology Bulletin*, Technical Series, no. 7 (1934): 1–24.

Meyer, Larry L. "D-Day on the Painted Desert." *Arizona Highways*, July 1986, 2–13.

Miller, S. A. "The Petrified Forest of Arizona." *Cincinnati Society of Natural History* 17 (April 1894): 56–58.

Muench, Joyce R. "The Enchanted Stone Forest." *Arizona Highways*, July 1958, 14–28.

Nash, Roderick. "The American Invention of National Parks." *American Quarterly* 22 (Fall 1970): 726–35.

"A Petrified Forest." *Cambrian* 15 (November 1895): 342.

"A Petrified Forest in Arizona." *Scientific American Supplement* no. 714, 7 September 1889, 11412.

"The Petrified Forest of Arizona." *Natural Science News*, 7 December 1895, 177–78.

"The Petrified Forest of Arizona." *Popular Science News*, September 1894.

"Petrified Forest National Park: Home of the Ancients." *Arizona Highways*, April 1963, 4–5.

Reed, Erik K. "People of the Petrified Forest." *National Park Service Region III Quarterly* 2 (April 1940): 22–24.

Righter, Robert W. "National Monuments to National Parks." *Western Historical Quarterly* 20 (August 1989): 281–301.

Rothman, Hal. "Forged by One Man's Will: Frank Pinkley and the Administration of the Southwestern National Monuments, 1923–1932." *Public Historian* 8 (Spring 1986): 83–100.

————. "Second-Class Sites: The National Monuments and the Growth of the Park System." *Environmental Review* 10 (Spring 1986): 45–56.

Rowe, Timothy. "*Placerias*: An Unusual Reptile from the Chinle Formation." *Plateau* 51 (1979): 30–32.

Rust, H. N. "The Petrified Forest." *Land of Sunshine*, February 1896, 123–25.

Sellers, Richard W., Alfred Runte, and others. "The National Parks: A Forum on the 'Worthless Lands' Thesis." *Journal of Forest History* 27 (July 1983): 130–45.

Smith, Ida. "Petrified Forest National Park." *Arizona Highways*, April 1963, 6–29.

Spamer, Earle E. "A Historic Piece of Petrified Wood from the Triassic in Arizona." *Mosasaur* 4 (December 1988): 1–3.

Stevenson, Charles. "The Shocking Truth about Our National Parks." *Readers Digest*, January 1955, 45–50.

"The Story of the Petrified Forest Wood Co.: A Unique Arizona-Based Industry." *Arizona Highways*, June 1975, 33.

Swain, Donald C. "Harold Ickes, Horace Albright, and the Hundred Days: A Study in Conservation Administration." *Pacific Historical Review* 34 (November 1965): 455–65.

————. "The National Park Service and the New Deal, 1933–1940." *Pacific Historical Review* 41 (August 1972): 312–32.

Trexler, Keith A. "Geological History." *Arizona Highways*, June 1967, 29–31.

Van Cleve, Philip F. "Petrified Forest National Park: Plant Fossils." *Arizona Highways*, April 1963, 31–33.

Walker, Wyman D. "F. X. Aubrey: Santa Fe Freighter, Pathfinder, and Explorer." *New Mexico Historical Review* 7 (January 1932): 1–31.

Wallace, Andrew. "Across Arizona to the Big Colorado: The Sitgreaves Expedition of 1851." *Arizona and the West* 26 (Winter 1984): 325–64.

Walton, Matt. "Geology of the Painted Desert and Petrified Forest." *Arizona Highways*, July 1958, 7–12.

Welles, "Collecting Triassic Vertebrates in the Plateau Province." *Journal of the West* 8 (April 1969): 231–46.

Wendorf, Fred. "Archaeological Investigations in the Petrified Forest: Twin Buttes Site, a Preliminary Report." *Plateau* 24 (1951): 77–83.

————. "Early Archaeological Sites in the Petrified Forest National Monument." *Plateau* 21 (1948): 29–32.

————. "The Flattop Site in the Petrified Forest National Monument." *Plateau* 22 (1950): 43–51.

Wild, Peter. "Months of Sorrow and Renewal: John Muir in Arizona, 1905–1906." *Journal of the Southwest* 29 (Spring 1987): 20–40.

Zullo, Janet Lewis. "Annie Montague Alexander: Her Work in Paleontology." *Journal of the West* 8 (April 1969): 183–99.

INDEX

ABOUT THE AUTHOR

George M. Lubick is an associate professor of history at Northern Arizona University, where he has taught since 1977. He introduced a course in American Environmental History to the curriculum in 1980, and he also offers graduate courses on that topic. He has written two articles on Petrified Forest. "Soldiers and Scientists in the Petrified Forest" appeared in the *Journal of Arizona History* in Winter 1988, and "Protecting Our Forests of Stone" in *Plateau* (no. 4, 1990). Northern Arizona University's Office of Sponsored Research provided funding that facilitated research at Petrified Forest National Park, the National Archives, and the Huntington Library.

Lubick received his Ph.D. from the University of Toledo and his M.A. and B.A. from the University of Montana. His research interests focus generally on the American West, with special reference to national parks and general environmental issues in the region. New research will focus on science and the national parks from the nineteenth century to the present. The topic has grown naturally out of the research on Petrified Forest.